*Rape, Rage and
Feminism in Contemporary
American Drama*

Rape, Rage and Feminism in Contemporary American Drama

DAVIDA BLOOM

McFarland & Company, Inc., Publishers
Jefferson, North Carolina

LIBRARY OF CONGRESS CATALOGUING-IN-PUBLICATION DATA

Names: Bloom, Davida.
Title: Rape, rage and feminism in contemporary American drama / Davida Bloom.
Description: Jefferson, North Carolina : McFarland & Company, Inc., Publishers, 2015. | Includes bibliographical references and index.
Identifiers: LCCN 2015037607| ISBN 9780786470358 (softcover : acid free paper) | ISBN 9781476623719 (ebook)
Subjects: LCSH: American drama—20th century—History and criticism. | Feminism and literature—United States—History—20th century. | Rape in literature. | Women in literature. | Feminist drama—History and criticism. | American drama—21st century—History and criticism. | Feminism and literature—United States—History—21st century.
Classification: LCC PS338.F48 B56 2016 | DDC 812.009/3552—dc23
LC record available at http://lccn.loc.gov/2015037607

BRITISH LIBRARY CATALOGUING DATA ARE AVAILABLE

© 2016 Davida Bloom. All rights reserved

No part of this book may be reproduced or transmitted in any form or by any means, electronic or mechanical, including photocopying or recording, or by any information storage and retrieval system, without permission in writing from the publisher.

On the cover: Notheastern University's 2009 production of *No. 11 (Blue and White)* by Alexandra Cunningham, directed by Jonathan Carr, featuring Amelia Bubin as Tammy, photography by Nora Lindsay McBurnett

Printed in the United States of America

McFarland & Company, Inc., Publishers
  Box 611, Jefferson, North Carolina 28640
    www.mcfarlandpub.com

For all the theatre artists who have,
and will, put the complex issues surrounding rape
and the need to transform our rape culture
center stage

Acknowledgments

A book, like a dramatic text, goes through an extensive revision process and there are many people who have helped me along the way. The first incarnation of this work was carefully guided by Lee Potts, Haiping Yan, Alison Jaggar, Karen Jacobs, and Merrill Lessley. I am also very grateful to Elaine Aston, who was the first to suggest I explore the intersections of the depiction of rape in dramatic texts and the various waves of feminism. I am indebted to my mother, Joan Bloom, and my sister, Claire Bloom, for their careful proofreading, and my father, Bernard Bloom, for his support and encouragement. The Interlibrary Loan librarians at the University of Colorado and the College at Brockport: State University of New York were essential to my research and I am most grateful for their hard work. And finally, I'd like to thank the two anonymous readers of my manuscript whose insights resulted in a much-improved work. On a personal note I would like to thank my son Keenan. You did not get as much of my time as you deserved because of this project. My sincere apologies. You have become an extraordinary young man and I am very proud of you.

Table of Contents

Preface 1

Introduction 5

One: Second-Wave Feminism and Dramatizing Rape 13

Two: Rape Myths and Rapists 25

Three: Female Rage 65

Four: Antifeminist Backlash 96

Five: Third-Wave, Postfeminism and the Commodification of Rape 114

Six: Female Rage Revisited 139

Conclusion 157

Chapter Notes 167

Bibliography 179

Index 197

Preface

Lynda Hart, in the introduction to the book *Acting Out: Feminist Performances*, writes, "Getting raped, going crazy, and, of course dying—this is what women appear to do most often in realistic theatre" (5). In this study I examine the depiction of rape in 36 American dramas, written between 1970 and 2007. As I will document, the portrayal of rape, raped women, and rapists in these dramas reveals much about the cultural gendering of sexuality and expectations of masculine and feminine identity in the United States. In addition, the gendering of rage in our culture is explored in relation to the portrayal of sexual violence and the representation of a raped woman's response to her assault. Furthermore, I expose the prevalence of commonly accepted rape myths in these plays, such as women who dress provocatively and invite men into their homes deserve to be raped, along with equally frequent occasions in which these myths are contested. Finally, since feminism and women's activism has markedly transformed American society and artistic output, including American dramas about rape, I begin my study with the portrayal of rape in contemporary dramatic texts in the 1970s, when the feminist movement focused attention on the issue of rape in our society. Throughout this study, I will demonstrate the impact of second-wave feminism, antifeminist backlash, third-wave, and postfeminism on the depiction of rape in these dramas.

Limitations, Terminology and Structural Overview

I have limited the scope of my investigation in several ways. First, I have limited this study to the analysis of the dramatic texts. While I do at times discuss productions of selected plays based on firsthand accounts (reviews or scholarly criticism about a performance), my primary focus is the text itself.

Second, for a play to be included in this study, the rape (or attempted rape) depicted or discussed in the play needs to meet the following definition of rape: A sexually penetrating act (not limited to penetration of the vagina or the involvement of a penis) perpetrated on a non-consenting woman through the use or threat of force, or other forms of coercion such as physical pressure or psychological intimidation. Also included is the situation in which a perpetrator engages in a sexually penetrating act on a woman who is incapacitated or otherwise unable to give consent.[1] In the case of attempted rape, as long as it is clear that the rapist intended to perpetrate a rape as defined above, the play was included in this study.

Third, I have limited my study to the examination of dramatic texts that depict female rape. While I acknowledge that male rape is a problem and its depiction worthy of investigation, I agree with Nicola Gavey when she writes, "Despite moves within official discourse to increasingly gender neutralize the categories of victim and perpetrator, I would argue that with reference to sexual violence they are still coded as female and male respectively, in the public imagination" (*Fighting Rape*, 116–117). In other words, many of the conclusions I draw in terms of the representation of raped women may also apply to raped males in dramatic texts, and I look forward to reading future research in this area.

Fourth, I have limited the scope of this study to the depiction of the rape of a female who is characterized as a young woman or older, as opposed to plays depicting child sexual abuse. As with male rape, the depiction of child sexual abuse in contemporary American dramas is an area ripe for further investigation.

Fifth, I have focused on dramatic texts written by American playwrights that take place in the United States, or if set in another country, that include a protagonist from the United States. And finally, I have limited this study to the depiction of rape in contemporary American *dramas*; therefore, musicals and other theatrical genres have been excluded.[2]

Scholars use the terms "victim" and "survivor" somewhat interchangeably, with no perceivable consistency throughout the field. I agree with Sharon Lamb's point that "the term *victim* is a product of social relations, culture, and language" (Introduction, 3). I would add that the term *survivor* has likewise been socially constructed. Given that there will be no consistent use of these terms by the scholars to whom I will refer in this book, I will use the term *raped woman* to avoid any unintended layering of socially constructed meaning. Furthermore, I have chosen to omit the hyphen which is often (but not universally) included in the word postfeminism. I have made this choice in order to avoid the implication that feminism has achieved its objectives and is no longer relevant.

In Chapter One, I present an overview of second-wave feminism, feminist anti-rape activism, and theatrical manifestations of this activism beginning in the 1970s. In Chapter Two, I discuss the prevalence of rape myths, in both American culture and American drama. Additionally, I look at the depiction of rapists in a number of plays. In Chapter Three, I describe the representation of raped characters' rage in selected plays, both in terms of how female rage is contained and how it is demonized. In Chapter Four, I return to the influence of feminism on the depiction of rape and I examine the ways in which the antifeminist backlash of the 1980s is evident in selected plays. Chapter Five continues the exploration of feminism as I shed light on both third-wave feminism and postfeminism and detail the ways in which these movements are apparent in plays about rape written since the late 1980s. In Chapter Six, I return to the expression of female rage focusing on texts in which the active expression of rage by a raped character is presented as part of their path to healing.

Throughout this study I revisit several overarching themes, including the gendering of sexuality, violence, and rage; the acceptance of cultural myths about rape, raped women, and rapists; and the ways in which movements within feminism are all evident in dramatic texts.

Introduction

Research has shown that approximately 12 percent, or one in every eight women, will develop breast cancer at some time in their lives. The ubiquity of pink ribbons and race-for-the-cure events keeps the issue of breast cancer on the front burner.[1] Research has also shown that approximately 20 percent, or one in every five women, will be raped at some time in their lives. Furthermore, it is commonly accepted that many rapes go unreported; consequently, these percentages are undoubtedly low.[2] I do not in any way mean to diminish the importance of breast cancer awareness and research, but the truth is there are no colored ribbons on yogurt containers to raise money to bring an end to rape.

In recent years rape has been a topic of interest on nightly news broadcasts, including rape allegations against Bill Cosby, 2013 Heisman Trophy winner Jameis Winston, and "hot yoga" guru Bikram Choudhury; alarming statistics showing that approximately seventy sexual assaults are committed daily within the U.S. military, or 26,000 per year; two documentaries by Kirby Dick and Amy Ziering, *The Invisible War* which focuses on rape in the United States military and was nominated for a 2013 Academy Award, and *The Hunting Ground* which presents an exposé of rape culture on college campuses; a report by the Department of Education noting that reports of sex offenses on college campus have almost doubled from 2009 to 2013; comments about rape and raped women by 2012 Republican candidates; and the horrors experienced by Michelle Night, Gina DeJesus, and Amanda Berry during their ten years of captivity in Cleveland.[3] It is clear that the goal of transforming our rape culture, articulated in the 1993 collection of essays edited by Emilie Buchwald, Pamela R. Fletcher, and Martha

Introduction

Roth, has yet to be achieved. I believe that the study of dramatic texts provides a window through which readers can better understand the society and time period in which the texts were written and therefore provides a barometer of cultural change. In this work I will shed light on the ways in which contemporary American dramas either have or have not participated in the efforts to transform our rape culture.

Barbara Ozieblo and Noelia Hernando-Real, in their book *Performing Gender Violence*, detail how "theatre, particularly women's theatre, has been a useful tool in awakening awareness of violence" (2). Lisa Fitzpatrick observes that "fictional and dramatic versions" of rape and raped women's testimony "inevitably engage with hegemonic patriarchal discourses of sexuality and gender relations" (186). In other words, dramatic texts illustrate culturally influenced attitudes about gender, rape, raped women, rage, and rape myths. Therefore, the depiction of rape in plays, as well as in other media such as film, television, music lyrics, etc., provides an opportunity to both observe and question a multitude of societal forces that shape our attitudes, beliefs, and identities. A playwright's representation of rape obviously does not occur in a vacuum, and I intend, through an analysis of the portrayal of rape, raped women, and rapists in contemporary American dramas, to examine the degree to which cultural forces are both reinforced and confronted in our American creative imagination.

Sally Burke writes, "A rapist ethic informs male/female relationships. This ethic, which always blames the victim, [and] provides a rationale for male behavior, is just as visible in modern American drama as it is in modern American culture" (96). This rapist ethic is enhanced by what I refer to as the gendering of sexuality—in other words, when masculine aggressive sexuality and feminine passive submission are eroticized. This gendering of sexuality informs male/female relationships by representing masculine domination as "natural." At the same time, the social construction of masculinity and femininity influences the construction of male and female characters in plays. Carla J. McDonough writes, "A study of gender presentation in American theater is relevant to an understanding of how gender is figured in the culture" (14). McDonough's contention that the study of gender in dramatic literature is relevant to an understanding of culture itself is at the core of my work.

In this study I focus on three major themes: first, I document how the depiction of rape in contemporary American dramas written between 1970 and 2007 supports and/or contests cultural myths about rape, raped women and rapists, highlighting the ways in which these myths reinforce the gendering of sexuality in American society. Second, I examine the depiction of raped women's rage, specifically in terms of how the expression of rage by raped women in dramatic texts is evidence of gendered rage in our culture; and finally I trace the evolution of feminism and document how this evolution is evident in plays about rape.

The Rape Script and the Gendering of Sexuality, Violence and Rage

Sharon Marcus, in her article "Fighting Bodies, Fighting Words: A Theory and Politics of Rape Prevention," views rape in terms of a social script. "The rapist does not simply *have* the power to rape; the social script and the extent to which that script succeeds in soliciting its target's participation, help to create the rapist's power" (391). In other words, Marcus defines rape as a scripted interaction derived from socially constructed masculine and feminine identities, along with other gendered differences that exist in our culture prior to an actual rape. I contend that the gendering of sexuality, violence, and rage is an integral part of this rape script. "To speak of a rape script," Marcus continues, "implies a *narrative* of rape, a series of steps and signals whose typical initial moments we can learn to recognize and whose final outcome we can learn to stave off" (390). Marcus suggests that by understanding rape as a scripted event, we can more effectively adjust our thinking to re-image women as "neither already raped nor inherently rapable" (387). This theory is especially useful when examining a rape that is literally scripted in the context of a play.

Marcus also references the gendering of fear and violence in our culture. "Whereas masculine fear triggers the notorious 'fight-or-flight' response, feminine fear inspires the familiar sensations of 'freezing'—involuntary immobility and silence" (394). This assumption that women will not fight back is an integral part of the rape script. Additionally, gendered rage leads to what Sharon Marcus identifies as grammatical positions for women in the rape script. The first is "a communicative stance of *responsiveness* [which] encourages women not to take the offensive in a dialogue with a would-be rapist but to stay within the limits he sets" and the other is an "interpretive stance of empathy." In fact, as Marcus points out, some writers (she cites Frederick Storaska) "advocate empathy as a mode of self-defense." These feminine empathetic and responsive impulses create situations in which women (and, as I will document, female characters) identify with the rapist rather than "force him to recognize her will and humanity" and respond with feminine-defined behaviors that ultimately mark them as rapable (393).

Finally, Marcus describes the importance of viewing the events that precede a rape as independent moments in the rape script, as opposed to an interpretation of rape "which makes one type of action, [for example] a verbal threat, immediately substitutable for another type of action, [a] sexual assault." When we substitute the threat with the action, Marcus explains, "the time and space between these two actions collapses and once again, rape has always already occurred" (389). Verbal threats, sexually harassing activities, and the like, Marcus contends, "should be countered and censured for what they are—initiatives to set up a rape situation. To make them metaphors for rape itself, however, occludes the gap between the threat and the rape—the gap in which women can try to intervene, overpower and deflect the threatened action" (389). As I will illustrate in this study, this gap between the threat and the rape is often overlooked by raped female characters in contemporary American dramas.[4]

Not only do characters in dramatic texts follow the rape script Marcus describes, they also mirror the sexual script described by Christopher Kilmartin and Julie Allison, in which men are socialized to employ a degree of coercion in their seductions. "We socialize the typical male to follow a sexual script in which he first tries to kiss a woman. If she is willing to kiss him, at some point he tries to touch her breasts. If she says 'no' or pushes his hand away, he should not interpret this refusal as meaning 'no,' but rather 'try again later'" (37). This pattern continues until the "seduction" succeeds. This sexual script is facilitated by the gendering of sexuality in our culture.

The gendering of sexuality begins with the social construction of gender itself. Teresa de Lauretis, in her book *Technologies of Gender*, details how the social construction of gender is both "the product and the process of its representation." Once we "marked the square by the F for female," she notes, we officially "entered the sex-gender system. Not only do other people consider us females, but from that moment on we have been representing ourselves as women.... We thought that we were marking the F on the form, in fact the F was marking itself on us" (5, 12). However, being marked as female goes hand in hand with being marked as sexual, as female gender stereotypes are typically sexual. Female passivity and vulnerability translates into sexual attractiveness, ineffective resistance, and sexual availability on male terms. Nicola Gavey elaborates on this point, describing what she calls the cultural scaffolding of sex as the "legitimized, normalized, and normalizing constructions of aggressive male sexuality and passive female sexuality that provide not only a social pattern for coercive sexuality but also a convenient smoke-screen for rationalizing rape (within heterosexual relationships, in particular) as simply just sex" (*Just Sex* 72). This construction of aggressive male sexuality is linked to conventions and expectations of masculinity. Aggression is, as Stevi Jackson argues, part of the male's "scripted" role in sexual scenes. "He is not only expected to take the lead but to establish dominance over the woman, to *make* her please him, and his 'masculinity' is threatened if he fails to do so. Sexual conquest becomes an acceptable way of validating masculinity" and, as is exemplified in dramatic texts, when flirtation slides into sexual conquest, seduction slides into rape, and the fluidity between gendered sexuality and gendered violence is evident (19).[5]

Finally, the gendering of rage is evident in societal attitudes pertaining to angry women. Traditionally women are expected to be friendly, good-natured, always smiling and deferring to others (especially males) or they run the risk of being thought of as "bitches." Unrestrained female anger is not part of the feminine ideal and it is often viewed as a dangerous and destructive emotion, and women who actively express anger are demonized for their behavior. Consequently, few options exist for raped women to "appropriately" express their rage. In a theatrical context we often see the consequences of the gendering of rage. Mary Brewer writes about the British play *Ficky Stingers*, "the play is problematic and deeply disturbing because the way it portrays the women's responses to being raped and their lives after being raped seems to offer women no options except silence or passive acceptance ... or madness" (112). This is characteristic of most American plays as well. As I will argue, a majority of contemporary American dramas present one of two primary options for the expression of rage by raped female characters: either their rage is stifled, or when manifested, it is so extreme that it results in the portrayal of a monstrous woman. This limited dramatic expression of female rage is evidence of the degree to which rage, like sexuality and violence, is gendered in our society.

Teresa de Lauretis claims "the cinematic contract that binds each individual spectator to the social technology of cinema is more complex than an exchange of money for pleasure or entertainment. For it produces, as a surplus, certain effects of meaning which are central to the construction of gender and subjectivity" (*Technologies* 96). The same is true of the theatrical contract. Plays about rape produce meanings that extend far beyond an engaging afternoon reading a script or an evening at the theatre as they contribute to the readers' or audience members' impressions of rape and raped women.

Feminism's Waves

Since the mid-twentieth century both female identity and feminism have gone through numerous incarnations. The return to domesticity and hyper-femininity during the post–World War II era mandated that a white middle-class woman's place was squarely in the home, girdled, made up, and greeting her husband with his evening cocktail, dinner ready on the table, and the children quietly out from underfoot. The revolutionary 1960s and 1970s spawned numerous social/political movements, including second-wave feminism, which ushered in new possibilities for women. However, second-wave feminism was criticized for its focus on issues pertaining exclusively to white middle-class women. Third-wave feminism began in the 1980s when more specific branches of feminist thought emerged, for example, black and lesbian feminist theories. Additionally, a new focus on gender studies incorporated other philosophical approaches to the previous investigations of female identity, such as queer theory, post-structuralism, post-colonial theory, and postmodernism. By the late 1980s, we saw third-wave feminists pursuing not only a more inclusive version of feminism, but, unlike their second-wave predecessors, they sought to include a valuing of femininity into the quest for empowerment and self-determination for which second-wave feminists fought. Concurrently, the 1980s witnessed a conservative antifeminist backlash. Almost as soon as many feminist possibilities had materialized, this conservative antifeminist backlash threatened to halt feminism's momentum in its tracks. By the 1990s many women, claiming that feminism was no longer relevant, shunned their mother's feminist title and ushered in the postfeminist era.[6]

Defining rape has been a challenge throughout time and has changed along with these various waves of feminism. In *Rape: An Historical and Social Enquiry*. Sylvana Tomaselli writes, "Rape will, depending on the point of view, be presented as either crime, vice, sin, ritual, physical violence, perversion, or just another word for sex" (10). Until the late twentieth century, the traditional definition of rape was the classic "stranger" rape. In other words, a woman attacked outside of her home by a deranged sex-starved violent stranger, who threatens not only her chastity, but her life as well. This definition changed as the awareness of non-stranger rapes increased, due in part to the efforts of second-wave feminists to heighten awareness of different forms of sexual violence. Currently, definitions of rape include acquaintance, date, and spousal rape. In these cases, however, the characterization of rape usually hangs on the complex issue of consent, often accompanied by a "he said, she said" debate. The raped woman is required to prove that force was used (and significantly more than might be expected in normative heterosexual relations when aggressive male sexuality is the status quo) and that she resisted. Since women are traditionally expected to monitor

Introduction

sexual activity, consent is inferred in the absence of definitive proof of force and resistance.[7]

In *Rape, Rage and Feminism in Contemporary American Drama*, I document the influence of societal forces in relation to gendered sexuality, violence, and rage, cultural attitudes about rape and raped women, as well as the influence of feminism on the depiction of rape in dramatic texts. Additionally, I explore the ways in which playwrights have participated in the efforts to transform our rape culture.

One

Second-Wave Feminism and Dramatizing Rape

Part One: Second-Wave Feminism

In the late 1960s and early 1970s, newly formed feminist organizations and public protests fueled the women's movement. Some of the first organizations were the National Organization for Women, NOW (1966); Women's International Terrorist Conspiracy from Hell, W.I.T.C.H. (1968); and Women Artists in Revolution, WAR (1969). Public protests during this time included the 1968 protest at the Miss America pageant in Atlantic City, at which over one hundred women threw items of domesticity, such as aprons, hair rollers, bras, and high heels, into a freedom trashcan; the 1969 storming of a bridal fair at Madison Square Garden by members of W.I.T.C.H., with chants of "Always a Bride, Never a Person"; and the 1970 Women's Strike for Equality. These organizations and events exemplify women's efforts to fight for equal rights and to disrupt widely held notions of female inferiority and passivity. Additionally, inspired in part by Betty Friedan's groundbreaking book, *The Feminine Mystique*, women recognized how the gendered division of labor, compulsory heterosexuality, and rigid standards of beauty functioned as societal forces designed to keep women controlled, docile, and silent. Whether society, patriarchy, or simply "just men" were identified as the problem, women's awareness of their marginalized status was due in part to these feminist organizations and their protests.

The women's liberation movement of the 1960s is referred to as second-wave feminism, with the first wave being a period of feminist activism in the late 19th and early 20th centuries. The feminist movement is not a single set of activist groups subscribing to similar beliefs.

It is more appropriate to speak of feminisms rather than feminism. Briefly, liberal feminism (the first activist movement of the mid- to late 20th century) sought to improve the status of women, fight for social and economic equality with men, and foster female empowerment and self-determination primarily through legislative reforms. Liberal feminists seek equality with men, and therefore do not highlight differences between the sexes. On the other hand, radical (also known as cultural) feminism sees women's oppression as rooted in the patriarchal domination of women, and rather than simply gain parity with men, radical feminists stress the superiority of female attributes and advocate for a separate female culture. This branch of feminism has been criticized for its premise that there is a fundamental female essence and that the main difference between men and women is their biological makeup. Materialist feminism (sometimes called Marxist or socialist feminism) minimizes the biological differences between the sexes and instead stresses that gender oppression is not the only material or historical condition worthy of examination; race, class, sexuality, and other forms of oppression must also be addressed. Material feminists seek a radical transformation of society to address these intertwined forces of oppression. Whereas radical feminism would emphasize the commonality between a white upper-class woman and an African American woman living in poverty, materialist feminism highlights the degree to which some women are triply or even quadruply oppressed by gender, race, class, and sexual orientation. Materialist feminists stress that "the advantages offered to white, upper-class, heterosexual women ... are purchased through the subjugation of women who are defined as outside that category. All women may be oppressed, but they are not equally oppressed" (Conboy 6).

Feminism's focus on rape emerged in the 1970s through consciousness-raising (CR) groups. These gatherings were effective methods for awakening feminist identification as communities of women joined in solidarity to share their experiences of victimization. Women realized the degree to which their personal problems had underlying social causes, rooted in potentially changeable power relations. Women's recognition that "the personal is political" paved the way toward greater activism, and fighting rape became part of the feminist agenda. As Jane

One: Second-Wave Feminism and Dramatizing Rape

Gerhard explains, "With the establishment of rape counseling hot lines, networks of battered women shelters, women's health centers, and abortion clinics across the country, feminists in the 1970s concretely politicized a range of what had previously been seen as private, and thus nonpolitical, aspects of women's sexual lives" (37).

Historically, women were viewed as male property and rape was treated as a crime against a women's father or husband. By the mid-twentieth century, this view was no longer overtly accepted; rather, it was customary to view rape as a violent attack by a deranged stranger and victims were often held responsible for their assault due to their risky behavior or underlying seething sexuality. When women, through their CR group conversations, realized that most of them had been affected by rape, rather than seeing it as a personal misfortune, rape was identified as a significant social problem, and many feminists linked sexual violence to an analysis of patriarchy. In her 1975 classic book *Against Our Will: Men, Women and Rape*, Susan Brownmiller contends that rape is violence not sex. The motivation for rape is not founded in sexual needs or urges, but rather in a desire on the part of men to dominate, control, and degrade women. "From prehistoric times," Brownmiller writes, "rape has played a critical function. It is nothing more or less than a conscious process of intimidation by which *all men* keep *all women* in a state of fear" (5).

Numerous scholars have observed the fluidity of rape's definition and concurrent historical implication, from a crime against a man (the raped woman's father or husband) to evidence of licentious impulses in women (most notably women of color) to the actions exclusively of mentally deranged men, to a means of social control of women whereby women's behavior is restricted due to the shadow of fear and intimidation embedded in a rape culture.[1] The view that rape is rooted in men's desire to control women through patriarchal power, and actual or threatened violence, rather than rooted in men's sexual desire was one of the primary revelations of second-wave feminism. Ultimately, rape became a political issue and beginning in the mid–1970s laws concerning rape were finally reformed, for example, removing the exception for spousal rape, broadening the definition of rape, lowering evidentiary burdens, and implementing of rape shield laws.

It is important to remember that in the early 1970s, at the same time women discovered the universality of sexual violence in CR groups, they were also experiencing the sexual revolution. Women's sexual desires and sexual fulfillment were accurately touted as being every bit as important as men's. However, with the availability of effective birth control, along with the "make love not war" mentality, women found it "politically incorrect" to refuse sexual invitations from comrades in the free love movement. While the sexual revolution announced a new day in social thinking and nonprocreative sexual enjoyment, as Imelda Whelehan notes, it did not instantly change "women's sexual identity or their power relationships with men." Women may have been "sold the idea of sex as liberation" but ultimately it left them with "new pressures to perform sexually at every occasion" (qtd. in Genz 58). Women ultimately began to wrestle with notions of consent and pressured or coerced sexual activity in which they may have felt pressured to participate.

Moving beyond the initial momentum of second-wave, politically active feminists, by the 1980s some women promoted an alternative view of rape—rather than rape being rooted in men's desire to control women through patriarchal power, and actual or threatened violence, rape was seen as existing at the far end of a continuum of heterosexual sex. In other words, they believed rape was sex not violence. Those who subscribe to this view argue that male aggression and female passivity are fundamental to socially constructed gender roles, in which a degree of coercion is considered normal, and dominance and submission are eroticized. "Sexual violence cannot be categorized away as violence not sex," argues Catherine MacKinnon, adding that male sexuality "centers on aggressive intrusion on those with less power. Such acts of dominance are experienced as sexually arousing, as sex itself" (*Feminist/Political* 66–67). Nicola Gavey notes rape was no longer "the deviant other to normal sex between a man and a woman; but something conceived as an always-possible potential within the very building blocks of ordinary sex." Rape in this definition was not rare; it actually "coexisted with a whole range of other forced [or pressured] sexual acts," and most of them, it turned out, "were committed by men at least known to, and often in a heterosexual relationship with, the women they abused" (*Just Sex* 34, 63). Ultimately by the 1990s, "normal" men, with whom women were acquainted, were recognized as potential rapists, and acquaintance, date, and marital nonconsensual sex were considered legitimate forms of rape.

Part Two: Second-Wave Theatrical Activism and Rape

In the early days of the anti-rape movement, feminist activists wanted to draw attention to the fact that rape was a social problem and additionally discredit the sexist victim-blaming attitudes circulating in society. Theatre practitioners were part of this movement. As early as the 1960s, theatre companies like the San Francisco Mime Troupe (1961), the Bread and Puppet Theatre (1962), and El Teatro Campesino (1965) sprang up seeking to politicize audience members by performing pieces about major forms of oppression. While these theatre companies shared a political sensibility with the women's liberation movement, their practices continued to be male-dominated, whether in their administrative hierarchical structures, or in terms of the subject matter of their plays. Finding this untenable, many women, radicalized by the women's liberation movement, established their own diverse theatre companies across the country. Usually, according to Elaine Aston, these women "organized their work democratically and non-hierarchically [and] sought to re-present women as subjects in their own right: to move women's issues, experiences and stories center stage" (*Feminist Theatre Practice* 6). Early feminist theatre groups included the New Feminist Theatre (1968), Women's Interart Center (1969), It's All Right to be a Woman Theatre Company (1970), the Westbeth Feminist Collective (1970), and the Alive and Trucking Theatre Company (1971). According to *Ms. Magazine*, by 1977 there were over fifty feminist theatre companies in the United States (qtd. in Leavitt, 21–22). Barbara Ozieblo reminds us that CR groups "used strategies borrowed from the theater to bring women to self-knowledge and self-esteem while converting their sessions into theatrical events which would eventually invade public spaces with performances" ("The Political," 15). This foundation led to scripts and performances that focused on women's value and strength, and allowed for unrestricted self-expression in a theatrical setting.

Rape, Rage and Feminism in American Drama

One of the first plays dealing with rape produced by a feminist theatre company was *Rape-in*, produced in 1970 by the Westbeth Feminist Collective. This company was started by members of a tenants' association set up to negotiate with the landlords at the Westbeth Artists Residence in New York City. Many association members were playwrights and they frequently presented staged readings of their plays. *Rape-in*, produced in 1971, consisted of a series of short plays performed in cabaret style, one of which was Dolores Walker's play *Abide in Darkness*, in which the post-rape trauma of the character Esther is examined. Charlotte Rae describes the production, noting how Esther, when visited by her new neighbor Ellen, exhibits "over-anxious behavior" saying, "I am sorry. I did not mean to be rude, asking who you were; but since IT happened, I am very careful." During the scene Esther keeps putting on more and more clothing until Ellen finds an excuse to leave (88). Esther's obsessive dressing can be interpreted as an indication of her traumatized state. This production was followed in 1972 by the Alive and Trucking Theatre Company's production of *Pig in a Blanket*. This play dealt with issues of sexual politics for both men and women. Audience members were often all female, or when mixed, male and female audience members sat separately. Dinah Leavitt describes the production, noting that scene five consisted of "a stylized enactment of a gang rape of one actress. The male-female segregated audience was usually quite moved, and at some performances the rape was halted by audience women" (35). Audience members were "overwhelming enthusiastic" about the production. "Women audience members were especially pleased to see issues relevant to them presented on the stage in an essentially woman-defined drama" (37). These theatrical productions, especially in the 1970s, encouraged political activism, stressing the political/social implications of rape.

The Rhode Island Feminist Theatre Company's production of *Persephone's Return* in 1974 (a theatrical piece that grew out of the collaborative writing efforts of company members) is another example of using theatre as a means of political expression. Date rape is among the important rape-related topics this play examines. While the term "date rape" appeared on a flyer for "speak-outs" on rape in 1974, and it was discussed in Brownmiller's 1975 book, it did not "carry over to the public agenda until the 1980s" and the term itself did not appear in a newspaper headline or lead paragraph until 1984 (Bevacqua, 154, 156). The reluctance to discuss date rape was also seen on college campuses as, according to Peggy Reeves Sanday, "in 1990 the subject of campus date and gang rape was virtually unknown" (*Fraternity* 199). *Persephone's Return* demonstrates the degree to which feminist theatre companies were on the cutting edge of anti-rape activism and public awareness campaigns.

Persephone's Return *(1974) by the Rhode Island Feminist Theatre Company*

Persephone's Return uses the myth of Demeter and Persephone to theatricalize how matriarchy was replaced by patriarchy. Additionally, the retelling of the myth is interspersed with modern scenes that demonstrate the oppressive effects of patriarchy on contemporary women. The play opens with a ritualized dance in praise of the Earth Mother, which serves as a "secret initiation and fertility rite" passed from mother Demeter to daughter Persephone (8). Hades comes from the underworld and by describing his loneliness easily convinces Zeus (Persephone's father) to let him kidnap Persephone. As the company writes in their introduction to the play, this action demonstrates a contemporary cultural practice, "men play a brief part in the life cycle; they remedied this by rape, abduction, separation and ownership (marriage). Men give their daughters away to men" (2). As soon as Hades abducts Persephone, who is screaming for her mother, the play immediately shifts to three short contemporary scenes involving Mr. Hadley, an older man who behaves inappropriately with Penthea, a junior high school girl; a Woman and a Rapist (the rapist is played by the same actor who plays Hades); and Hank and Seph, a couple on a date. During these three scenes, we watch Mr. Hadley engage in flirtatious conversation with Penthea, and ultimately grab her, kiss her and sneak his hand onto her breast; the Rapist attack the woman, throwing her to the ground as she screams; and Hank attempt to date rape Seph. These scenes demonstrate an attitude of male entitlement, described by Robert Golden and Fred Peterson as a perceived right "to sexualize women," and to expect "sex if they have paid for something, if women kiss or touch them or otherwise lead them on" combined with a belief that "being in a romantic relationship entitles them to sex whenever they want it" (101). Seph struggles and is ultimately able to free herself from Hank's aggressive embraces, but his intentions are clear in the scene.

After these scenes the Rapist puts on the mask of Hades, indicating not only Hades' rape of Persephone, but also the continuance of sexual violence against women since that time. The play continues with the reenactment of the myth interspersed with other modern-day scenes, including Hal, who can't understand why his wife Petra is more interested in finishing her book than having sex with him. He feels unappreciated, and ultimately forces his wife to have sex with him when she is clearly unwilling. Only one of the rape scenes from the play depicted the conventional view of rape at the time—in other words, an attack by a violent stranger. The variety of other scenes of sexual assault or harassment in this play revealed to the audience what women in their CR

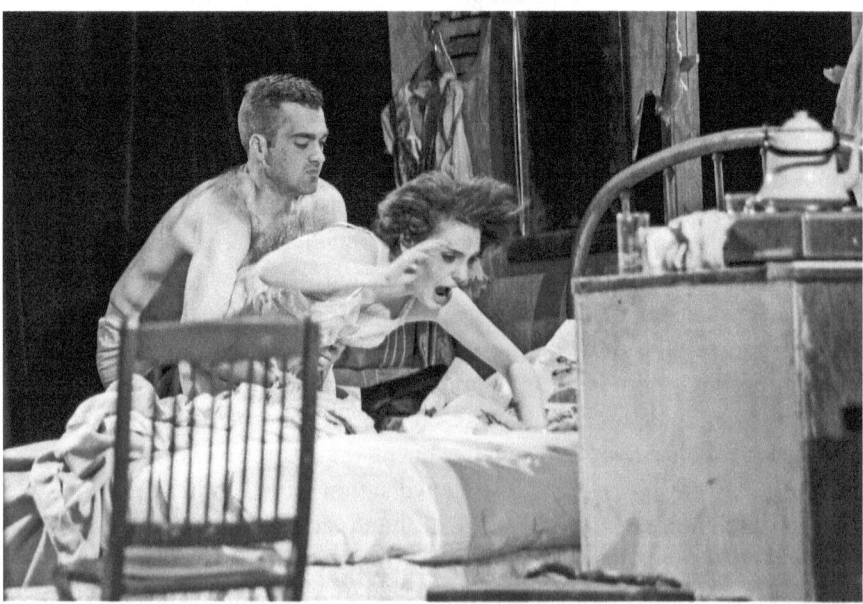

Tye date rapes Jane in the Raven Theatre's 2014 production of *Vieux Carré*, directed by Cody Estle. Featuring Joel Reitsma as Tye and Eliza Stoughton as Jane (photograph by Dean La Prairie).

groups had come to realize, the prevalence of rape in many different forms.

While not in the headlines until 1984, many dramatists depicted rape within a relationship much earlier. Some of these were by well-known playwrights, produced for a more mainstream audience than those produced by feminist theatre companies. For example, Tennessee Williams's 1978 play *Vieux Carré* includes a scene between Jane and her live-in lover Tye. She has made it very clear that she is not interested in sex, when he "*grasps her arm and draws her to bed*." She screams "no" repeatedly and he says "yes" and "*throws her onto the bed and starts to strip her; she resists; he prevails*" (85–86). In their next scene she says clearly, "You forced me, you little pig, you did, you forced me." Tye callously replies, "You wanted it" (96). Another example is Ntozake Shange's 1975 choreopoem, *For Colored Girls who have Considered Suicide When the Rainbow is Enuf,* which opened on Broadway in 1976, which includes an explicit discussion of date rape. The women in the play, each indicated by the color of their dress (blue, red, purple, etc.), tell the audience, "a friend is hard to press charges against/if you know him you must have wanted it." They state that a legitimate rapist must be "a stranger" and "someone you never saw/a man wit obvious problems." But, they stress, "The nature of rape has changed." And along with it, the nature of rapists, "we can now meet them in circles we frequent for companionship/we see them at the coffeehouse/wit someone else we know/we cd even have em over for dinner & get raped in our own houses" (17–21). Long before date rape was in the headlines, playwrights depicted/discussed this frequent form of sexual assault in their plays.

In an interview with Neal Lester, Shange suggests that child molestation and rape "have to become as heinous to us as lynching was; we have to understand them as political crimes.... Violence in domestic relationships is *not* an option!" Violence against women "should in fact be considered treason" (722, 726). In her play *boogie woogie landscapes* (1978), Shange includes a group of characters who are the nightlife companions of Layla, an "all american colored girl." These nightlife companions ponder the condition of women's safety in the face of rape. "What are they gonna do," they ask, "take the windows & doors from our houses/leave us lil boxes no man can enter for fear of electrocution/

bar us from the streets?" Remarking on the lack of interest in solving the problem or public attention given to rape, they proceed to list several alternatives to be considered in hopes of focusing attention on the issue of rape. Included in these options are the idea that all men should be "sent to new jersey" or send men to Cuba and they could "come back with stories about how the yng women in cuba walk abt with no fear in their streets" and let people know there is "no rape in cuba" or insist that self-defense classes are "offered free by the state" and "every convicted rapist must be in a parade thru times square." Additionally, the companions request that "all women who died or who demonstrated remarkable courage & integrity during rape attacks are given congressional medals of honor, or the purple heart," shouting "EXTRA EXTRA/ READ ALL ABOUT IT." However, the nightlife companions continue "(*confidentially to the audience*) the ny times has never asked me what I think abt a goddamn thing" (123–124). While the alternative options are at times comical in Shange's piece, the disenfranchisement of women, particularly women of color, is profoundly serious.

Even though well-known playwrights such as Williams and Shange have had plays involving rape produced in large venues, most of the political, social-activist plays about rape have been produced by small theatre companies or groups of students, often performed on college campuses where date and acquaintance rape was (and is) a significant problem. These activist plays, which have continued to be produced past the era of second-wave feminism, often have an educational focus, seeking to use theatre as a way to provoke discussion, and alter behavior. In 1981, for example, the Other Theatre Company, based in Madison, Wisconsin, wrote and toured the play *Obadiah's Image: The Training of a Rapist*. This piece, which focused on the social messages and cultural myths about rape that serve to train a man to be a rapist, will be discussed in the next chapter. In 1992, Carolyn Levy worked with her students at Macalester College in Minnesota to develop and subsequently perform a series of short pieces about violence against women entitled, *Until Someone Wakes Up*. Levy writes, "If I looked hard at the society and culture in which we are living, if I really examined forces at work on our students as they grow up, then the rape statistics were not a surprise. The climate is ripe for such things to happen" (229). In one of the

One: Second-Wave Feminism and Dramatizing Rape

short pieces, there is an interchange between a mother and her son, who are speaking the words to a familiar nursery rhyme: "Georgie Porgie, pudding and pie, kissed the girls and made them cry!" After which a narrator says, "One in twelve of the male students surveyed had committed acts that met the legal definition of rape or attempted rape" (230). Another sequence included this conversation between a waiter and customer:

> WAITER. Would you like some coffee?
> WOMAN. Yes, please.
> WAITER. Just say when. (*Starts to pour*)
> WOMEN. There. (*He keeps pouring*) That's fine. (*He pours*) Stop! (*She grabs the pot; there is coffee everywhere.*) What are you doing? I said stop.
> WAITER. Yes, ma'am.
> WOMAN. Well, why didn't you stop pouring?
> WAITER. Oh, I wasn't sure you meant it.
> WOMAN. Look, of course I meant it! I have coffee all over my lap! You nearly burned me!
> WAITER. Forgive me, ma'am, but you certainly looked thirsty. I thought you wanted more.
> WOMAN. But—
> WAITER. And you must admit, you did let me *start* to pour.
> WOMAN. Well, of course I did. I wanted some coffee.
> WAITER. See, there you go. A perfectly honest mistake [232–233].

This comical interaction is an absurdist parallel to date-rape situations in which men claim they simply misunderstand women's attempts to say "no." *Until Someone Wakes Up* had a profound impact on audience members, not unlike the experience women had 20 years earlier in their consciousness-raising groups. "We thought we were prepared for the response," Levy notes, "but we were amazed at the outpouring of emotion from spectators. They greeted the play with joy and pain. For some, it reaffirmed that they were not alone in their experiences" (233).

Other noteworthy examples of anti-rape awareness being promoted through a dramatic text include Amy Seham's play *One Night at Alta Bates*, which was developed and performed in 1993 at the University of California Berkeley campus; Eve Ensler's *The Vagina Monologues* (1996), one of the most effective theatrical productions aimed at raising awareness about and funds to combat violence against women and which continues to be produced every year, both on college campuses and in more professional venues; and Sound Off Theatre's performances at the College at Brockport, part of the State University of New York system, which uses theatre to educate college students about rape. During their freshman orientation, incoming students see performance pieces about date rape and other important issues for college students, such as eating disorders, suicide, and binge drinking. These performances serve as a catalyst for discussion among students on these important issues. Maine-based Add Verb Productions tours widely with Cathy Plourde's play about dating violence, *You the Man*, which "uses live theatre to empower students—both male and female—to step out of the bystander role and practice safe peer interventions."[2]

Finally, Nicole Quinn's short one-act play (2007) *Information* is typical of these educational performances geared toward college audiences. In this short piece we are introduced to several college students who have experienced some form of sexual abuse. Among them, Kelly was assaulted in her dorm bathroom, Jenna was given a date-rape drug and subsequently raped by an upperclassman who was supposed to be showing the freshmen around, Dave was forced to have oral sex with another man during a fraternity hazing, and Pilar was fondled by her professor. Ultimately, these students speak out about their victimization and suggest ways colleges can "acknowledge and confront the reality of harassment, abuse, and assault on their own campuses" (*Information* 58).

Beginning in the era of second-wave feminism, depictions of rape in dramatic texts served to reinforce the awareness women gained in their CR groups about the political and social implications of sexual violence and the need to transform our rape culture and eradicate the rape script. This kind of theatrical activism has continued into the twenty-first century. One of the features all of these activist productions share is a commitment to highlighting the prevalence of myths about rape and raped women in our culture.

Two

Rape Myths and Rapists

According to researchers, a strong belief in cultural myths about rape and raped women is a characteristic many rapists have in common, so it is not surprising that most of the rapist characters in contemporary American dramas demonstrate a belief in these myths.[1] While I have separated these two issues in this chapter, their connections are significant. It is important to note, however, that a belief in rape myths exists throughout American society, not just among rapists, and the same is true for numerous characters in American dramas, rapist and non-rapist characters alike.

Part One: Rape Myths

The term "myth," as Joanna Bourke explains, "does not simply connote 'untruth.' Rather, the use of the word 'myth' is a shorthand way of referring to a structure of meaning permeating a particular culture.... [Myths] create unified communities by clarifying positions and transforming commonplace assumptions into objective truths" (24). Myths about rape, raped women, and rapists, when widely accepted, can change unsubstantiated suppositions into widely held beliefs.

Martha Burt was one of the first to use and define the term "rape myth" in her 1980 article, "Cultural Myths and Supports for Rape." Initially, Burt defined rape myths as "prejudicial, stereotyped, or false beliefs about rape, rape victims, and rapists" that create a "climate hostile to rape victims" (217). By 1991 researchers and the public were well aware of the statistics on acquaintance and date rape, and Burt refined the definition to include the awareness that "rape myths have the effect of denying that many instances involving coercive sex are actually rapes." Burt stressed the cultural foundations of rape myths, noting that they are spread in the same manner that people "acquire other attitudes and beliefs—from, their families, their friends, newspapers, movies, books, dirty jokes, and, lately, rock videos" ("Rape Myths," 26, 28). Dramatic texts can likewise participate in spreading the acceptance of rape myths. It is disheartening to realize, as research on cultural myths about rape reveals, the degree to which belief in these myths has persisted. It may have been in 1980 that Martha Burt first documented the fact that many Americans accepted rape myths as truths, but Sarah McMahon's research in 2010 demonstrates the continued acceptance of rape myths. McMahon notes that "victim-blaming beliefs still persist as well as [beliefs] excusing the perpetrator" (9).

Since 1980 researchers have identified several myths that pertain to raped women. These myths can be grouped into the following five major categories:

- Nothing happened, no harm was done.
    It is impossible to rape women who resist an attack. A woman with her skirt up runs faster than a man with his trousers down. A raped woman might as well relax and enjoy it.
- Women lie about being raped.
    Women "cry rape" to cover up an unwanted pregnancy or to get back at men who have jilted them or refused their advances. Women lie about rape when they regret consensual sex after the fact.
- Women invite it, want it, and like it.
    Women never mean no. Her mouth says "no" but her eyes say "yes." Women have an unconscious rape wish.
- Women deserve to be raped.
    Women put themselves in bad situations by dressing a certain way, drinking alcohol, or flirting with men. If you let a man into your apartment, or go to his apartment on the first date you are "asking for it." Women who walk in the wrong part of town at night are "asking for trouble."
- Rape only happens to certain women.
    Only bad girls get raped.
    If she was raped, she must have done something to bring it on, she must be a "bad girl."[2]

Two: Rape Myths and Rapists

I have identified an additional myth that applies to raped women, the myth that raped women are contaminated. This myth of contamination is evident in the testimony of raped women, as well as in plays involving rape.[3] In some instances, a raped woman may in fact contract a sexually transmitted disease due to a rape, as in Bruce Norris' play *The Pain and the Itch*, in which Kalina, acquired a "sickness" when soldiers raped her as a young girl, and therefore she was quite *literally* contaminated. However, for the most part, the impression that raped women are contaminated is actually *figurative*, and it is a powerful myth that has an impact on the self-image of raped women and on how they are perceived by others. As one raped woman said, "When I realized he was gone, I wanted to pour Lysol all over me. I wanted to be cleansed" (qtd. in Russell, *Politics of Rape*, 19). In many cultures, including our own, raped women are often considered impure or spoiled goods. In a theatrical context this myth of contamination, combined with the other myths I've listed, serve to increase the shame and humiliation often exhibited by characters who have been raped. Additionally, these myths increase the tendency of other characters to blame raped female characters for their attack, as well as the tendency of raped women to blame themselves. Charlotte Canning attests that "women who were raped were made to feel responsible by society.... The attitude was reinforced by making rape something shameful so that women did not dare voice their experiences" (152). This silence based on numerous rape myths contributes to the under reporting of rape.

Researchers have also identified the following myth that pertains to rapists:

- Male sexuality is an uncontrollable physical force.
    Rape is a result of uncontrollable male passions. Men can't control their sexual urges. Rapists are sex-starved, insane, or both.[4]

This last myth allows men to feel "entitled to sex" due to these "uncontrollable" needs. Even Ann Landers, in a 1991 letter entitled "A Male's Theory on Date Rape," wrote:

> The problem is that for many men, there is only one way to end arousal and that is ejaculation. At the height of ecstasy, does the female partner

> think the man is going to excuse himself, go … and take a cold shower? No way. He *wants the final act*.… If the female partner has made up her mind that there is NOT going to be penetration, she should put a stop to the proceedings at the very first sign of male arousal. A female who doesn't want the total sexual experience should have healthy respect for a flashing warning light. [A woman who] agrees to hours of petting but does not want to complete the sex act is asking for trouble and she will probably get it [qtd. in Bourke, 440].

In other words, men are simply victims of their irrepressible sex organs and women who tempt them get what they are asking for. This myth of uncontrollable male sexuality was perpetuated in the movie *There's Something about Mary*, albeit in the service to the movie's comic genre, when Dom (played by Chris Elliott) advises his friend Ted (Ben Stiller) to "clean the pipes" before going on a date with Mary (Cameron Diaz). "It's like going out there with a loaded gun," Dom warns. Song lyrics as well perpetuate this myth. Myriam Miedzian remarks that lyrics "by the heavy metal group Poison, which reached number three on the Billboard pop charts and sold over two million copies, include lines like "I want action tonight.… I need it hot and I need it fast. If I can't have her, I'll take her and make her" (*Boys*, 158).

While the myth of uncontrollable male sexuality may justify a sexually aggressive act in the mind of the rapist, women also believe this rape myth. Many women who have been subjected to date and acquaintance rape discuss the fact that they have allowed nonconsensual sex to take place because they were told, and in fact believed, that they had aroused their partner past the point of no return, and that it would be unfair, and unwise, to ask him to stop. This sentiment is also expressed by female characters in contemporary American dramas.[5]

Rape Myths in Dramatic Texts

The degree to which rape myths permeate our society is illustrated in contemporary American dramas, as virtually all the plays about rape in this study include lines indicating that some of the characters believe these cultural myths. However, in a significant majority of the plays either the raped female character disputes these myths or other characters have lines which serve to discredit the rape myths that are articulated in the dramas. In relation to rape myths, it appears that characters in dramas over the past forty years have, for the most part, been actively refuting widely held beliefs about rape, raped women, and rapists. I will begin, however, with examples of texts in which the characters exhibit a belief in rape myths.

Extremities (1978) by William Mastrosimone

Extremities is an example of a play in which certain characters believe some of the widely accepted rape myths. In this play, the character Marjorie has successfully thwarted an attempted rape, but her roommates, Terry and Patricia, clearly believe she asked for it based on the provocative way she dresses. Terry complains, "Every time I'd have a guy over, I'd have to shout in to see if you're decent." Patricia agrees with her, stating, "You parade around this house like it was a centerfold, ... and then you complain about the advances you provoke" (82). Even the would-be rapist Raul admits that that it was Marjorie's sexy clothing that caught his attention in the first place. This common rape myth blames the raped woman for her assault because men cannot control their "natural" impulses when in the presence of such a provocatively dressed female.

In the play, we learn that Terry was raped as a teenager. She was at a Halloween party wearing a Tinkerbell costume "one size too small." Her girlfriend's father agreed to drive her home, and taking what he said was a shortcut, he raped her in a cemetery. Terry insists, because of her outfit, that "it was all my fault." When she arrived home, without her skirt, her father called her a whore. Terry herself excuses her rapist when she says, "Maybe they just need to do that sometimes, men" (40). While Terry did not consent to have sex with the father of her girlfriend, she believed that he couldn't control himself. She blames herself for arousing him to the point where his sexuality was uncontrollable and he had no choice but to rape her.

Twice Shy (1989) by Debra Neff

Belief in the myth that women can lead men on to the point that they can't control their sexual urges can result in women reluctantly consenting to sex. This is the case in Debra Neff's 1989 play *Twice Shy*, whose protagonist Louise had been raped two years prior to the events of the play at a fraternity party. Louise confesses that the only reason she agreed to have sex with her new potential love interest, Steven, after their first date was because she "didn't want to seem like a tease" (148). I am not arguing that Steven in this instance should be categorized as a rapist, but rather that by this admission, Louise not only demonstrates the power of the myth that men, once aroused can't, and shouldn't be asked to control themselves, but also that Louise's sentiments are evidence of the gray areas between consensual sex, un-expressed reluctant nonconsensual sex, and rape. Louise's experiences are not unique. Sarah Walker notes women consenting "to unwanted sex is not a rare phenomenon, as some studies report that more than two-thirds of sexually active college women have at least once consented to intercourse they did not really want" (157).

The Rape of Emma Bunche (1987) by Jules Tasca

A play that perpetuates the myth that women lie when they accuse men of rape is *The Rape of Emma Bunche*. Kira Cochrane reports, "Recent research on this subject puts the number of false allegations in rape cases at 3 per cent—the same proportion you would expect to find in any crime." However, in other crimes victims are not accused of lying, "No one talks of people 'crying burglary' or 'crying mugging' and yet the term 'cry rape' is firmly established and featured in countless tabloid headlines last year. When it comes to rape, the perspective that 'women lie' is ingrained in our culture" (23). *The Rape of Emma Bunche* is one of eight pieces that comprise the full-length play, *The God's Honest: An Evening of Lies*. In this play Emma invites Malcolm to her home in order to apologize for her past behavior. She had recently accused him of raping her and he was arrested and sent to jail. The next day, Emma told the judge that she had "overreacted" when she "used the word rape" and Malcolm was released (13). In the play, Tasca presents two totally different versions of the events. According to Emma, Malcolm did in fact rape her, but she felt sorry for him and therefore lied to the judge when she said he did not rape her. According to Malcolm, the sex was consensual. When Emma says that Malcolm "got carried away," he admits that he was excited, but that he "had some help." Emma replies, "Who told you to get so excited. You tore my blouse," adding, "I didn't want to have sex. You forced yourself on me" (10–11). She insists that she said "no," and that she "told him to stop," but Malcolm replies, "When a guy's in ecstasy he doesn't even hear a bomb going off, Emma; you could level a city and he wouldn't hear" (13). Max blames Emma because he believes, like Ann Landers, that men are unable to stop once they reach a certain level of excitement, and therefore a woman who is not willing to proceed to the logical outcome and "leads him on" is ultimately to blame if he proceeds without her consent. Max is depicted as a character who clearly believes in the power of uncontrollable male sexuality.

But things take a turn when, following Emma's apology, Malcolm is about to leave and Emma begins to kiss him. She tells him that her parents are away and won't be back until the next day. They move to the couch where things get more passionate. All the while, Emma is sending mixed signals. At the same time that she is kissing him, she also says, "Leave my sweater alone, Malcolm. I really don't want you to do this to me." And yet she immediately says, "Kiss me again." The play ends with Emma saying, "Malcolm, no, you're tickling me." The stage directions indicate that she begins to laugh while repeatedly saying, "No, Malcolm" (16–17). While the ending leaves open the possibility that Emma may have actually lied about being raped, this short piece demonstrates the ways in which mixed signals and miscommunication can be precipitating factors in date and acquaintance rape. Nonetheless, the myths that women lie about being raped, and that men can't control their sexual urges, are communicated loudly and clearly in this play.[6]

From thinking that women invite rape via their wardrobe, or lie about being raped, or that male sexuality is uncontrollable, characters in many dramas take rape myths as truths, much like (as research demonstrates) some of the general population. Fortunately, as stated above, the majority of plays involving rape contain characters who actively refute these myths.

Contesting Rape Myths

In many instances (including some of the plays already mentioned), playwrights actively contest culturally accepted rape myths. When a character in a play indicates that they believe a rape myth, and other characters refute the myth, an alternative point of view is presented. As the following examples from four selected plays will demonstrate, playwrights, for the most part, appear to be actively contesting cultural myths about rape.

Obadiah's Image: The Training of a Rapist (1981) by the Other Theatre Company

Members of the Other Theatre Company, based in Wisconsin, worked together to create the play *Obadiah's Image: The Training of a Rapist*. This play dramatizes the multitude of cultural forces that facilitate rape, including various characters' belief in numerous rape myths. The issues discussed in this 1981 drama have persisted. In 1990 Peggy Reeves Sanday researched fraternity gang rape, concluding, "Guys can't be who they are but must cast themselves in the image of the sexually successful male who 'scores'" (*Fraternity* 218). Mark Moss observes in his book *The Media and Models of Masculinity*, written in 2011, thirty years after the play was written, that "enormous pressure still resonates within society for men and boys to exhibit what are often termed traditional masculine qualities" (xv). This mandate for socially determined masculine behavior, including the requirement for sexual success, is highlighted in the drama.

During the play, the main character, Obadiah, who is stuck in a dead-end waiter job, rapes Elizabeth—another server at the restaurant—after they go to a concert together. Obadiah tells Elizabeth that they will be going as "friends, just friends" and prior to agreeing to go with him, Elizabeth confirms "just friends, right?" (27). Nonetheless, due to the numerous cultural messages Obadiah has received about gender roles, he expects more from her than platonic friendship. Many of these messages are communicated through jokes the male characters in the play share, which serve to create the atmosphere in which treating women

Two: Rape Myths and Rapists

as sexual objects is acceptable. Among the cultural messages and rape myths this play exposes are images of gendered sexuality in the media and the myth that women want to be raped.

The play begins with offstage voices chanting numerous rape myths, for example, "the way she was dressed," "she asked for it," "men have needs," and "boys will be boys" (1–2). The play contains several parodies of TV shows and commercials, and while they are humorous, they also effectively demonstrate how the media is complicit in perpetuating rape myths and images of aggressive male sexuality. For example, there is a parody of a cowboy/western TV show in which the villainous bad guy who has abducted Chastity, the innocent heroine, ignores her demands that he stop, and her cries for help. He says, as he continues to hold her down, "Relax… I know just what you need… You'll like this… I know how to take care of a lady… Trust me." When the masked hero rescues our heroine, as he is untying her he also says (with intentional irony), "Just trust me. Relax. I know just what you need. You'll like this. I know how to take care of a lady. Trust me" (3–4).

There is also a mock preview for the movie *Sabine Love Slaves*, which the announcer tells us is a "story of war and its rewards." Sextulus and his soldiers conquer the Sabine men and then abduct their women. The women are depicted as enjoying their attack, swooning at the feet of the conquering heroes, as the announcer says, "They didn't return because they were slaves, and they loved it." The Sabine men refer to their raped women as "soiled" and "whores" (24–25). The very next scene, titled "Obadiah Masturbates," involves an enactment of the images in Obadiah's head, including a Macho Voice repeating, "Get it. Get it. Get it. Hips, hips, ass, tit." and a Caveman voice chanting, "Grab it. Grab it. Have it, Have it. Hips, hips, ass, tit. Grab it, take it, feels so good." All the while the Sabine women surround Obadiah saying, "So good. Feels so good. So good. Obe has got the power" (25–26).

Given these cultural forces, it comes as no surprise that Obadiah repeats these sentiments when, as he drives Elizabeth home after their concert "date," he traps her in the car. He tells her she is "really very beautiful." When she protests and insists that he take her home he says, "Don't talk. Don't ruin the moment…. Everything's all right. There's no need to be up tight." He feels he deserves at least a kiss, after all, "I know you like me. So just relax." When she refuses his advances, he says, "Quit acting so innocent. Come on—I saw you in those jeans." The stage directions note that he "*pushes Elizabeth down on the car seat. Holding her down with one hand, he unbuckles his belt with the other*" (38-39).

The final scene returns to the cast chanting the same rape myths that were chanted in the opening scene. Elizabeth repeatedly stresses that Obadiah raped her. He insists that he didn't, "We were on a date... You were asking for it... You loved it." In one last bid to maintain his innocence, Obadiah says, "It's not my fault. It's their fault. It's what they taught me. How was I to know?" (40). As the play's title suggests, rape myths that are ingrained in our society, influencing men's behavior, contribute to the "training" of potential rapists.

We Keep Our Victims Ready (1989) by Karen Finley

Performance artist Karen Finley's work, as Stephen Watt and Gary Richardson observe "continually interrogates society's devaluation and persistent victimization of women," including exposing some of society's myths about rape and rape victims (1026). In *We Keep Our Victims Ready*, Finley exposes both the widely held attitudes that women deserve and want to be raped, and the sense of contamination that remains after a rape. "Everyone says I deserved it—I'm a hussy. I'm a tramp. I'm a whore—'cause I wear lipstick? Work at nights? And drink bourbon straight?" She then voices the raped woman's anger, "When I said NO you didn't listen to me. When I said NO, You fucked me anyway... When I said NO I wasn't playing hard to get. And I never meant yes." Ultimately, the need to be cleansed is articulated by the character, "You raped me. I took a shower, a hot one, but I couldn't get clean—his sweat, his semen, his skin smells near—another bath another shower... I just cried—I just cried" (1039).

One Night at Alta Bates (1993) by Amy Seham

One Night at Alta Bates describes Michelle Langdon's experiences after having been raped at gunpoint. In this play several characters clearly believe cultural myths about rape. For example, after the attack

Two: Rape Myths and Rapists

Michelle goes to the emergency room with her friend Jane. Two other women in need of the emergency room, Jamie and Sissy, arrive later and see from the list of patients that there is a rape victim waiting to be seen. They try to guess which woman in the waiting room is the raped woman, and pick out Michelle, "not very pretty" they say, adding, "She might have changed her clothes or something. Tried to dress down before reporting it to the police." They go on to gossip about a mutual acquaintance, Connie, who accused their friend Jack of rape, "It's ridiculous." Sissy laughs, "If she didn't want it what was she doing in his room?" (7). Seham's depiction of these two characters shows that they too believe several rape myths, for example, women lie about being raped, women ask for it, and that women invite rape by their wardrobe choices. Additionally, the security guard at the hospital believes that women have rape fantasies, and wonders if raped women actually "enjoy it" (28).

Ultimately, an alternative point of view is presented through Michelle's vivid description of her sexual assault, as well as through the dialogue of other characters, such as the admitting nurse, Manuela, who supports Michelle and refutes rape myths when they are articulated by others. When another nurse, Scott, admits that he doesn't think Michelle was raped because she didn't looked stressed, Manuela counters saying, "People react differently to different things," and that Michelle "probably hasn't even started dealing with it yet" (37–38).

Through the course of the play Michelle's friend Jane realizes that a sexual encounter she had in the past may have actually been rape. Jane was twenty-one at the time and a virgin. She brought a man back to her room, and while initially she admits, "I was so inexperienced—and he was doing a lot of really sensual stuff that was kind of scary and exciting," she admits that when he became more aggressive, she "really got scared." She said no, and she pushed him away, but he continued (39). From the rapist's point of view, according to Irina Anderson and Kahy Doherty, he may have been "merely treating the woman's resistance as part of 'natural' courtship behavior." And for the raped woman, the "problem, she will be told [is] therefore with her—with her perception of the events or with her inability to communicate clearly enough that her resistance was real and not 'feigned'" (7). Furthermore, in terms of the rape myth that women deserve to be raped, whether a woman invites a man into her residence, or goes into his, the message is clear, as Kellie Bean contends in her discussion of the Kobe Bryant rape accusation, "Like the refrain of a bad song, we heard the same question repeated over and over again: "What did she think was going to happen?"—as if her mere presence in a man's hotel room meant rape was inevitable and excused anything Bryant may have done to harm her" (157).

Jane, in reliving the event, confronts the line between rape and seduction, unsure where her experience falls. She feels responsible, admitting that she "had taken him all the way up into my bedroom." But, she stresses, "I said no and I never said yes. And I was pulling back and pushing—pushing him… But I still am not sure—in my own mind… I feel as if I don't know if I get the badge. You know, my girl scout, 'I've been raped' badge" (39). Jane finally accepts that she should not blame herself for the assault, but the degree to which she nonetheless harbors feelings of self-blame are a testimony of her own acceptance of rape myths.

In *One Night at Alta Bates*, Amy Seham has created a variety of characters, some articulate rape myths, some refute them, and others, like Jane, struggle with their own tendency to accept cultural myths about rape and raped women.

Information (2007) by Nicole Quinn

Finally, *Information* provides an example of a play with several scenes in which characters articulate cultural myths about rape, which are subsequently contested. Max, a student accused of rape by a woman he plied with alcohol-filled jello shots, accepts rape myths and insists: "Women lie about being raped all the time," and his friend Sammy agrees, "You can tell she wanted it." Even the raped female students in the play blame themselves and refuse to acknowledge that their attacks could be defined as rapes. Ashley says, "I wanted to be with him, I wanted to hook up, I just didn't want to go that far … it was my fault … I was drinking" (54; ellipses in orig.).

Despite the fact that many characters in this play accept rape myths, Donna, a peer counselor who was herself raped when she was fourteen, presents an effective counter-argument with the help of a Mad Scientist character (complete with Freudian accent) who spouts frequently held rape myths. For example, "Ze rapist is oversexed, committing his crime on impulse und out of uncontrollable passion," and "Ze victim provokes ze attack, or asks for it, or should have known better zan to do something zat would illicit zis behavior. She is somevhat at fault" (55–56). Donna successfully refutes these and other rape myths and ultimately the students insist that changes be made on campus to transform the status quo.

The previous discussion of rape myths as depicted in American dramas shows the extent to which rape myths are taken as truths by numerous characters; the mere fact that virtually every play includes characters who accept rape myths speaks to the prevalence of such beliefs. But to the credit of the playwrights, almost every play includes characters who dispute these myths. What does stand out is the fact that the rapist characters in these plays invariably believe rape myths, and as I previously mentioned, researchers have documented the connection between rape myth acceptance in men and the likelihood that they will (or have already) committed a sexual assault. The depiction of the rapist character in contemporary American dramas reveals a great deal about our imaginative impressions of men who rape.

Part Two: Rapists

A rape-supportive culture, in which rape myths are prevalent and widely believed, gives rise to generation after generation of potential and actual rapists. Rape can be thought of as a learned behavior, and we see the results of this learning process in many American dramas. Socially constructed definitions of masculinity and gendered sexuality, with a focus on male aggression and female passivity, allows for scenes of seduction that include coercive sexual activity and silent acquiescence to be interpreted as consent. This can be seen as a logical outcome in a society that views male domination and female submission as characteristic of erotic encounters.

There appears to be an active debate among scholars and researchers about the true nature of rapists. On the one hand, some subscribe to the belief that rapists are pathologically unstable, due in part to their upbringing—for example, having been sexually abused as a child—and that they do not belong in any category of "normal" males.[7] Rapists in this model are more likely to fit the stranger-in-a-dark-alley version of rape. On the other hand, some researchers argue that most rapists are in fact "normal" men, who may exhibit enhanced aggressive sexuality, but who are not in any way deranged or mentally unstable.[8] Since the 1970s feminist activists and theorists have worked to focus attention from the former to the latter point of view. This can be attributed to the increased awareness over the past forty years of date, acquaintance, and spousal rape. The tendency to pathologize rapists may be due to the fact that incarcerated rapists are the main source of data for researchers, a population that may not represent the majority of date and acquaintance rapists. "Evidence indicates," as Diana Scully and Joseph Marolla note, "that rape is not a behavior confined to a few sick men, but [rather that] many men have the attitudes and beliefs necessary to commit a sexually aggressive act" (59). In fact, close to 80 percent of raped women are acquainted with their rapists.[9]

This debate about the true nature of rapists in no way minimizes the role mental health practitioners can play in efforts to eliminate rape, but as Scully and Marolla point out, psychopathological models used to explain rape and rapists behavior that are based primarily on atypical rapists, inform the public's view and this "leads one to view sexual violence as a special type of crime in which the motivations are subconscious and uncontrollable rather than overt and deliberate as with other criminal behavior" (58–61). Consequently, with the psychopathological model, the primary focus becomes treatment of the individual offender rather than a focus on the broader social and cultural forces that facilitate rape itself.

Most American playwrights appear to agree with the opinion that rapists do not have a psychopathological condition, since only a small percentage of contemporary American dramas have a pathologically sick or deranged rapist character. In fact, most contemporary dramas highlight the numerous cultural forces that perpetuate the attitudes and beliefs that are necessary to commit a sexually aggressive act, for example, the acceptance of rape myths, gendered sexuality, and the social construction of masculinity. Rape in these plays cannot be easily categorized as simply violence, power, or sex. In fact, the multifaceted depiction of the rapist characters speaks to the complexity of motivations involved in an act of rape. Additionally, many dramatic texts portray situations in which the rape of a female character has nothing to do with the raped woman, but is in fact about the relationship between the male characters in the drama.

Dramatizing Rapists: Rape and Relationships Among Men

Bovver Boys (1990) by Willy Holtzman

Bovver Boys depicts the rape of a young woman that is actually motivated by the relationships among the *men* in the play. The play is set in 1970 in Dundee, Scotland. The protagonist, Gene Biddle, is an American conscious objector who has been assigned to work at a community center for his alternative service. He encounters a gang of Scottish skinheads, the Suedes, who frequently "bovver" (a Scottish term for rumble) with a rival gang, the Shams. The young men are all about to turn eighteen and their limited life choices are closing in on them. These choices are joining the army, drinking away their welfare checks, or working at some thankless job. The play explores the impact of an endless cycle of poverty and violence on this community, especially among the young men and women.

Early in the play, Gene learns of a forthcoming brawl between the two gangs and takes it upon himself to teach the boys about non-violent conflict resolution and somehow prevent the bovver from taking place. Gene befriends the leader of the Suedes, Allie, and says that if Allie were to give up the gang, he could take over Gene's job at the community center when Gene's alternative service is done. Christine, Allie's girlfriend, offers to find out the location of the upcoming fight, in hopes that Gene can alert the police and prevent the violence. But as she approaches the Shams' territory, Christine is beaten and raped, although she does not reveal the fact that she was raped until later in the play.

Christine claims that she doesn't know who did it, but she assumes that it was a member of the Shams. "It was dark, and I was alone," she explains to Joyce, the secretary at the community center. Christine blames herself for the attack. "Maybe I wasna paying close enough attention to where I was.... I tried to get away. Maybe I didna try hard enough." Her shame, humiliation, and sense of being contaminated is evident in the scene, and she insists to Joyce that she won't tell anyone else what happened. This is not uncommon, as a student of Peggy Reeves Sanday admits, "Most incidents go unreported because of shame, no one wants to deal with it, some people are afraid to admit that they were actually abused.... One-fourth of my friends have been raped, assaulted, violated in some way" (qtd. in Sanday, *Fraternity*, 213). It is easier for Christine to let people believe whatever they want about the attack, rather than reveal the truth of her rape.

Joyce understands the gang mentality and wants to help Christine. Joyce explains, "It's one thing if you're beat. If you're beat, you're a hero. But if you're done, you're a whore. That's how they see it." Christine insists that she is not a whore, that in fact she had been a virgin before the attack, adding, "I'm fifteen years old, Joyce. Fifteen" (53–54).

When Allie and Christine meet after the incident we learn that he views Christine's assault as a personal attack on himself and his gang. "I say it was a Sham done it, and that's what matters. Because we'll hammer the lot of them. Believe that! Think they can do that to the Suedes." Christine replies, "Did it to the Suedes, did they? I see. It's your pride was hurt. The pride of the bloody gang. Fuckall anyone cares about me" (63). Allie insists that he will fight them as a way of showing her that he cares. When Allie kisses Christine, she pulls away from him, which raises his suspicions. "He didn' just beat you, he done you as well. And you let him" (66). Christine admits she was raped, but she continues urging Allie to give up the "whole bloody gang business" stressing that if he is determined to fight the Shams, he shouldn't use her as his excuse, because she never even made it into the Shams' territory (67).

It turns out that Ennis, another member of the Suedes gang, was the man who beat and raped Christine in order to prevent her from finding out the location of the bovver. When confronted he admits it, insisting, "It's the gang comes first" (78). When Allie confronts Ennis, he says, "She wanted to stop the bovver. She's nothing to you. She's only a bird. She's only a fuckin' bird." Ennis ultimately leaves for the fight, telling Allie, "We'll be waitin' for you" (82). Eventually Allie realizes that he needs to think about his future, rather than the future of the gang, and he accepts the community center keys from Gene as an indication that he will take charge of his future.

In Holtzman's drama Christine's rape was actually about the relationship between Ennis and Allie. Ennis, who sensed that Allie might leave the gang, was desperate to keep the gang together and he hoped that Christine's rape would function to solidify the bonds between the men in the Suede gang. This theme of rape serving to cement bonds among male characters occurs often within the sample of plays examined in this study.

Good Boys and True (2007) by Roberto Aguirre-Sacasa

Good Boys and True is one of two plays in this section in which the rapist is a high school athlete. This is an important subject for playwrights to explore since Michael Messner's research on rape by student athletes indicates that in high schools, "male athletes perpetrate many of the most egregious examples of sexual assault" (29). Additionally, in Rebecca Feasey's work on masculinity and television, she notes "there have been numerous cases in recent years where athletic, physically dominant and assertive sportsmen have used and abused their muscularity outside of the sports arena in all manner of physical and sexual assaults" (101).

Good Boys and True is my first example of a star high school athlete rapist, although in this case the rape could be considered somewhat ambiguous, somewhere on a scale between nonconsensual sex and undeniable rape. The athlete character, Brandon, is referred to by several characters as a rapist, but the raped character does not acknowledge her assault as a rape. This is not unusual as Mary Koss's research has shown; "only 27% of the women whose experience met legal definitions of rape labeled themselves as rape victims" (44). In other words, 73 percent of raped women did not think of themselves as having been raped. Additionally, in this play, as was the case with *Bovver Boys*, the sexual assault is shown to actually concern the relationship among the male characters in the play, rather than a relationship between the rapist and the female character.

This play takes place in the late 1980s. Brandon Hardy is a white, privileged, upper-class, senior at a private college-prep high school. He is captain of the football team, as was his father when he attended the same prestigious high school. He has been accepted into Dartmouth for the fall, and his future looks bright. He has a girlfriend, Erica, but he is also having a secret sexual relationship with Justin Simmons, another football player at the school.

The coach of the football team, Coach Shea, contacts Brandon's mother, Elizabeth, and lends her a video tape of a young man having sex with a young woman. It is clear that the young woman on the tape does not know that the sexual encounter is being videotaped, and that the young man does. Coach Shea thinks the young man might be Brandon, but his face is never clearly visible on the tape, so he asks Elizabeth to view the tape and speak with Brandon about it. The young woman's face is visible, and it is clearly not Brandon's girlfriend, Erica. Elizabeth admits that the sexually aggressive young man looks somewhat like Brandon, but he looks any number of young men from the school. When confronted by his mother about the tape, Brandon adamantly denies that he is the man on the tape.

The tape was first found in the locker of a member of the football team and subsequently the entire team watched it, including Brandon and Justin. Copies of the tape quickly circulated not only throughout the private high school but to other schools in the area. After repeatedly insisting to everyone that he was not the man on the tape, Brandon is ultimately identified by the young woman once her identity is discovered. Brandon's bright future is shattered as he is suspended from the school and his acceptance to Dartmouth is revoked.

When Brandon finally admits his guilt to his mother, the audience learns of the events that took place. Brandon had gone to the local mall and picked up the young woman, Cheryl, at the food court and asked her out for that evening. He had set up a hidden camera and a mattress

Two: Rape Myths and Rapists

Brandon picks up Cheryl in the Raven Theatre's 2014 production of *Good Boys and True*, directed by Cody Estle. Featuring Will Kiley as Brandon and Sophia Menendian as Cheryl (photograph by Dean La Prairie).

at the vacant home of a friend whose family was moving, and he brought Cheryl there. Elizabeth describes to Brandon what she had seen on the video tape. "*I saw you*—lead that girl onto, what? Not even a bed, onto a *mattress*, on some floor ... I saw her smiling at you because she didn't know what you were about to do." Brandon listens quietly as his mother continues. "I saw you grab her hair—and pull on it—and push into her harder and harder ... I saw you slap her. I saw you force her face into the mattress, so—why, so you wouldn't have to *hear* her?" (30; ellipses in orig.). Brandon says nothing in response.

Elizabeth, Coach Shea, and Brandon's father are baffled as to why Brandon would risk his future by videotaping himself having sex with a young woman, sex that appears to be nonconsensual. In a scene with Justin, Brandon insists that the reason he put the tape in the locker of fellow football team member was simply because Mitchell's locker was unlocked. But Justin has a different, more compelling theory as to why

Brandon and Justin discuss the video tape in the Raven Theatre's 2014 production of *Good Boys and True*, directed by Cody Estle. Featuring Will Kiley as Brandon (left) and Derek Herman as Justin (right) (photograph by Dean La Prairie).

Brandon would have wanted the football team to have seen a video of him having sex with Cheryl. We learn that Mitchell had recently gone to the varsity pool at the school one night, and he had seen Brandon and Justin. As Justin recounts, "We were naked, ... I was jacking you off" (40–41). It becomes clear Brandon arranged to videotape himself having sex with Cheryl in order to prove to the team that he was heterosexual, and because he wanted to counteract any rumors that might be circulated by Mitchell to the contrary. Rebecca Feasey illuminates this choice when she notes that "different models of masculinity have been said to form a hierarchy of acceptable, unacceptable and marginalized models for the male" (2). Clearly for Brandon, any questioning of his heterosexuality would be unacceptable. Therefore, Brandon forcing himself on Cheryl, and videotaping it, had nothing to do with her; it was really about his relationship with the other members of the football team and his own homophobia. Cheryl was merely a pawn in his plan to deny his sexual relationship with Justin. As was the case in *Bovver Boys*, this script provides an example of nonconsensual sex taking place because of the relationships among male characters in the drama, and the depiction of a rapist whose motivations cannot simply be attributed to a violent nature, a need for power over women, or a simple desire for aggressive sex.

Tape (2000) by Steven Belber

In this drama we once again see the degree to which rape is depicted in terms of the relationship between male characters. *Tape* depicts an aspect of male relations in which "heterosexual men are encouraged to use women as badges of success to protect and enhance their standing in the eyes of other men," as well as a means of competing with each other (Johnson 34). *Tape* is about a competitive relationship between Jon and Vince, who were best friends in high school. Jon is a struggling filmmaker and Vince is a volunteer fireman who earns his living dealing drugs to fifty-year-old ex-hippies in the San Francisco area. They meet up in Lansing, Michigan, where one of Jon's films is being shown as part of the Lansing film festival. Vince has learned that Amy, a woman he dated in high school, now lives in Lansing, and he, unbeknownst to Jon, has called and invited her to join him for dinner. Prior to Amy's arrival the men begin to argue about her primarily because ten years earlier Jon began seeing Amy shortly after she and Vince broke up. Jon apologizes and admits that this might have hurt Vince's feelings. Vince responds, "That's not what I'm talking about." Vince wants to know what happened between Jon and Amy. "We slept together," Jon admits, to which Vince replies "How?" (16–17).

It becomes progressively clearer throughout the play that Amy's body was the battleground on which the competition between Jon and Vince was fought. Jon is the victor, from Vince's point of view, because he actually slept with Amy, and Vince never did. The relationship between the three characters exemplifies Jill Dolan's assertion that rape is "a property crime of men against men in which women are victims in the homosocial exchange" (*Feminist Spectator* 93) and Peggy Phelan's comment that women are "the currency with which men strive to out-purchase one another" (104). The key issue for Vince is not to get Jon to admit that he slept with Amy, but that he *raped* her. Vince thinks he is eliciting the confession so that Jon will apologize to Amy, but in fact Vince merely wants his moral victory from the high school battleground. Vince first asks, "Did you rape her?" Followed by, "Was it like date rape?" Jon consistently says, "No," to which Vince says, "Did you 'kind of' force her to have sex with you?" (18). Jon admits that things "got a little out of hand," and were a bit "rough," but he totally discounts any feelings Amy may have about the event. He excuses his behavior, saying he was a "dumb, drunk high school senior who thought she was just being a little prudish and needed some coercion. It was bad and I regret it but it was a far cry from rape" (19).

Not only does Vince want Jon to confess to the rape, but he has hidden a tape recorder in the room and tapes the confession. The stage directions indicate that the anger and competition between the two men becomes physical just before Amy arrives, as "*Jon charges Vince and tackles him onto the bed.*" The two "*wrestle ferociously.*" Playwright Steven Belber explains in the stage directions that the "*fight is not so much about the tape as about their anger with each other, which is intense, deep-rooted and filled with violent tendencies*" (28). Ultimately, Jon does admit that he "coerced her to have sex with him ... by applying excessive linguistic pressure." He discloses that things became "aggressively playful" and finally admits, "I pinned her arms back and stuck my dick in" (20–23).

Amy, now ten years after high school, is a successful assistant district attorney in Lansing. When she arrives at the motel room to meet Vince for dinner she notices the tension between Jon and Vince. Amy confronts the high school buddies by pointing out that the root of this confrontation over the date rape is their competition. "It's never too late to one-up your best friend by telling him once and for all that you raped the love of his life in high school." After a pause Amy continues, "Especially if you get to do it in front of her" (40). Amy clearly understands the way in which her sexual encounter with Jon was, and continues to be part of the competitive relationship between Jon and Vince.

Amy quickly determines that the reason Vince is obsessed with get-

Two: Rape Myths and Rapists

Jon, Vince, and Amy reunite after many years in the Lilac City Performing Arts 2014 production of *Tape*, directed by Meghan Kirwin. Featuring Blaine Nicholls as Jon (left), Zachary Tinker as Vince (center) and Cori Olson as Amy (photograph by Milton Harper).

ting Jon to confess to date rape is not because he feels Amy deserves an apology. She understands that what she feels is not at all Vince's concern; rather, she realizes he wants a confession because that is the only situation under which he can imagine that Amy would sleep with someone else. When Amy questions why Vince thought Jon had raped her, he says, "Because why else would you have slept with Jon when you were supposed to be dating me?" Amy clarifies that she and Vince had "already broken up" to which Vince replies, "I know, but *we* hadn't even slept together, so what the hell were you doing sleeping with him?" (41). It appears that Vince is eager to obtain Jon's rape confession so that he can claim the moral high ground, and justify for himself why Amy would have slept with Jon when she would not sleep with him. The issue of Jon's sexual conquest of Amy, and the context in which it took place, is all about the competition between these two men.

The "Boy Next Door" Rapist
No. 11 (Blue and White) (1998) by Alexandra Cunningham

No. 11 (Blue and White), which premiered at the Humana Festival in Louisville, Kentucky, depicts a rapist who is clearly a hypersexual young man, one who does not fit a stereotypical psychopathological description; instead he resembles the boy next door. As Michael Scott Moore wrote in his review of a recent production, the number 11 is the jersey number of "a popular senior and lacrosse star at an East Coast prep school. Reid Callahan is a tall, handsome, pampered athlete admired by his friends and desired by almost every girl. He's also a brutal rapist" (*Culture/Stage*, n. p). *No. 11* is based on the real life case of Alex Kelly, a high school wrestling star who served ten years of a sixteen-year sentence for raping two high school girls in 1986. Shortly before his trial for rape, Alex fled the country and spent eight years as a fugitive. He was finally captured in 1995 and ultimately found guilty two years later.

In Cunningham's play the Alex Kelly character is named Reid Callahan. Reid is a charismatic high-school senior and star lacrosse player. As previously mentioned, Reid's status as a star senior-high school athlete is fitting, given that athletes and fraternity members are the most representative groups among rapists on college campuses.[10] One of Reid's morning ritual includes "beating off in the car," because it helps him "concentrate." His friend Brian explains, if "Reid gets his rocks off and over with now, he won't feel the need to do it in the library stacks during third period study hall" (54). This comment reinforces the myth that male sexuality is uncontrollable, and mirrors Kathryn Ryan's contention that "rapists may actively feed their sexual arousal by engaging in excessive sexual preoccupation, while viewing their excessive arousal as something that is not under their own control" ("Further" 584). Brian's reference to Reid's morning ritual sets up a justification for his "uncontrollable" sexual assaults.

In the play, Reid manages to juggle a very active social life; his "official" girlfriend is Jenny, another high-school senior, but he is also dating Kristin, a college freshman. His friends at school include fellow lacrosse players, Brian and Danny; and three female students: Tammy, Paige, and Alex, whose homework he is constantly trying to copy. In the play Reid

Lindsay and Tammy, both raped by Reid in Northeastern University's 2009 production of *No. 11 (Blue and White)*, directed by Jonathan Carr. Featuring Marlee Delia as Lindsay (above) and Amelia Bubin as Tammy (below) (photograph by Nora Lindsay McBurnett).

brutally rapes two women, Lindsay, a woman he meets at a party who accepts his offer of a ride home, and Tammy, his friend from school. In both cases the rapes take place in the car Reid is driving.

Cunningham's play does not follow a linear chronological plot structure; for example, the audience sees a scene between Lindsay and her father which depicts their conversation *after* she had been raped, *before* they learn the details of the rape itself. Lindsay had lied to her father the night of the party, telling him she was on a date with Justin, a friend of hers from school. After raping Lindsay, Reid tells her to get out of the car and walk home. When she arrives at the door alone her father is furious. He assumes that Justin, Lindsay's supposed date, didn't walk her to the door. Her father badmouths high school boys, "what passes for a date these days," he says, stressing to Lindsay "if you all put your foot down, this crap would stop. If you told them how you wanted to be treated, they'd have to go along with it." He tells his daughter that she shouldn't "put up with it." Ultimately, according to her father, Lindsay and other young women are to blame for their dates' disrespectful behavior. Lindsay is clearly ashamed and says nothing to her father about what had just happened to her, and the next time she is seen on stage she is lying "in a heap on the floor" in her dark bedroom, a symptom of her sense of shame and contamination (73, 77).

Cunningham employs a similar non-chronological structure when depicting Tammy's rape. Before the assault Tammy is onstage, shivering in the cold, waiting for her mother to pick her up after a school hockey game, when Reid shows up. They have a friendly conversation and the scene ends with them both laughing. In the next scene with Tammy (which depicts events *after* her rape), we see a defiant, angry young woman speaking with her mother as they drive home, "I guess you didn't have to come pick me up, Mom, you're right. I guess you could have just blown it off, I guess you could have let me stay at the rink all night." Tammy begins to cry, "or I guess you could turn around and take me back there and just *leave* me" (78). Tammy's hostile emotions in this scene are explained when we later learn that Reid had offered to let Tammy wait for her mother in his warm car, but once she got in, he drove to a secluded place, raped her, and then returned her to the school. When Tammy's mother finally came to pick her up, Tammy is unable to

Two: Rape Myths and Rapists

Reid offers Tammy a ride home in Northeastern University's 2009 production of *No. 11 (Blue and White)*, directed by Jonathan Carr. Featuring Amelia Bubin as Tammy and Chris Nourse as Reid (photograph by Nora Lindsay McBurnett).

tell her mother about the rape; instead her emotions come out in an angry outburst directed at her mother.

Once word gets out that Reid may have raped Tammy and Lindsay, his friends are convinced that the two women are lying. Jenny, Reid's girlfriend says, "Look at him. Does he look that desperate? I'll tell you who looks desperate. Those two bitches, *that* is *who*" (88). Paige thinks Lindsay is lying just to get attention. "Pretty fucked up way to try to get some spotlight on you... I saw you, I saw you 'Oh (*Fake giggling*) whose Jeep is that, I love it.' I don't know who you think you're fooling" (89). Tammy hopes that Alex (Reid's female friend) knows the truth, but Alex denies any knowledge of the rape and says to Tammy, "I know you asked him out while Jenny was gone and he turned you down. He *told* me that, *that's* something I *know*" (92). Finally, Reid's coach also thinks the accusations of rape are false. He describes how "little cupcakes" wait outside the locker room and "fawn all over" the athletes. "All I know is, if a bunch of little cookies weren't there giving it away, these young guys wouldn't come to start thinking it was free" (89).

These characters all believe the myth that women lie about being raped. The raped characters' vivid descriptions of the violent rapes, however, leave no doubt that they are telling the truth, but most of the characters in the play doubt their accusations and go to great lengths to both discredit and demoralize the two young women. Lindsay receives suspicious phone calls from Reid's friends, and consequently, when Tammy calls to solicit her help, Lindsay repeatedly hangs up on her. Tammy is harassed in many ways at school by Reid's supporters; for example, a class assignment worth one third of her grade is stolen, and Brian hovers by her locker, slamming it shut every time Tammy opens it. The cruelty these students display may be based on their loyalty to Reid, but it is also evidence of their acceptance of cultural myths about rape. As reviewer Moore states, "The essence of *No. 11* excavates the dark side of a popular jock, and shows—harrowingly—how a group of parents and friends will protect him. It's a story of denial in a very American mode, and it looks less like a funny experiment than like everyday life" (*Culture/Stage* n. p.).

By the end of the play, Alex has serious doubts about Reid's innocence, and her own complicity in the events of the play. She knows he has obtained a passport and is about to leave the country, and she tells him, "You can't hide. I'm sure you're still trying, but don't kid yourself. The worst thing you've ever done—that's who you are," implying that he will ultimately be defined by his actions, rather than his friends' impressions of the accusing women (104).

The rapist characters in *Bovver Boys, Good Boys and True, Tape,* and *No. 11 (Blue and White)* have a variety of motives for their sexual attacks, but they are not depicted as psychopathological rapists. There are, however, some plays in this study in which the rapist is portrayed in such a manner.

The Pathological Rapist

While most of the plays in this study depict a rapist who does not fit a psychopathological model, there are some dramas, which I will briefly describe, in which the rapist is depicted as psychologically unstable. In these plays the raped women are not only assaulted sexually, but they are murdered or if they survive, the rapist clearly intended to murder them.

Down the Road (1989) by Lee Blessing

Lee Blessing's 1989 play, *Down the Road*, is about a journalist couple, Iris and Dan Henniman, and their efforts to write a biography about William Reach, an imprisoned serial rapist and murderer. Reach has murdered at least 19 women, most of whom he also raped. Reach, the rapist character, has been sentenced to life without parole for his crimes and Iris and Dan interview him at the prison for their biography. Iris and Dan find Reach quite unsettling, and most likely audience members would as well.

During his interviews, Reach admits that what he enjoyed most was knowing that he had control over everything. After describing stabbing one of his victims seven or eight times, raping her and throwing her body down a hill, Iris asked him how he felt. Reach replied "Perfect... Like God" (61). He explains that he was careful to choose women who were well dressed and clean. In fact, once when he had picked up two young women who were hitchhiking in the rain, he took one of them home because she looked "messy" (69). Reach's need for control fits the model of rapists described by Golden and Peterson. "They are consumed with issues of control, power, aggression, and self-gratification. Unfortunately, many believe that these traits are acceptable for males" (8). Terrence Crowley concurs, noting, "Men learned to define our masculinity in terms of our differentiation from what we felt was feminine as well as our ability to control women. The dichotomy was absolute: I was either in control or I was a pussy" (343).

Reach had been previously convicted of rape, although he is quick to point out to Dan that he had plea-bargained for a lesser offense and never went to jail. He was, however, required to see a court-appointed therapist. In fact, he had the head of a woman he had murdered and subsequently raped in the trunk of his car when he went to his final appointment with the therapist. "What did he say to you, that last day?"

Dan asked. "He said he thought I'd made real progress," Reach replied (71).

Iris and Dan delve into Reach's background and find nothing remarkable, no abuse, beatings, molestations, etc. Iris realizes, "Somewhere along the line Reach got the idea that unless you succeed—*really* succeed, become famous—you don't exist... Before he started killing women, there was no Bill Reach." Iris ultimately concludes that Reach was "a man with no identity, but a real gift for the twentieth century—[he] found a goal: to become unforgettable, at any price" (80–82). Iris and Dan are left with the understanding that, as his biographers, they are in fact participating in the fulfillment of Reach's goal.

The Glory of Living (1999) by Rebecca Gilman

Clint Needham, the rapist in *The Glory of Living*, had been in and out of trouble since he had been arrested for car theft at the age of fifteen. He is described by reviewer Jennie Webb as "a pathological, sexually violent criminal who has his now-wife completely under his control" (21). His wife, Lisa, whom he met when she was fifteen, is obviously a battered woman, and it is implied that she has been subjected to both physical and sexual abuse by Clint over the course of their relationship. This drama, according to playwright Gilman, "came from a real Alabama murder during my senior year of college. The criminal was a young girl [similar to the character of Lisa] who had not been taught to value her own life, so she could not be expected to value anyone else's" (qtd. in Jones 27).

Lisa is profoundly passive in the face of Clint's aggressive masculinity. This gendered behavior is symptomatic of cultural mandates reflected in Marcus's rape script, specifically the communicative stance of responsiveness, in which the women allow the needs of others to supersede their own. This behavior is seen in Lisa, as she does whatever Clint asks of her. In fact, Clint's power and control over Lisa is so extreme that she picks up women for him to rape, and then the two of them take the raped women to a secluded location and Lisa murders them. Lisa believes that even if she were to run away, Clint would find her and kill her. This passive response on Lisa's part allows Clint to successfully control her, as well as other women he has raped, which ultimately serves to establish his masculine identity.

Only three of the women Clint intends to attack are actual characters in the play, but Lisa confirms that there have been more. Once Clint and Lisa are arrested, Lisa is asked by a detective if Clint had raped women, and Lisa replies, "Yeah... It wadn't nothin' new. He did shit like that all the time" (50). In one scene we learn that an unnamed and intoxicated female character, around fifteen years old, who has been handcuffed to the bed, was raped by Clint. After he leaves she limps off to the bathroom and tells Lisa, "He hurt somethin' in me" to which Lisa replies, "He's real big. He made my gash bigger" (26). Lisa offers to give the girl a ride, reassuring her that she won't be seeing Clint anymore. This pleases the girl, but she is unaware that Lisa will be driving her to a pre-arranged rendezvous with Clint, where they will murder her.

Clint is depicted as a dominating, aggressive, and violent man who is both physically and sexually abusive to women. He shows no remorse for his crimes, and although he apologizes to

A young girl is raped and chained to the bed in the School of Theatre and Dance at Illinois State University's 2012 production of *The Glory of Living*, directed by Matt Campbell. Featuring Colleen Besler as the girl (photograph by Pete Guither).

Lisa at the end of the drama, he nonetheless allows her to spend the rest of her life in prison for murder, while he merely serves an eighteen-month sentence.

Michael Solomonson, in his article "Rebecca Gilman's Exploration of Gender Conditioning as a Factor in Violence Against Women," examines *The Glory of Living* and *Boy Gets Girl*, also by Gilman. He argues that Gilman "suggests that cultural conditioning of both men and women play a part in the violence that occurs." This "patriarchal conditioning," Solomonson notes, "involves empowering men to objectify women as something to be looked upon and, if sufficiently pleasing, to be possessed as a type of sexual commodity." While I am focusing now on the character of Clint, Solomonson's comments are worth noting in relation to the dynamic between Clint and Lisa. "Part of the process of objectifying women involves a conditioning whereby women are encouraged to be compliant to the male gaze, to be looked at by men, appreciated by them, and to be pursued, often in a boorish and crude manner" (200–201). In addition to the depiction of a psychopathological rapist character, we see the gendering of sexuality as well as gendered violence playing out in this drama. Clint is violently aggressive toward all the women he encounters over the course of the drama, and Lisa not only refuses to fight back, she in fact participates in the violence.

Self Defense or Death of Some Salesmen (2001) by Carson Kreitzer

Self Defense or Death of Some Salesmen also includes a rapist character who fits a psychopathological model. This play was inspired by events in the life of Aileen Wuornos, a prostitute and female serial killer who admitted to killing seven men, but claimed it was in self-defense after the men became abusive. Aileen was sentenced to die in the electric chair for the first murder in 1992 and was ultimately executed in 2002.

In the play, the Aileen Wuornos character is named Jolene Palmer, also referred to as Jo. *Self Defense* includes a scene in which Jolene testifies at her own trial. In this testimony, she describes the events that led up to her killing Tom Waldren. During this testimony we learn of Jolene's brutal and violent rape. Her accounts of the event make it clear that

Two: Rape Myths and Rapists

Tom had every intention of killing Jolene when he was through raping her. In addition to Jolene's description of Tom's behavior and demeanor, which clearly indicate a psychopathic personality, two other prostitutes who had met Tom describe his suspect personality. One woman says, "He could be so sweet, and then the next minute he'd turn around and … scare the hell outta you" (280; ellipsis in orig.). The other woman acknowledged that he had "bad impulse control," adding he was the kind of guy who "wants what he wants." She was not surprised he "met with an untimely death"; after all, "You never know what's gonna set somebody off" (316).

After the trial, a reporter character is quick to point out the irony that neither the police nor Jolene's public defender were able to find evidence to support Jolene's claim that Tom Waldren had raped her, while he [the reporter] had easily found prison records indicating that Waldren had previously served ten years for attempted rape and assault. Kreitzer also includes an additional piece of evidence in her drama to support the premise that Tom Waldren was a psychopathological rapist/murderer (as well as the other six men Jolene claims to have killed in self-defense): the fact that unsolved prostitute murders had decreased significantly since Jolene had killed these men in self-defense.

We see in these dramas a wide range of rapist characters, from the typical "boy next door" student athlete, to characters that fit the psychopathological rapist/murderer profile, all of which are character types documented in the literature about actual rapists. Additionally these characters mirror the research in respect to their belief in numerous rape myths circulating in our culture. This characterization is not limited to dramas in which a rape is perpetrated by an individual rapist, it exists as well in dramas depicting rape by groups of men.

Gang Rape in Dramatic Texts

The depiction of women being assaulted by a group of men provides an additional opportunity to examine the creative construction of rapist characters. Scholars have noted that group think and de-individuation are contributing factors in gang rapes, when a contagious mob mentality predominates. Often, gang rapes take place in situations in which men are required to prove both their masculine status as well as their loyalty to the group.[11] Thus, as Kathryn Ryan argues, "gang rapists are bonding with the other rapists. The rape victim is merely an object in this ritual" ("Further" 595). Just as Ennis's rape of Christine in *Bovver Boys* was really about his desire to solidify the gang, and Brandon's videotaped rape of Cheryl was intended to confirm his heterosexuality in the eyes of the other football players, the gang rapes in the following dramas serve as a bonding event for the participants.

Rosalee Pritchett (1970) by Carlton and Barbara Molette

Carlton and Barbara Molette depict a gang rape in their 1970 drama *Rosalee Pritchett*. Rosalee Pritchett (an African American) is married to a prominent physician who is respected by both whites and African Americans. She lives in an affluent part of town (by African American standards) and regularly plays bridge with three other affluent African American women. In spite of the race riots that are taking place in the downtown area, they feel safe in their suburb. Rosalee (Rose) is gang-raped by four white National Guardsmen who are patrolling her neighborhood. Ironically, it is Rose who mentions, "Out here, a woman is safer at night than she would be downtown in broad daylight" (6). Rose thinks that the curfew doesn't apply to people living in their area and when the possibility of the National Guard patrolling their neighborhood comes up, Rose says, "For what? We're law abiding citizens. The riots are not in our area. I don't think we have anything to worry about." Although she does mention that she feels "a lot safer with them patrolling the streets at night" (6–11).

When describing the National Guardsmen, playwrights Carlton and Barbara Molette note, "they do get a thrill ordering people around at gun point—the pride of absolute power and authority" (12). The four men are Barron, the leader of the group, a forty-two-year-old insurance executive who has two teenage daughters; Lowe, a thirty-nine-year-old gas station owner and hunter who has four healthy boys; King, a thirty-seven-year-old accountant who is also a deacon in his church; and Wittmer, a twenty-six-year-old unmarried shoe salesman. The men are not happy that they have been called into active duty due to the riots and hope that the assignment will end soon.[12]

The men's gendered and aggressive sexuality is obvious in their dialogue. For example, shoe salesman Wittmer complains that he is missing out on an opportunity to date a "little redhead" that came into the store today. His lines are accompanied by bumps and grinds. He adds to the other men, "Now, all I can do is sit here, with a hard on, sweat, and think about it." King calls him "a horny old sonofabitch" to which Wittmer replies, "It's just my manly nature. When this is over, I'll be able to keep all my women happy again" (13). Gas station owner Lowe's preoccupation with sex is also obvious when he learns that King has an African American accountant working at his office. The man and his wife have even had dinner at King's house. Lowe immediately asks King what the wife looks like, adding, "Did you get it?" When King asks, "Get what?" Lowe replies, "That dark meat, boy! They sho-o-ore got some good pussy!" (16).

In her book, *Women, Race & Class*, Angela Davis discusses the sexualization of African Americans, both men and women, noting the "fictional image of the Black man as rapist [which] has always strengthened its inseparable companion: the image of the Black woman as chronically promiscuous." In fact, Davis remarks, "the entire race is invested with bestiality," and consequently, "Black women must certainly welcome the sexual attentions of white men. Viewed as 'loose women' and whores, Black women's cries of rape would necessarily lack legitimacy" (181–182). We see this myth played out in Lowe's savoring of the "dark meat" and "good pussy," and the play documents the lack of legitimacy Rose will experience after her encounter with the National Guardsmen when she is on her way home after playing bridge with her girlfriends.

The four men question Rose, and despite her protestations that she lives in the neighborhood, they tell her that she is under arrest for violating the curfew. The men's aggressive sexuality comes out as they taunt Rose. Wittmer says Rose should buy shoes from him, adding, "I'll give you something that'll make you feel good!" Lowe chimes in, "Yeah, let me sell you some gasoline sometime. I'll be glad to fill you up." The men won't let her leave, and ask her to "entertain" them. Rose tells them to keep their hands off of her, and Wittmer says "we're just being friendly" (19–21).

The leader of the group, Barron, tries to break things up, but Lowe and Wittmer accuse him of being a "nigger lover." This peer pressure is sufficient for Barron to change his tune, and the men throw Rose to the ground and the lights fade as Rose screams for help (21).

Patriarchy is generally used to describe relationships between men and women, but Allan Johnson asserts that "patriarchy has more to do with relations among men than with women, for it is men who control men's standing *as men*." Johnson contends it is because of this male-centered status quo that "when a man suspects *himself* of being less than a real man, he judges himself through a patriarchal male gaze" (31). Therefore, Barron's capitulation to the desires of the other men could be due to the fact that men who participate in gang rapes need to prove their loyalty to the group, as well as confirm their masculine status within the group.

Under a Western Sky (1996) by Amparo García-Crow

Male bonding, or in this case male initiation into a group, as well as the interplay between rape myth acceptance and rapists is reinforced in *Under a Western Sky*. This play centers on the residents of a small town in South Texas, where Yolanda Vasquez, an eighteen-year-old Mexican-American woman, is brutally gang-raped at an illegal cockfight. The rape is first reported to the sheriff by Javier Zuniga, a thirteen-year-old boy who witnessed the attack. He tells the sheriff that he has "seen something ... bad" (ellipsis in orig.) and that the men "went crazy," adding, "I never been to one of those rapes before." He begins to describe the events of the evening, saying, "They acted like they done it before or something" (176–180).

Carla J. McDonough, when summarizing Ray Raphael's study of American men's "struggle to become men" writes, "Raphael argues that although the female body may be used in male rites of passage, female recognition of masculinity is not of ultimate importance. What is most desired and most needed is recognition from other men, because the belief is that while women can create boys, only men can create other men" (13). It appears that the gang rape was to have served as Javier's initiation to manhood, and the confirmation of his masculine status since one of the rapists, Monkay, grabbed him and threw him on top of Yolanda, saying, "This is what you can look forward to" as the other men laughed at him (182). The rape serves as a bonding experience for the men, and given that it appears to Javier that the men have done this before, there is an expectation that this bonding ritual will be repeated.

Characters' belief in rape myths is evident in the drama. Even many of the women in the town think that Yolanda must have invited her attack—after all, some of the men accused of raping her have beautiful wives at home. The myth that women lie about being raped is believed by Carmen, the sheriff's daughter, who wonders why Monkay would "want to do it with Yolanda when he'd got her [his beautiful wife] at home?" Carmen insists that Yolanda was cheating on her husband and someone caught them, so the rape is just a "cover up" (195–197). The myth of uncontrollable male sexuality is evident in the "boys will be boys" attitude of an older man in town. He is upset that the sheriff is taking this all so seriously, and passes off the entire affair as "bad judgment" on the part of the rapists (207). After all, he remarks, "the whole town here knows that she knew all the men better than she should have" adding, "a teenager has many nights like that if he's normal" (204, 207).

Patriarchy, according to Allan Johnson, is really about competition and comradeship among men, and women play into this merely as a way to advance men's standing. As Johnson points out, this is especially true of marginalized men who "are allowed to dominate women as a kind of compensation for their being subordinated to other men because of social class, race, or other forms of inequality" (37). And most of the characters in *Under a Western Sky* are marginalized, lower-class Mexican-Americans.

Finally, it appears that along with male bonding, the phenomenon of group think functioned to motivate the male characters to commit these rapes. This is true as well in the following four plays I would like to briefly mention in which a gang rape is depicted.

The Widow's Blind Date, White People, Ma Rainey's Black Bottom, And I Ain't Finished Yet

In *The Widow's Blind Date* (1989) by Israel Horovitz, we learn that Margy Burke was gang-raped when she was seventeen. She has returned to her hometown, twenty years later, because her brother is gravely ill, and she arranges to meet two of her seven rapists, Archie and George. According to Archie, a group-think mentality was to blame. Archie insists, "Nobody planned it, Margy, it just happened!" He explains that as boys they always talked about wanting to have sex with any number of girls, adding that Margy was so beautiful that "*everybody* was always sayin' they'd love ta do it with *you*." He tries to excuse his behavior, saying, "When George here, well, *started*, everybody ... wanted to, too. Everybody liked you." Margy responds to Archie's attempt to explain the events by stating, "And that's how you showed me you *'liked'* me?" (100–101; ellipsis in orig.). Archie's memory of the events indicates how the momentum of one became the momentum of the group and the seven boys all lined up to take their turn.

Group think may also have played a part in the gang rape in J. T. Rogers' 1998 play *White People*. This is an example of a gang rape which Robert Golden and Fred Peterson describe as one in which the white young men are demonstrating "that their group is dominant, powerful, and superior" over the African American couple (54). We learn about the rape through a series of monologues by the character of Martin Bahmueller. Martin has recently been informed by the police that his insolent fifteen-year-old son, Steven, was one of a gang of six young white men who had attacked an African American couple. The man was beaten severely and the woman was violently beaten and raped. Additionally, the violent nature of the rape shows the degree to which rape, in this context, is not an expression of passion, but rather an expression of violence and power.

Martin struggles to understand his distant son and recounts his efforts to make contact with him in the past. He notes that Steven would just sit there, "hunched over, moving the zipper on his jacket up and down. Not a word. Just like always. I'm watching Steven, headphones on, cutting me out, thrashing about. I am watching my son. Where does this anger come from?" (21). Given Steven's apparent anger, the violence of the gang rape may also be an indication of the gendering of anger in American culture. Martin explains that when the police arrived, the attackers ran, all but Steven who stood "paralyzed" at the scene. Martin's anguish at his son's actions, and his own sense of impotence as a parent is clear when he shares his thoughts with the audience, "What keeps going through my head, [is] why was he still standing there? Why didn't he follow those older boys? Did he understand what he'd done? Was he accepting responsibility? Or did he just wanna get in one last kick?" (33).

Two final plays are examples of gang rape being used to punish and intimidate African Americans who in the late 1800s and early 1900s dared to purchase land. We learn in August Wilson's 1981 play *Ma Rainey's Black Bottom*, which is set in the 1920s, that band member Levee's mother was gang-raped when he was just eight years old. As Levee explains, people called his father "an uppity nigger 'cause he done saved and borrowed to where he could buy this land and be independent." A group of white men came into their house when his father was getting seed and fertilizer, and "took hold of her just like you take hold of a mule and make him do what you want" as a way to punish the couple for their transgressions (62). Similarly in Eve Merriam's *And I Ain't Finished Yet* (1981), the character Hannah Tutson describes how a group of men attacked and raped her, insisting that she and her husband were "living on another man's premises." Hannah insisted they had bought the land. She explains in the drama how one man in particular, George McRae, "acted so bad, and I was stark naked, ... he pulled my womb down so that sometimes now I can hardly walk.... It was my land. I had paid for it.... No one is going to move me from here" (43).

The use of rape as a form of retribution and intimidation is also a common feature of dramas depicting rape in war and military conflicts outside of the United States, and sadly it is commonplace even into the 21st century as Lauren Wolfe, from the Committee to Protect Journalists, documents in a 2011 report titled "The Silencing Crime." In her report, Wolfe discusses Lara Logan's attack in Egypt's Tahir Square that year, as well as numerous cases of rape and the threat of rape being used to silence journalists worldwide.

An analysis of dramas by American playwrights over the past forty years demonstrates, as does sociological research since the 1970s, that acceptance of rape myths is a continuing problem in our culture. However, many playwrights have succeeded in refuting these myths in dialogue spoken either by the raped female characters or by other characters in their plays. Playwrights have also crafted rapist characters that do not fit a stereotypical psychopathological model, which is important, given that women are far more likely to be raped by someone they know than by a deranged stranger. Additionally, these dramas illustrate the ways in which societal expectations of powerful masculinity and peer pressure can have devastating consequences for women.

Three

Female Rage

In their book *Female Rage*, Mary Valentis and Anne Devane write, "Behind 'backlash,' behind 'self-esteem,' behind 'loving too much,' behind our 'erotic silence' and our 'foolish choices' is a reservoir of female rage, denied and, yes, repressed" (8). As I will point out in this study, behind the behaviors of female characters in plays involving rape, there is also a reservoir of female rage. This reservoir may be tightly covered or overflowing; in some instances it is frozen and in others it contains geysers that shoot off unexpectedly. I will explore this reservoir through an examination of the representations of female rage in post-rape or attempted rape situations in contemporary American dramas.

Three primary patterns emerge when analyzing the post-rape anger of raped female characters in dramatic texts. The first pattern, which is the topic of part one of this chapter, is when the raped characters' rage is stifled or contained, for example, through the pathologizing and trivializing of the raped female character and her rage. This pattern of contained rage exists throughout the entire time period under examination. The containment of female rage is evidence of the gendering of rage that has persisted over the past four decades in American culture. It is important to note that when the rage of a raped character is contained, and therefore in some way silenced, this may be intended to highlight the societal forces in American culture that facilitate the silencing of raped women's voices, as opposed to an indication that playwrights are unconsciously supporting these forces. In some cases the silencing of rage is indicative the raped characters' acceptance of some of the rape myths discussed in the previous chapter and the intense shame and sense of contamination they exhibit.

The second pattern, which will be discussed in part two of this chapter, is when raped characters actively express their anger in the post-rape situation. Specifically, I document dramatic texts in which the characters' anger is so exaggerated and extreme that the raped women are ultimately demonized through their portrayal. This particular pattern emerges primarily in the late 1970s and 1980s and, as I will argue, is associated with the antifeminist backlash of that era. The third pattern, which I detail in Chapter Six, "Rage Revisited," is when playwrights depict the active expression of anger in post-rape situations as part of the healing process for the raped female character.

Part One: Female Rage Contained

Given that in our culture, aggressive expression of anger is considered unfeminine, the containment of such anger in the depiction of raped characters is evidence of the gendering of rage in our society reinforced in the dramas. Several conditions exist in these plays that serve as containing devices of the raped characters' rage. These devices include (1) the reinforcement of the myth that raped women are contaminated and the portrayal of the raped characters' rage as being turned inward rather than being actively expressed; (2) trivializing the raped character and her potential or actual rage and pathologizing the raped female character so her expression of rage, or lack thereof, is attributed to a mental illness; (3) conflating rape with seduction, thereby invalidating the rage that would have been felt by female characters had they recognized their assaults as rape; this also allows the rapist characters to deny that their actions are sexual assaults, since, from their point of view, they are merely expressing affection for the raped woman; and 4) allowing male characters to voice the rage rather than the female raped character, hence appropriating female rage.

Despite my efforts to isolate these rage-containing conditions, it is important to note that plays often exhibit multiple rage-stifling devices. For example, the play *Hush* by Laura Gagliano is an example of female rage contained due to the depiction of the raped female character's perceived contaminated status. Consequently, she is so ashamed that her rage, rather than being expressed, is turned inward. However, in this play the raped character's rage is also appropriated and expressed by other characters in the play. A similar situation exists with the play *Under a Western Sky,* by Amparo García-Crow. This play is an example of female rage appropriated because the raped woman's rage is expressed by her husband; however, the myths of contamination and uncontrollable male sexuality are also evident in this play.

The First Containing Device: Female Rage Turned Inward

Hush (1992) by Laura Gagliano

Teresa Bernardez observes, "Anger silenced contributes to the making of the most ubiquitous 'symptom' of women today: depression" (4). Renee Curry and Terry Allison concur. They point out, "Female reluctance to assume the male prerogative of rageful revenge" is a "demonstration that female rage often turns inward onto the female self" (7). Julie Brickman describes a common occurrence among rape survivors: "they may develop the compulsion to inflict new suffering on themselves in order to keep former suffering repressed" (22). This turning inward of rage is one way in which rage is contained. In Laura Gagliano's play *Hush,* date-rape victim Kim's post-rape behavior is an example of rage turned inward.

The play begins after the Kim has been raped; however, the audience witnesses the event through a series of flashbacks. Immediately in the opening stage directions, we read that "*Kim appears depressed*" (5). Her best friend Sara notices that "something's definitely wrong" with Kim, but Kim passes it off as lack of sleep. Kim is described in the stage directions as being "*listless,*" "*listening passively,*" "*looking exhausted,*" and "*quiet and unresponsive.*" Sara is surprised when her friend shows no interest in reviewing for a big math test and appears to no longer care about her college plans. At the end of the short first scene, Kim vigorously rejects Sara's brother John's attempts to give her a friendly hug and exits, leaving John and Sara confused by Kim's behavior (6–8). In the next scene, Kim is described as "*walking without really caring where she is going, [her] arms are crossed as though she's cold and as she cries we can see that she's remembering something painful"* (9–10).

In the first of several flashback scenes, Kim's appearance is dramatically different. She is described as appearing *"fresh and neat"* and *"relaxed and at ease"* (10). Kim's physical appearance and demeanor steadily decline and ultimately, after much prodding, she describes to Sara (via another flashback) the events leading up to and including being raped "a few weeks ago" by her boyfriend Rob. Kim begs Sara not to tell anyone (19). Her obsessive need to keep this secret is evidence of her shame and sense of contamination.

Throughout this first scene in Act One, Kim never expresses anger. The depression Bernardez speaks of is all we witness. Revealing her secret does not alleviate this depression, and Kim goes from walking without really caring where she is going to wandering *"aimlessly."* She is *"disheveled and totally absorbed in what's going on in her mind"* and looking *"miserable"* (28). Shortly after this description, we learn that she has tried to commit suicide.[1] In order to appease her family and friends, Kim agrees to see a therapist, but still, there is no acknowledgment of anger, merely self-blame and degradation. Even toward the end of the play when Sara confronts Kim, asking, "Aren't you angry? Don't you want to yell or scream or throw things?" Kim is passive. John and Sara end up fighting about whether or not it would be a good idea for Kim to confront her former boyfriend (49–50). At the end of this explosive exchange between John and Sara, Kim quietly comforts her friends, assuring them that she will be okay with time and that they shouldn't worry about her. John *"takes Kim's hand and the three of them begin walking off together"* as the play ends (51). In this play, Kim's shame and self-blame (byproducts of her internalized contamination) lead directly to her rage being turned inward.

I do not dispute Laura Gagliano's representation of Kim's reaction to her rape; many survivor accounts mirror this portrayal, however, the uplifting and touching ending serves to undermine any accuracy in the depiction of Kim's post-rape reactions. More importantly, what I find troubling about this and other plays in this study is the degree to which they merely reproduce existing rape myths. They mimic the societal containment of female rage rather than actively contest these cultural forces or in any way present alternative behavioral patterns, despite the fact that some of the characters do try to refute the culturally accepted rape myths as discussed in the previous chapter.

I'd like to return to the rape script described by Marcus. Sharon Marcus argues that a woman's passive responses to a threatened rape is evidence of rules governing socially acceptable feminine behavior—in other words, polite empathetic responses which are ultimately self-defeating. Kim's behavior in the rape scene is similar to what Sharon Marcus identifies as a stance of responsiveness, and Kim is unable to take the offensive and interrupt the flow of Rob's aggressive sexual advances. Additionally, the rape script casts females in the role of the empathetic partner, identifying with the would-be rapist's needs rather than their own. Kim has come over to Rob's house to avoid a tense situation at home with her feuding parents, and while she does allow him to kiss her, when things get more intense, she pushes him away and leaves the room. However, Kim returns to apologize saying, "I'm just tense, what with my parents and all.... I'm doing everything I can to drive everyone away from me," adding "I'm being stupid." Rob continues his romantic advances and, as the stage directions note, "*Kim gives in to him to avoid a fight.*" When Rob "*grows more insistent,*" Kim simply tries to change the subject with excuses such as "Don't you think we should be going downstairs?" or "Won't your sister need help with her math?" (23–24). By the time Kim actually asks Rob to stop, he already has her pinned and proceeds to rape her.

The gap between the threat of a rape and an actual rape (as described by Marcus), a gap in which there is an opportunity for effective resistive actions, is overlooked. While Kim's dialogue shows her attempts to defuse the situation, these attempts are ineffectual in part due to her continual gendered response to the situation. In addition to exemplifying the rape script detailed by Marcus, this scene represents the gendering of sexuality that Alyn Pearson describes, "Women smile more than men, … we apologize before stating an opinion, and we strive day in and day out to perfect our bodies for the male gaze. This is the rape culture. When men decide that they want, we give. When we say no, we apologize. Our no's are interrupted by their yes's" (63).

In addition to mirroring the rape script, we see again a rapist whose belief in rape myths serves as an excuse for the attack. Rob justifies his actions by placing the blame on Kim and revealing the degree to which he subscribes to numerous rape myths. "She knew what was going on," Rob says to John. "She may say she said no, but I was there, I know what happened. She had her head on my shoulder, looking up at me with those big eyes, fooling around just like always." Rob begs John to believe him, adding, "She didn't do anything she didn't really want to do" (32).

In this drama, Kim's pain and shame are vividly depicted, but her rage is contained. This effective containment of Kim's rage, along with the character's complicity with cultural rules of gendered behavior, reinforces her self-destructive tendencies and denies her potential resistive agency.

The Second Containing Device: Female Rage Pathologized and Trivialized

Rosalee Pritchett (1970) by Carlton and Barbara Molette

In *Rosalee Pritchett* by Carlton and Barbara Molette, which was discussed in the previous chapter, the titular character is gang-raped by several National Guardsmen who are ostensibly protecting her neighborhood from rowdy black rioters. In this play, Rosalee's rage is silenced, pathologized and trivialized. Her pathologized status is communicated in part through the staging of the play as described by the playwrights in the stage directions.

The play begins with a dark stage. Slides of Rose in *"very middle class social situations"* are shown while we hear her voice. She explains, "I'm in here ... in the hospital, because I had a nervous breakdown. I guess you might say I had a nervous breakdown because of the riots" (5; ellipsis in orig.). When the lights do come up on stage, Rose is isolated stage right on a platform and, according to production reviews, she is costumed in a hospital gown. In fact, as indicated by the playwrights, Rose is never *"physically present in the scenes. She participates in the dialogue just as though she were and the other characters react to her as if she were*" (3). For example, during the pre-rape bridge playing scenes, Rose speaks her lines from her isolated area of the stage and her friends look at the empty chair as if she were there. Even during the on-stage rape scene, the National Guardsmen converse with and attack an *imaginary* Rose, while the actor playing Rose remains in her designated stage area. This physical distancing and hospital gown costume serve to reinforce her month-long hospitalization and function as a staging device to pathologize her and her rage. The playwrights also literally silence her rage in that Rose has no spoken lines in the play after her rape.

An effective way to shut down rage, or any emotion for that matter, is to trivialize it. This leaves anyone who continues expressing the trivialized emotion open to humiliation. The fact that Rose is dimly lit on the side of the stage and is not physically present with the National Guardsmen during her rape scene is one way in which the impact of her rape and consequently her rage is diminished. As reviewer Mel Gussow notes, "Rosalie [*sic*], confined to a hospital with a postrape breakdown, recounts the entire story from a platform behind a scrim and does not take part in the action. The rape, without a victim, loses impact" ("Condemning" 19). Gussow's comments are important; however, I believe the containment of Rosalee's rage, through the trivializing reactions of her bridge-playing friends in the last scene of the play, also diminished the potential impact of the character.

By the end of the play, Rose's absence due to her extended hospitalization results in her place at the bridge table being taken by Thelma, a newcomer to the group. According to the stage directions, even though we witness the foursome playing cards, we still see Rose dimly lit on the other side of the stage in her hospital gown. The women play cards, they discuss recipes, diets, a debutante ball they have just organized, and a spring dance they are planning. Rose's absence from the group and her hospitalization come up from time to time in the conversation. We learn that no one knows who raped her. Some of the women seem to doubt Rose's story about the National Guardsmen, since they never saw any Guardsmen in their neighborhood. They mention that Rose was incoherent and not making sense after the attack, adding that "Rose always did fantasize a bit" (23). As soon as the conversation gets uncomfortable, the women return to the safer topics. For example, when Doll mentions that she hopes Rose will "recover from her hysteria" in time for the spring dance, Dorry says, "Has she really been hysterical? I guess she would be after being raped like that. Oh well." Dorry then quickly changes the subject asking the other women, "Guess where *we're* going for our summer vacation?" (25). The women continue talking about summer trips and bathing suits as the lights fade to a blackout.

There are many ways in which this dialogue functions to trivialize Rose's already pathologized and silenced rage. First, the mere fact that a substitute has been found for Rose at the table is an indication of her replaceable and diminished status among the group of friends. Second, it is clear that the women are not convinced of the validity of Rose's version of what transpired, and who actually raped her which serves to support their belief in the myth that women lie about being raped. Finally, the quick change of subject whenever Rose's condition is mentioned is another trivializing factor. The women's discomfort in discussing the rape combined with their distrust of Rose's description of the events that transpired is an indication of Rose's contaminated status in their eyes. It is arguable that the depiction of Rose's friends as women who trivialize her rage actually documents the degree to which these women are themselves manipulated by cultural attitudes about rape. Nonetheless, Rose's rage is contained, and her agency denied.

We see again components of the rape script outlined by Sharon Marcus in this text, as Rosalee's polite feminine behavior at the initial phases of the threatened rape disallow more resistive responses to the men. Her initial response to the men seems consistent with the situation; they are white, uniformed National Guardsmen, and she is an African American female out after the curfew, although as evidence of their intentions is presented, her passive gendered behavior persists. This is reinforced, of course, due to the fact that the men are actually interacting with a dummy representing Rosalee, as the character herself is sitting on the other side of the stage. In keeping with the interpretive stance of empathy component of the rape script, Marcus points out, some writers advocate an empathic response as a self-defense strategy. In other words, according to these writers, if a rapist is attacking a woman due to his low self-esteem, by responding empathically to a potential rapist the woman may thwart his attack. However, Rosalee's polite response to the

Three: Female Rage

National Guardsmen, even long after it was obvious that she was in danger, did nothing to prevent her rape.

The Third Containing Device: Female Rage Appropriated

Under a Western Sky (1996) by Amparo García-Crow

Yet another way that female rage is contained is when the rage is voiced by male characters in the play rather than, or in some cases in addition to, the raped woman herself. This appropriation and replacement of female rage is rooted in the gendering of rage, which accepts the notion of a male's active expressions of anger while denying women the same prerogative. This can result in a female character rendered silent when the post-rape rage is voiced by male characters.

In *Under a Western Sky*, which I discussed briefly in terms of the depiction of gang rapists in the previous chapter, the raped female character, Yolanda, does not actively express any post-rape rage. Instead the rage is voiced by her husband, Frankie. In this case the appropriation of anger is not depicted as being due to a universal cultural gendering of rage; in fact, Yolanda is portrayed by Frankie as a woman who does not shy away from voicing her anger. Prior to the rape, Frankie, when speaking to another male character remarks, "I got to pick up Yolanda. She'll kill me if I'm late. She locks me out. She throws all my stuff out the front door when she gets mad at me" (184). However, once she is raped, Yolanda's anger is muted; she is silent and all rage is expressed by Frankie.

After Yolanda is gang raped, the local sheriff interviews her about the attack. Frankie is present and he constantly interrupts the flow of the sheriff's questions. For example, as Yolanda is reciting a list of the men who raped her, Frankie continually interjects with comments indicating his anger. "Roel Paiz? He just fixed my van. God, no," and "Armando Rodriquez.... That son-of-a-bitch, smiling right to my face." After learning that Luis Salazar was among the rapists, Frankie says,

"No, man, I cain't believe it. Not him, too.... I cain't believe it. These are my friends. Were. What did I ever do to them? I cain't ... (*wants to say fucking*) believe it" (225–227; final ellipsis in orig.). Frankie can barely restrain himself. He begins to get violent, standing up, kicking the furniture and yelling when he learns of yet another name, "I cain't believe it. He was my best friend. In Junior High but still, my best friend." When the sheriff asks if that was everyone and Yolanda shakes her head, the stage directions indicate that "*Frankie bolts up and kicks the chair again and storms out.*" Yolanda, we are told, simply "*looks at her feet*" (229–230).

Frankie's rage and desire for revenge is portrayed in several other scenes in the drama, and at the same time, Yolanda does not expresses her rage. Allan Johnson describes Frankie's behavior as typical of patriarchal men, as the "path of least resistance for a man whose wife is raped isn't to take care of her, but to wreak heroic revenge on the rapist." This is because, in a patriarchy, a woman's welfare is secondary to a man's "rights and standing as a man in relation to other men." From the man's point of view, the rapist doesn't just rape a woman, he "violates a man's proprietary rights of sexual access and casts doubt on that man's ability to defend his sexual property against other men" (142). This is similar to Allie's reaction to Christine's assault in *Bovver Boys*, which he views as a personal attack on himself and his gang. Frankie, in *Under a Western Sky*, is outraged that *his* wife was the victim of the gang rape, and that *his* so-called friends would wound *him* by their actions. Frankie assumes this male prerogative, and his character expresses the post-rape rage while Yolanda adopts a stance of feminine-gendered silence and passivity, with no productive way to express her anger. Clues are provided in the script, however, to explain Yolanda's post-rape silence when a narrator character announces at the end of the play, "Yolanda dreams that she is in a church attending a funeral without her clothes on. Everyone in the town has turned up for the funeral ... they stare and point at her. She sobs so loudly in her dream, she wakes her husband up with a gasp" (278–279). Yolanda's dream shows that her contained rage is not only a result of the gendering of rage after her rape, which allows for Frankie to voice the rage rather than Yolanda, but in addition, her rage is contained due to her sense of shame and contamination.

Three: Female Rage

The Fourth Containing Device: Conflating Rape with Seduction

Selkie, Getting Out, *and* The Widow's Blind Date

The fourth containing device I would like to discuss is the when a rape is depicted as, or considered by the characters to be, a seduction. This ultimately invalidates the raped female character's rage and allows rapists to believe that their assaults were expressions of affection. Ellen Rooney notes the frequency with which the two terms, rape and seduction, are "partnered by the 'or' that marks undecidability." She attributes this to "our failure to escape the 'old Patriarchal system,' the system that bound seduction to rape. The singular subject 'seduction or rape' is grounded in the notion of a female passivity that operates both within seduction and within rape" (1271–1272). Susan Estrich details how in many legal cases the line between seduction and rape is frequently shaded in the direction of calling an incident a seduction rather than a rape, thereby exonerating the rapist.[2] In other words, not only does the depiction of rape as seduction stifle female rage by invalidating it, it perpetuates many of the myths about raped women that were discussed in the previous chapter, such as "all women want to be raped" or "she was asking for it," and consequently, rapists can deny that their actions were assaults.

The gendering of sexuality makes the conflation of rape and seduction very tempting, and, as Donnalee Dox details in her discussion of rape in the musicals *Oklahoma*, and *Man of La Mancha*, "romanticized representations ... make watching a rape acceptable as entertainment" (210). Additionally, it is not unusual for a sexually powerful and aggressive male character to be constructed as the romantic hero in a story. Once rape is equated with seduction, the fact that so many women, both in dramas and in the real world, marry their rapists does not seem abhorrent. From Biblical law, to Greek myths and dramas, to the contemporary play *Selkie* by Laurie Brooks Gollobin, women who marry their rapists is a commonplace occurrence.[3] One of the most famous examples of a woman marrying her rapist occurred on the television soap opera *General Hospital*. As Mary Buhl-Dutta notes, "Luke raped Laura, but when he later married her, the series retroactively redefined her rape as a choreographed seduction" (35). Deborah Rogers argues, "Most viewers are oblivious of the fact that reinterpreting soap rapes and brutality as romance denies—if not legitimates and glorifies—male violence by reading it as love" (qtd. in Buhl-Dutta 38).

The conflation of rape with seduction is evident in several plays in this study, among them *Selkie*, *Getting Out*, and *The Widow's Blind Date*. In the first play I'll discuss, *Selkie*, the raped female character's rage is contained due to the depiction of her rape as seduction. In *Getting Out* and *Widow's Blind Date*, the raped female characters *do* express their rage, so in these cases the conflation of rape with seduction does not contain the raped woman's rage. I am including these examples nonetheless because in these plays the conflation of rape with seduction functions, for the rapist characters, to justify the assaults they perpetrate on the female characters.

Selkie (1994) by Laurie Brooks Gollobin

Selkie was selected for this study in part because it appears in an anthology entitled *Theatre for Young Audiences: 20 Great Plays for Children*. Plays written for young audiences are rarely critiqued outside of specific journals and organizations focused on these materials, hence many theatre scholars are not familiar with this particular canon of plays.[4] And yet, given that many of these young audience members will become the theatre-going audience of the future (not to mention the adult citizens of our society), a critical examination of the plays *they* witness is an important part of all theatre scholarship. I believe that the issue of rape as depicted in a play written for young audiences is so important that I have chosen to include this particular play in my study despite the fact that, while written by an American playwright, it does not take place in the United States and its protagonist is not an American.

Peggy Phelan, in her book *Unmarked: The Politics of Performance*, discusses the importance of discovering "the blind spot within the visible real" (3). In other words, when rape is presented as seduction, the seduction becomes the visible real, and the rape is the invisible blind spot that

Three: Female Rage

must be recognized. Linda Higgins and Brenda Silver discuss this point as they describe the challenge of re-reading rape in literary pieces in which rape is depicted as seduction, which requires a "conscious critical act of reading the violence and the sexuality back into texts ... where it has been turned into a metaphor or a symbol or represented rhetorically as titillation, persuasion, ravishment, seduction, or desire" (4). Therefore, in my analysis, I will read the violence back into the text of *Selkie*.

Because in this play the abduction/rape is depicted as seduction, the rape could be viewed as not conforming to the definition I detailed in the preface to this study. We are given no details about the sexual acts that occur between Duncan and Margaret, the characters I have identified as rapist and raped woman. Nonetheless, I will argue and present evidence to support my contention that Margaret was an unwilling recipient of Duncan's penetrative sexual aggression.

Selkie is based on myths of the Seal People. Laurie Brooks Gollobin has set her story in the Orkney Islands north of Scotland. The play is narrated by the character of Pa, and begins on a midsummer's evening. Pa explains that this midsummer night is the one night each year when female seal people change into beautiful lassies. His son, Duncan, a young man about eighteen years old, has come to observe this magical transformation. When three selkies enter, Duncan hides behind some rocks and watches. The stage directions indicate that "*joyously, the three throw off their skins [and] are transformed into beautiful young women [who] do a wild dance on the beach.*" Duncan is especially attracted to the brown-haired selkie and he ultimately steals her pelt, so she will be unable to return to the sea, and he "*leads her*" to his home (583).

Several lines in this text make it obvious that we are witnessing an abduction rather than a seduction. First, in setting up Duncan's decision to steal the pelt, Gollobin describes the selkies as dancing "*wildly.*" This appears to be a euphemism for erotically, given Duncan's reaction to the dance, which is described by the narrator as a "powerful feelin'" driving him to "take" the brown-haired selkie to be his "sea-wife" (583). This section perpetuates the rape myth that male sexuality is a physical force that cannot be resisted to child audience members. Duncan is *driven* to abduct the selkie. He is presented as not being in control of his actions.

After Duncan takes the pelt, the brown-haired selkie is depicted as having no recourse but to go with him. She "*reaches out her arms*" and pleads with him to return the pelt. When he "*firmly*" refuses to give her the pelt, she merely "*collapses on the beach crying*" (583). And Duncan simply leads her offstage. The brown-haired selkie does not indicate a willingness to go, but nor does she resist.

The next scene takes place fourteen years later and the selkie is now called Margaret. She and Duncan have a thirteen-year-old daughter, Ellen Jean. It is clear from the stage directions that these have not been easy years for Margaret, as her body "*is bent and she wears a shapeless homespun dress with an apron. She moves with an odd, shuffling gait, as though her limbs are too heavy for her body*" (584). In addition to her appearance Margaret's lines indicate that she is unhappy and longs to return to her true family. She is a loving mother, but there is no indication that she has grown to love Duncan. Duncan, on the other hand, continues to claim his proprietary rights over Margaret. He grows progressively more and more uneasy as midsummer's eve approaches and the selkies' cries grow in volume. Duncan calls out the window, "Be off noo! Stop your callin'! ... Go back tae the sea an' leave us alone. She belongs tae me. Do ye hear? She belongs tae me!" (593).

On a midsummer's eve, Ellen Jean finds her mother's hidden pelt. She takes it to the sea and meets the black- and red-haired selkies from the first scene. They explain that they are crying "fer one ta'en by a crofter fourteen years ago an' kept from her home an' family in th' sea" and Ellen Jean realizes that her mother is that selkie woman (596). The selkies urge Ellen Jean to give the pelt back to her mother so that she can return to her family. When Ellen Jean does return the pelt, Margaret is overjoyed and she tells her daughter that she (Margaret) has been a "captive on the land" for fourteen years. "In that time I have grown old and stiff. Me skin is dry and cracked fer want o' the sea. Me bones are as brittle as driftwood lyin' on the shore. Ye have brought me what I need. It is me time tae return home" (600). Not only does Margaret return to the sea, but Ellen Jean goes into the sea with her as well.

The following year, Ellen Jean returns. A young man, Tam, with whom she had a budding romance, waits on the shore, hoping that she will appear. We see a stark contrast in this scene between Ellen Jean's active decision to return to the land and be with Tam, and Margaret's abduction depicted in the opening scene of the play. In this scene, as the stage directions indicate, Ellen Jean *"holds out her hand to Tam"* and the two do a joyous version of the "wild dance" Margaret and her friends had danced at the beginning of the play. Pa explains to the audience, "And so it was tha' the sea married the land" (602).

Jeanne Klein, when asked to direct a production of *Selkie*, discussed some of her concerns, noting that the play is "about rape and holding a woman against her will, all in the name of a 'children's' traditional folk tale." This Klein found troubling. Duncan, she argues, "gets off scot-free with just a little emotional madness over losing his prized property that he stole in the first place.... [The] play's focus on their child, Ellen Jean, downplays Duncan's rape of Margaret and renders it invisible offstage" (e-mail).

Despite the fact that ultimately we are shown a woman, Ellen Jean, who actively chooses to be united with a man, Margaret's initial abduction is minimized in the text, which could easily lead the audience to assume she was seduced, rather than raped. She expresses no rage in the play, merely remorse. Duncan is the only character who expresses anything close to rage and this is when he insists that Margaret belongs to him.

In the following plays, *Getting Out* and *The Widow's Blind Date*, only the rapist character perceives the sexual assault as a seduction. The raped female characters correctly identify the attacks as rape. Their rage is not contained, but the conflation of rape with seduction, from the male characters' point of view, allows them to feel justified pursuing their sexual assaults.

Getting Out (1977) by Marsha Norman

Getting Out was Marsha Norman's first play. It was originally produced in 1977 by the Actors Theatre of Louisville. This drama depicts the first twenty-four hours in the life of Arlene Holsclaw after she is released from the Alabama Pine Ridge Correctional Institute, where she served an eight-year incarceration for the second-degree murder of a cab driver. After her release, Arlene accepts a ride back to her home in Kentucky from Bennie, a widower prison guard who befriended her in prison. Bennie still calls Arlene by the name she used when she was first incarcerated, Arlie. As soon as they arrive at the apartment she has rented, Arlene asks Benny to leave, saying, "You go on now," but he replies, "Go on where, Arlie?" Initially, Benny mentions that he just wants to stay until he knows that she is "gonna do all right," adding that she has no one to take care of her. He says he's been looking after her for the past eight years while she was in prison and he got used to it. She says, "Well, you kin just git unused to it" (6–7).

Arlene keeps dropping hints that he should leave, suggesting he should visit Fort Knox on his way home. When the stage directions indicate that Bennie "*gives her a familiar pat*" Arlene "*slaps his hand away.*" Bennie proceeds to call her "sweetie" to which Arlene replies, "I ain't your sweetie" (9). Arlene consistently repels Bennie's advances, but his true intentions are revealed when he acknowledges that he has actually retired, and he has no plans to return to Alabama. "And you drove me all the way up here spectin to stay here?" Arlene asks. Bennie replies, "I was thinkin' on it." He even tells her to "take off them clothes and have yourself a nice hot bath." He offers to get the two of them some food, adding, "I'll take my time sos you don't have to hurry fixin yourself up" (13). Bennie is clearly setting the stage for a romantic evening, an evening that he feels he deserves after driving her all the way to Kentucky.

We see in this play an example of the sexual script described in the introduction. Benny makes repeated attempts to initiate a romantic encounter with Arlene, which she rejects, and he refuses to hear her "no" and just keeps trying to proceed with his seduction. After Arlene and Bennie eat, he offers to rub her back, and she says no. He tries again, grabbing her shoulders; Arlene tells him it hurts and asks him to stop. Bennie persists, saying, "Be lot nicer if you was laying down." Arlene asks him once more to leave but Bennie "*grabs her and throws her down on the bed*" and continues to rub her back. Finally, after more protestations and struggling, Bennie releases Arlene, innocently saying, "I ain't holdin you down." He offers to stay with her, make sure she is all right. He starts to leave, then asks for a kiss. Arlene feels trapped and tells him to stay away and slaps him. But Bennie continues with his seduction/rape attempt. "Ain't natural goin without it too long. Young thing like you. Git all shriveled up." Arlene starts hitting him but he overpowers her. Bennie "*kneels over her on the bed*" and "*unzips his pants*" (34–36).

Three: Female Rage

Bennie's actions are similar to a man on a date, buying dinner, offering a relaxing backrub, and suggesting several reasons why Arlene should take advantage of his romantic invitation. Bennie is following societal expectations of masculinity in which a man is supposed to persist even in the face of rejection by the female. As Michael Kimmel declares, "A man's job is to wear down [a woman's] resistance. Sometimes [the humming of male desire] can be so loud that it drowns out the actual voice of the real live woman that he's with. Men suffer from socialized deafness, a hearing impairment that strikes only when women say no" (142). Bennie is simply following the sexual script and expects to claim his reward.

Finally, Arlene is able to get past his selective hearing when she correctly identifies the truth of his actions, "This how you got your [wife] Dorrie, rapin?" Bennie replies, "That what you think this is, rape?" Arlene continues, "I oughta know… First they unzip their pants, some-

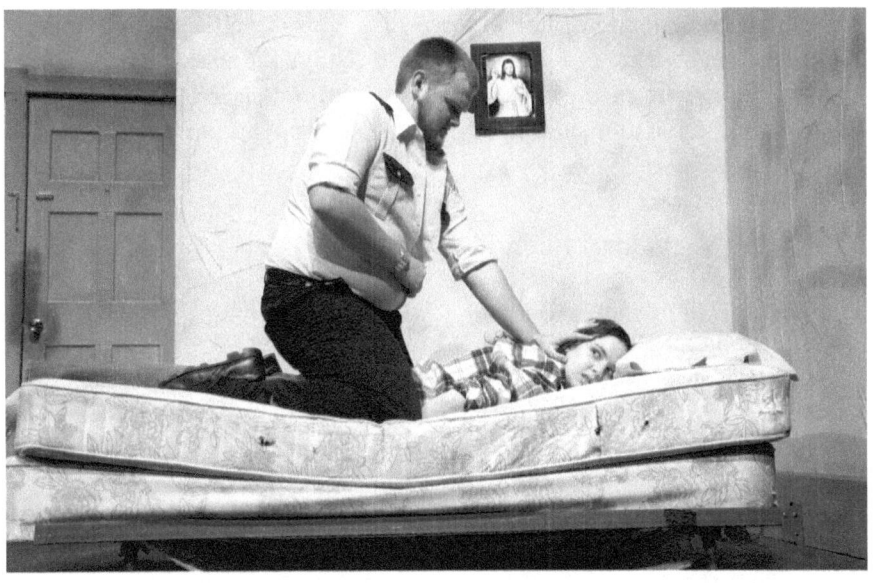

Bennie attempts to rape Arlene in the Adams State University Theatre Department's 2013 production of *Getting Out*, directed by Jenna Neilsen. Featuring Jake Webb as Bennie and Clarissa McNamara as Arlene (photograph by Linda Relyea).

times they take off their shirt. But mostly, they just pull it out and stick it in." Bennie stops, "*one hand goes to his fly*" but he finally registers what she has been saying. He straightens up, obviously shocked. He puts his arms back in his shirt and tells her, "Don't you call me no rapist. I ain't no rapist," and he "*begins to tucks his shirt back in and zip up his pants*" (35–36).

Bennie did not initially identify his actions as rape and clearly expected a different response to his sexual invitation. In fact, he was dangerously close to taking his seduction to its expected conclusion. It wasn't until Arlene called his actions "rape" that he actually heard her words. As Noelia Hernando-Real attests, once "Bennie comes to see himself as a rapist, [the] traditional discourse on manhood is deconstructed" (49). Bennie does return and attempts to apologize and reconcile with Arlene, but she rebuffs his advances. She is determined to start her life on the "outside" with no baggage from the past. Arlene does express her rage, but since Benny views his attempted rape as a seduction, he feels justified in persisting. This is similar to Rob's persistence in the face of Kim's attempts to change the subject in the play *Hush*. However, in the case of Kim, she did not clearly articulate the truth of the situation, and Rob's persistence (from his perspective) paid off.

The Widow's Blind Date (1989) by Israel Horovitz

This play was briefly discussed in relation to the group-think phenomenon that often accompanies gang rape. One of Margy's rapists was Archie, a man who has loved her since he was in elementary school. George, another one of the rapists, proudly forces Margy to remember that he (George) was the first to rape her. When Margy can't seem to remember the second rapist, Archie admits that he followed George, but he declares that he had nothing but love in his heart while he was raping her, "I was talkin' to you all the way … all the way …. whisperin' in your ear … tellin' you 'I love you, Marg.' I did. I do." Later, Archie explains, "The only reason I got in line, Margy, was I 'cause I didn't think you'd have me any other way…. That's why, Marg. Ever since the second grade I've carried a torch for ya … som'pin' wicked" (96, 100; ellipses in orig.).

Three: Female Rage

Stevi Jackson explains, "The masterful male and yielding female form a common motif of our popular culture.... Sex is seen as a means of forcing a woman into loving submission" (20). According to Archie, he participated in the gang rape because of his overpowering love for Margy, and he considered the gang rape an opportunity to express that love. He apologizes to Margy, but still doesn't accept his actions as rape. "What they [the other rapists] did was *dirty*, Marg. What I did was *making love*, and that's the truth" (102). Margy's reaction to the rape will be discussed in Part Two of this chapter, but suffice it to say, her rage was not contained by Archie's conflation of rape with seduction. Nonetheless, from Archie's point of view, the sexual encounter he had with Margy did not in any way constitute rape.

Part One of this chapter has detailed numerous ways in which female rage is contained in dramas about rape. I do not intend to trivialize the trauma of rape, which is vividly depicted in many of the plays discussed in this chapter. However, the shame felt by the raped female characters in these plays is evidence of the degree to which they have internalized the myth that raped women are contaminated. Furthermore, their self-doubt and self-blame is often due to their acceptance of the myth that depicts masculine sexuality as an uncontrollable physical force, in addition to the societal gendering of rage which disincentivizes women from actively expressing anger.

Part Two: Female Rage Demonized

"The unkindest cut of all." "The ultimate crime against manhood." "Vengeance of a high-voltage nature." "Men everywhere crossed their legs and collectively winced." "A selfish psycho." "So long as we can call ourselves civilized, she isn't." "'Primitive' was the word that kept coming to my mind." "Barbaric and uncivilized." "This woman does not deserve any support."[5]

These statements all refer to Lorena Bobbitt. Katie Roiphe writes, "After cutting off her husband's penis, Lorena Bobbitt has become a symbol of female rage"—not just female rage, but more importantly, female rage demonized (Bobbitt A29). The demonization of Bobbitt in 1993 had actually been foreshadowed years earlier in the depiction of female rage in post-rape situations in dramatic texts. The monstrous female characterizations in plays about rape are evidence of a powerful metaphor circulating in our culture, the metaphor that vengeful, angry women are monsters. Through the analogy between vengeful, raped women and monsters, raped female characters are demonized in several plays.

Metaphors demonstrate numerous assumptions that have been naturalized and are simply taken for granted as truths. As George Lakoff and Mark Johnson stress in *Metaphors We Live By*, metaphors can actually be "self-fulfilling prophecies," that "create social realities" (156). The fact that metaphors are used frequently and often unconsciously is a significant aspect of their power. The successful perpetuation of the metaphor that angry women are monsters stems from the invisible power metaphors wield and from the gendering of rage in our culture. Violent, explosive anger is seen as the territory of men. Margo Wilson and Martin Daly argue: "Most men who kill in jealous rage are not considered insane. Not only is jealousy 'normal,' but so, it seems, is violent jealousy, at least if perpetrated by a man and in the heat of passion" (207).[6] However, when women exhibit these emotions, they are suspect.

Susan Harris Smith, when discussing misogyny in plays by three well-known American playwrights (David Rabe, Sam Shepard, and David Mamet), marks how their depiction of violence toward women is "distorted, grotesque," and "concealed." She contends that in their plays, they "protect the audience from seeing women as victims either by removing them entirely from the stage or by substituting an image of woman as object or as comic butt; the women are de-graded and distorted by 'the male gaze'" (121). I will argue that the female raped characters in *Extremities* (1978) by William Mastrosimone, *Blood Moon* (1984) by Nicholas Kazan, and *The Widow's Blind Date (1989)* by Israel Horovitz are likewise not seen as victims, because they are depicted as monsters. The power of the "angry woman as monster" metaphor ultimately replaces the rage-filled raped woman with a "monstrous" female character who is demonized for her actions.

All three plays begin with or include a compassionate depiction of the raped characters; however, due to the actions generated from their expressed rage and the progressively sympathetic depiction of the rapists, the focus shifts to the emotional process of the rapists and away from the raped woman. At the same time, the earlier characterization of the raped characters is replaced by their monstrous status. In other words, due to their extreme and monstrous expressions of rage, they are demonized.

Extremities (1978) by William Mastrosimone

This play, which was discussed earlier in relation to rape myths, follows the actions of Marjorie after a vividly portrayed attempted rape by Raul, a sleazy character who gains entry to her farmhouse by pretending to look for his (non-existent) friend Joe. Marjorie is able to thwart his attempted rape by spraying him in the face with bug spray. What to do with him becomes the primary debate of the play once Marjorie's two roommates return home.

Marjorie sprays Raul with bug spray in Randolph College's 2012 production of *Extremities*, directed by Lisa Cesnik Ferguson. Featuring Matt Cornpropst as Raul and Rebekah Baumgartner as Marjorie (photograph by Ken Parks).

Mastrosimone himself, in describing early versions of the play, discussed the "victim-turned-avenger" character saying, "At first I felt like Dr. Frankenstein—that I had created a monster" (qtd. in Klein 1). Mastrosimone's monster remains alive and well in subsequent revisions. In fact, his creation's monstrous tendencies are evident in the opening scene during her encounter with a wasp. Simply killing the wasp with bug spray is not sufficient. Marjorie not only over-saturates the insect with the poison, but burns its already dead body with her lit cigarette, demonstrating that she is able to go well beyond what might be appropriate in terms of guaranteeing that the wasp is dead.

The attempted rape is graphic, brutal, and shocking, allowing the audience to initially sympathize with Marjorie. Over the course of the play, however, Marjorie not only sprays Raul's face with insect repellent, she hog-ties and blindfolds him with extension cords and other household items, and imprisons him in the fireplace. Subsequently, she scalds him with boiling water; fashions a makeshift noose around his neck, which she frequently tightens; pokes him repeatedly with fireplace implements; douses him with ammonia (having told him it was gasoline) and strikes matches near his face threatening to

Marjorie tortures Raul in Randolph College's 2012 production of *Extremities*, directed by Lisa Cesnik Ferguson. Featuring Matt Cornpropst as Raul and Rebekah Baumgartner as Marjorie (photograph by Ken Parks).

burn him alive; promises to starve him and make him lay in his own filth; declares that she will kill him and even digs a grave for him in the backyard; douses him with Clorox bleach; bangs his hand with a hammer and threatens to do the same with his skull; spits in and slaps his raw, burned and blistered face; runs his knife over his body and threatens to castrate him; and finally, using her hand and not the knife, "slits" his throat.

The dramatic text actually brings up many valid issues surrounding rape and the treatment of raped women by the criminal and legal systems in the drama. For example, Marjorie realizes that she will be hard pressed to prove that Raul tried to rape her. She has no bruises, no semen, and she contends, "Before they believe a woman in court, she has to be dead on arrival!" (61). However, Marjorie's actions ultimately are so extreme that even her roommates, Terry and Patricia, question her side of the story, and, as several reviewers point out, during the progress of the play audience members are compelled to wonder who is the actual victim in this play.[7] Additionally, the identity of the true victim is compounded when in the midst of his suffering at the hand of Marjorie, Raul compares himself to Christ (36, 78).

Raul is portrayed as a pathological liar and psychopath. He is clearly constructed as a mentally unstable individual who in the final moments of the play tries to comfort himself by singing children's nursery rhymes. Tracy Davis observes, "Raul deserves and gets sympathy because he acts out of illness" (91). This sympathetic depiction elicits the sympathy of Marjorie's roommates, in fact, by the end of the play, even Marjorie has sympathy for Raul. He asks, "Don't leave me alone?" and Marjorie says, "I'm right here." He then asks, "Don't let 'em beat me?" and Marjorie says, "No." She leads Raul back to the fireplace where he curls up, starts rocking, and begins singing, as Marjorie, according to the stage directions, "*weeps*" (89–90). At the end of the play, as Alisa Solomon points out, we "shed tears understanding tears for little boys who grow into ... rapists and murderers" ("Weeping" 79).

Marjorie's vengeance is made to seem extreme and unjustified, not simply because we ultimately sympathize with the rapist, but also because Raul's character is the one that provides the few moments of comic relief in the play; consequently, he becomes less threatening, Mar-

Raul in the fireplace in Randolph College's 2012 production of *Extremities*, directed by Lisa Cesnik Ferguson. Featuring Matt Cornpropst as Raul and Rebekah Baumgartner as Marjorie (photograph by Ken Parks).

jorie's actions appear progressively more monstrous. I suggest that the transfer of compassion from Marjorie to Raul succeeds, in part, due to the culturally accepted metaphor that angry women are monsters.

Mastrosimone himself seems to think that he has written a pro-feminist anti-rape piece when, in an essay accompanying the play he writes, "Down through the ages *Extremities* has been performed millions of times in the psyches of raped women [who have] in the privacy of their nightmares, wielded hammers and broomsticks and brought about a justice that society denied them. I am only the one who wrote it down" ("Interview" 105). Mastrosimone implies that he is doing women a favor by writing this play, when in actuality he is perpetuating the monstrous female metaphor and, as several reviewers have noted, eliciting sympathy for the rapist.[8]

I would like to return once again to the cultural rape script outlined by Sharon Marcus. As previously discussed, Marcus identifies two grammatical positions for women in the rape script; the first is "a communicative stance of *responsiveness* [which] encourages women not to take the offensive in a dialogue with a would-be rapist but to stay within the limits he sets" and the other is an "interpretive stance of empathy" (393). This implies that when a woman/character follows the rape script, she stays within the confines of feminine-gendered rage and sexuality and identifies with the rapist rather than defend herself. Marcus notes, this aspect of the rape script "places all human agency on the male side: to avert rape, a woman must make a man feel like a full human being, rather than force him to recognize *her* will and humanity" (393). In fact, as Marcus points out, some writers "advocate empathy as a mode of self-defense." In other words, according to these writers, if a rapist is attacking a woman due to his low self-esteem, by "responding lovingly" to a potential rapist, the woman may thwart his attack. Judith Herman's research has shown that women's "generally high sociability, however, was often a liability rather than an asset during a rape attempt. Many women tried to appeal to the humanity of the rapist or to establish some form of empathic connection with him. These efforts were almost universally futile" (*Trauma* 59). The plays in this study support Herman's findings and Marcus's contention that these grammatical positions available to women in the rape script lead to the woman being raped. In none of the rapes depicted in the plays examined for this study did "responding lovingly" thwart a rape attempt. In *Extremities*, in which the attempted rape is vividly portrayed, Raul demands that Marjorie speak to him as a lover would, saying that she loves him and wants him. It is clear in this scene that her politely complying with his demands would not have prevented her rape, or her murder, which Raul has planned. In this play, we see a vivid example of a raped female character's rage demonized, as well as evidence of the rape script detailed by Sharon Marcus.

Blood Moon (1983) by Nicholas Kazan

Blood Moon's protagonist, Manya, an only child, is a nineteen-year-old young woman whose parents have recently died. She is a college student and decides to visit her uncle Gregory in New York City during the Thanksgiving break. Gregory introduces Manya to his friend Alan and, subsequently, due to Alan's urging, leaves the two of them alone in Alan's apartment where Alan rapes Manya. The first act details the events leading up to the rape and the rape itself. As in *Extremities*, the rape scene is vividly depicted and leads to a sympathetic depiction of Manya and her situation. Following her assault, she speaks to the audience, describing that after the rape she took a cab to her uncle's home and never told him about the assault. She returned to school and managed to make up a variety of excuses for not returning to visit her uncle, and in fact she did not see her uncle for over a year. "During that time," Manya discloses to the audience, "I was obsessed with one question: What do I do? Do I leave it at that ... or do I, somehow, respond?" (43–44). The second act concerns Manya's response.

Reviews of productions have dubbed this response "gory," "savage," "menacing," "fiendish," "gruesome," "definitely not for the queasy," "cold-blooded," "shudder-inducing," "perverse," "heinous," and "sufficient to turn your stomach."[9] Mel Gussow observes "at the performance I attended, as the play reached its gruesome climax, several voices in the audience cried 'Oh, no!'" ("Blood Moon" C6). It is in Manya's response to her rape that she is demonized.

Early in the second act, which takes place one year after the rape, Manya sets the table for her dinner guests, Alan and Gregory. Once they arrive, and much to the shock of both guests, she explains that one year ago, Alan had raped her. When Gregory questions Alan about it, he says, "She wanted it. I gave her ... what she wanted" (60; ellipsis in orig.). Manya goes on to describe her subsequent depression, weight gain, and the realization that she was pregnant. By the time reality hit her, it was too late for a legal abortion, and she convinced two medical student friends of her to help her perform the abortion herself. She describes the ordeal in vivid detail to the men as they eat dinner. Alan, who has three daughters from various marriages, asks whether Manya knew if his baby was a boy. Manya does not answer his question. Finally, at the end of the meal, she reveals the details of her monstrous revenge plot.

Alan remarks that on a few occasions Manya mentioned a "plan" for the evening. She simply replies that she wanted to "have you here to dinner, to tell you my story." After further prodding, she reveals to Alan and Gregory that she had frozen the aborted fetus and the placenta. The stage directions indicate that Manya "*looks back and forth between the men ... relishing it.*" Gregory asks "What did you do with them?" Manya, after a long beat, gestures toward the dinner table. The men both become ill, and as Gregory rushes off stage apparently to vomit, Manya calls to him, "It was a boy" (80–83; ellipsis in orig.).

After her revelation, Manya moves toward the audience and asks, "Am I a monster? Was I? I don't know" (83). Manya may have doubts about her monstrous status, but she is depicted in that role. Who else but a monster would feed a man his aborted fetus? Manya is demonized for this outrageous behavior, and her expressed rage becomes her undoing as she is no longer taken seriously or acknowledged. In fact, reviewers of productions of *Blood Moon* have called Manya demonic, as well as psychopathic, cold-blooded, and perverse.[10]

The Widow's Blind Date (1989) by Israel Horovitz

The Widow's Blind Date opened in New York in 1989. Sally Burke rightly observes that this play "ostensibly holds sympathy for the rape victim yet ultimately victimizes her again" (103). Similar to *Extremities* and *Blood Mood*, this *second* rape occurs on two fronts: first, the raped woman, Margy, is demonized, and second, the rapists George and Archie are ultimately depicted in such a way as to elicit audience sympathy. Margy, who is thirty-seven years old and works at New York University, has returned to her Wakefield, Massachusetts, home because her brother is dying. She runs into Archie, an old high-school acquaintance, and accepts his invitation for dinner. She meets him at the newspaper baling plant where he and George (whom she also knew in high school) work. When Margy was in her twenties, she married, left Wakefield, and had two children. Her husband subsequently passed away. When Margy was seventeen years old, she was gang-raped by George, Archie, and five other boys from her high school.

The relationship between Archie and George is complex and competitive. They have known each other since grade school and have a close male friendship, including an intense and violent competition with respect to Margy, who they both remember as having been their sweetheart in grade school. Archie is quick to brag about his dinner date with Margy, and George counters by inviting Margy to their upcoming twentieth high school reunion. Archie, upset by this, asks George, "That s'posed ta be funny?" adding, with reference to the past, "George Ferguson messing with Archie Crisp's girls ... can't find none of his own. He's got to move in on his buddy" (38–39; ellipsis in orig.). This competition escalates over the course of the play, and we later learn that during the gang rape, Archie was supposed to go first, but George took his place in the line.

Margy passionately expresses her emotions as the events of the past are revealed. In a poignant monologue, Margy shares with George and Archie what she felt at the time. She clearly believed many of the rape myths previously discussed and blamed herself for her assault. She asks the men why they chose her. "Was I too provocative? Was it the way I smiled? Did I look available? Did I look like an easy lay?" She describes how for years she walked around "like a zombie, wondering was I really, deep down, underneath it all, *looking for it?*" Margy stresses that she was only seventeen, and "you hit me and then you and your kind did what you did. You line up.... *LINE UP* ... and you did what you did!" When George replies, "You loved it," Margy spews out her anger, screaming, "I DID NOT LOVE IT! I HATED IT! I HATED IT!" (98–99; ellipsis in orig.) But Margy's true purpose is revealed when she responds to

Three: Female Rage

George's question if she came back to get even, by saying, "You bet your ass I'm gonna get even! ... Wicked awful even! I'm gonna get sooo even with you, George, I can taste it!" (100).

Margy's monstrous status is solidified in a unique way twice in the play when her actions result in violence (ultimately fatal) between the two men. In the first case, her attitude is used by Archie as justification for hitting George. Archie's anger is aroused when Margy teases him, calling him "a goat," his childhood nickname. He tells Margy that he doesn't like it and proceeds to slap George, telling Margy, "Every time you make a smart remark that runs me down, I'm gonna hurt your friend here more." When Margy asks, "To which smart remark, precisely, do you refer, Archie?" he once again hits George. The teasing continues to

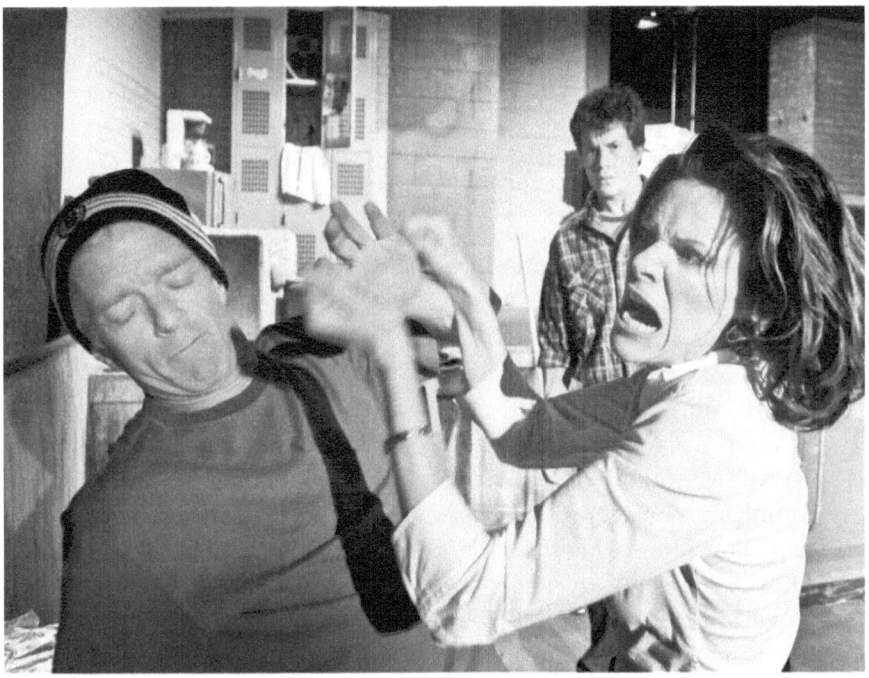

Margy's anger erupts in the Firehouse Theatre Project's 2008 production of *The Widow's Blind Date*, directed by Bill Patton. Featuring Ford Flannagan as George (left), Landon Nagel as Archie (rear) and Jennifer Massey as Margy (photograph by Jay Paul).

the point that Archie begins choking George. Archie ultimately releases George, but the violence is clearly initiated and continued due to Margy's remarks (49–50).

In the second instance, the situation is reversed and George uses Margy's behavior as an excuse to hit Archie. The tension onstage has increased and George is about to sexually assault Margy. He advances toward Margy, unhitching his belt, and says, "What's wanted here is more lovemakin'." Margy hits him and George declares, "Every time you hit me, Marg, I'm hitting this one." And he violently hits Archie (103–104). This pattern repeats numerous times and, as Sally Burke points out, "this action makes Archie, not Margy, the victim" (104).

In the final moments of the play, the fight escalates and George is killed when he is flipped by Archie into the baler and George's face "*explodes.*" Blood is everywhere. Margy "*looks at blood on baler door. She touches blood, pulling her hand down through stain, enlarging it.*" She takes her jacket, turns to Archie and says, "(*simply, clearly*) I'll be back Archie. It's a long list" (107). Archie cradles George, and tries to coax him back to life, ultimately screaming, "*Oh,* Jesus! Kermie? Kermie? Don't be dead, Kermie, don't be dead!" But George is dead, and the lights fade onstage, all but a single light on Archie. Prior to the final blackout the stage directions indicate "*a moment of absolute silence*" (108).

This last tableau could easily elicit sympathy for Archie and George. Margy is depicted as the cause of their suffering, rather than the reverse, and she is ultimately demonized. By the end of the play, as Burke remarks, "the audience is free to view Margy as the provocative whore who spawned all this bloody violence and ran away, leaving one buddy to mourn another" (104). Margy is no longer the injured party but a criminal, a monster, who promises even more bloody vengeance as she meticulously proceeds down the list of those who raped her, seeking the ultimate revenge.

It is worth noting that *The Widow's Blind Date*, as well as *Blood Moon* and *Extremities*, in which the raped characters are demonized due to their monstrous actions, were written during a time of antifeminist backlash in this country. This will be discussed further in the next chapter, but it points to my contention that playwrights' depictions of rape and raped characters do not occur in a vacuum. The cultural forces

Three: Female Rage

affecting the characters in dramatic texts—for example, adherence to myths about rape, the eroticizing of male sexual aggression and female passivity, the gendering of rage which facilitates the containment of female rage and the demonization of women who express aggressive rage—can likewise have an impact on the playwrights who craft these characters. Admittedly, in this chapter I have discussed the two extremes of this impact, rage contained and rage demonized, and a middle ground on which raped female characters can express their rage without being demonized should, and does, exist and will be the subject of Chapter Six.

Four

Antifeminist Backlash

Part One: Dramatizing Antifeminist Backlash

Susan Faludi, in her study *Backlash: The Undeclared War Against American Women*, describes antifeminist backlash as "a recurring phenomenon: it returns every time women begin to make some headway toward equality, a seemingly inevitable early frost to the cultures brief flowerings of feminism" (61). Bonnie Dow continues the argument, defining backlash as a "wholesale rejection of feminist ideals, an attempt to demonize women's liberation and return women to the subordinate roles of a bygone era" (87). I will argue that the vivid depiction of the monstrous female metaphor—the monstrous "liberated" female—in *Extremities, Blood Moon,* and *The Widow's Blind Date*, written between 1978 and 1989, is evidence of the influence of the antifeminist backlash within the United States at the time.

From a socio-political perspective, the depiction of the raped female characters in these plays is in keeping with the antifeminist backlash that was gaining momentum during the 1980s. Susan Faludi documents how attitudes about rape served to undermine feminist advancements of the 1970s. Faludi notes, for example, the U.S. Attorney General's Commission on Pornography "proposed that women's professional advancement might be responsible for rising rape rates" (xii), and echoes of the familiar refrain, "a woman's place is in the home" along with a procreative mandate, were commonplace.

In concert with these antifeminist sentiments against career women, we find in *The Widow's Blind Date* that sympathy is created for George and Archie, as well as distaste for Margy, due to the male characters' working-class status in contrast to Margy's liberated, educated, and upper-class status. Archie has been working at the baling plant since he was twelve, and both he and George are clearly trapped in these minimum-wage jobs. Kevin Kelly in his review of the play notes how sympathy is created for George by Horovitz "in our recognition that he's [George] never had a chance, that his hopes have long since been strangled by the socioeconomic system" (Stunner 21). Horovitz's language choices also highlight this oppression as Margy, who now works at New York University, has lost her regional dialect and word usage, whereas Archie and George have not. Margy in fact repeatedly corrects their grammar, flaunting her educational superiority (56, 57, 68).

Antifeminist backlash included a negative reaction to women's minor progress in the workplace. Men were threatened by the few women who were promoted to management positions, and this, coupled with the economic insecurity in the 1980s, led them to blame women and feminism for their problems, as they assumed that women's advancement led directly to their suffering. While Margy's gang rape happened in the past when she was seventeen, prior to her rising above the men in status, the men's violent reaction to her in the present is indicative of this antifeminist backlash. George even threatens to rape her again, saying, "You think you can just hop back inta town and be another person from what you are?" The stage directions indicate that he advances toward her, unhitching his belt, saying, "What's wanted here is more love-makin'" (103). In addition to dramatizing feminist backlash, *The Widow's Blind Date* dramatically exemplifies many of Allan Johnson's contentions about patriarchy related to backlash. Johnson describes a patriarchal society as one that is "male-dominated, male-identified, and male-centered," adding that the aspect of male identification "gives even the most lowly placed man a cultural basis for feeling some sense of superiority over the otherwise most highly placed women." This is why, according to Johnson, "a construction worker can feel within his rights as a man when he harasses a well-dressed professional woman" (5, 8).

Two of the rape myths previously discussed in Chapter Two were reinforced and perpetuated by antifeminist activists. The first of these is the myth that women invite sexual attention, and in fact are asking to be raped, as a consequence of their wardrobe choices and flirtatious behavior toward men. Camille Paglia, who some consider the spokeswoman of the antifeminist backlash, writes,[1] "Women must take responsibility for their share in this exchange, which means they must scrupulously critique their own mannerisms and clothing choices and not allow themselves to drift willy-nilly into compromising situations." Pagila discusses wardrobe choices, such as "Madonna's harlot outfits," saying, "if you advertise, you'd better be ready to sell!" (36).

A second rape myth upheld by antifeminist backlash is the myth of uncontrollable male sexuality. In a critique of antifeminist backlash, Andrea Dworkin, in *Right-Winged Women*, describes the belief among these conservative antifeminist women that men "suffer arousal passively—against their will or regardless of their will. They then act on what a woman, or any sex object, has provoked.... When a man has an erection and commits a sexual act because of it, or in response to it, he is acting in response to a provocation by a woman" (208).

In *Extremities*, as previously discussed, Marjorie's roommate Terry affirms the myth that women ask to be raped by their wardrobe choices, both in terms of her own rape as a teenager, and in terms of Raul's attempted rape of Marjorie. Additionally, Terry believes she excited her friend's father to the point where he had no control over his sexual functions because of her "too tight" outfit, so consequently it was really *her* fault that she was raped. Similarly, in *The Widow's Blind Date*, Horovitz justifies the actions of George and Archie by evoking the myth that women invite sexual assault by their behaviors. George, for example, repeatedly paints Margy as the school whore. When Archie tells George about his upcoming dinner date with Margy, revealing that she called him, George remarks, "Still the aggressive one, Margy, huh?" (4). He brags how Margy used to let him "look down" her blouse, adding that "everybody was!" (74–75). This depiction of a woman who would allow men to look down her blouse lends credibility to the rapist's actions and facilitates the demonization of Margy's rage when it is released. In an intense moment in the drama, when the secrets of the past are revealed, George reminds Margy that she is no longer in Worcester, or New York, or Paris, but that she is back home. "And when you're home, sistah, you are what you are. *What you are!!* Gangbanged at Fisherman's Beach and she comes up smilin' and beggin' for more ... beggin' for more! (93;

ellipsis in orig.). By characterizing Margy as morally loose, George uses her behavior as a justification for the gang rape.

In *Blood Moon*, raped character Manya is referred to by her rapist, Alan, as "exquisite" and "the freshest flower of spring, with a scent so faint, so delicate, yet so irritatingly sweet the reaction it provokes is almost uncontrollable" (25–26). As it turns out, Alan's reaction was not *almost* uncontrollable, however, as the myth would have us believe—it was *literally* uncontrollable. However, this play presents, perhaps even more powerfully, another antifeministy issue, that of abortion. Faludi documents the attempts to curtail women's access to reproductive choice during the '80s, some that even "called on raped women not to have abortions" (418). Consequently, in keeping with the antifeminist sentiments of the decade, Manya's demonized status is initially solidified by her willingness to have an abortion, and subsequently compounded by her vengeful actions in terms of her choice of dinner entrée.

A pattern emerges within these three plays. Initially, we are on the side of the raped women, but ultimately these female characters are retroactively held responsible for their rapes—after all, given their monstrous behavior, it is what they deserved! Eventually the rapists' actions are justified. We are led to see the raging raped characters as hateful and the male rapist(s) as laudable because all they desire is love (Archie), class mobility (Raul, Archie, George), or fulfillment of their uncontrollable sexual desire (all of them). The raped woman's rage is understood as humanly negative, hence monstrous, and the rapists' desire is understood as humanly flawed, hence excusable.

In these plays, the portrayal of the raped female character's anger leads directly to her demonization. As I have argued, the gendering of rage creates road blocks to women expressing their anger, and therefore, when rage is expressed in these plays, the emotion and the women are depicted as monstrous, leaving Marjorie, Margy, and Manya squarely the position of someone who can be legitimately demonized. In short, the monstrous female metaphor disempowers and discredits raped women's rage. Additionally, in each play the women are also demonized due to their feminist or perceived feminist stance: Marjorie's single, liberated status, and perceived overt sexuality due to her wardrobe choice; Manya's decision to have an abortion; and Margy's educational and career achievements and perceived flaunting of her higher-class status. The descriptive adjectives used to describe Lorena Bobbitt's "monstrous" actions quoted at the beginning of the previous chapter indicate that this demonization happens offstage as well as onstage. Lorena Bobbitt, according to newspaper and magazine accounts, withstood years of spousal abuse and rape. Her rage erupted in a violent retribution, an action that was deemed monstrous, and consequently, her voice and her rage were denied agency. In fact, her defense attorney knew full well the power of the "vengeful woman as monster" metaphor when he based her defense on temporary insanity. As Linda Pershing writes, Lorena's attorneys knew she "would be found guilty if the jury interpreted her actions as retaliation rather than as an irresistible impulse. [Therefore] the defense built their case on the contention that Lorena's actions were a hybrid of insanity and self-defense, not rage" (21). The actions of the three raped women in *Extremities*, *Blood Moon*, and *The Widow's Blind Date* were constructed as pre-meditated retaliation, and consequently the verdict handed down was clearly guilty.

Part Two: Antifeminist Backlash and the Demonization of Karen Finley's Rage

One further example of antifeminist backlash and the demonization of angry women can be found in the reception of Karen Finley's dramatic texts and performances. I believe the events surrounding the National Endowment for the Arts (NEA) funding for Finley can be viewed as an antifeminist effort on the part of government officials to demonize Karen Finley due to her aggressive, raged-filled performances, similar to the ways in which rage-filled female characters were demonized.[2]

Female performance artist Karen Finley's works in their *form* present a sharp contrast to dominant theatrical traditions, and descriptions of the *content* of her works span a wide spectrum from "obscene" to "inspired."[3] Scholars have described the potential of performance art to contest traditional representations of women and reveal the oppressive nature of such representations. The mere fact of a female subject embodied in the works of female performance artists allows these artists to defy and subvert the status quo of a male subject. Additionally, these artists deconstruct previously held assumptions about gender and sexuality, and expose systems of oppression by providing a voice, often a very loud (non-feminine) voice, for their female subjects, specifically in terms of creating a dramatic vehicle for the expression of rage about sexual violence.

One point illuminated by Teresa de Lauretis in her work on feminist cinema is how the "representation of woman as spectacle—body to be looked at, place of sexuality and object of desire—so pervasive in our culture" has "served to keep women in 'their place'" (*Alice* 4). De Lauretis continues her argument in *Technologies of Gender*, noting, "the subject of feminism, is a movement back and forth between the representation of gender (in its male-centered frame of reference) and what that representation leaves out or, more pointedly, makes unrepresentable" (26). This movement between a male-centered fantasy version of female representation and its female counterpart is evident in the performance art of Karen Finley, as she embodies multiple characters in her works.[4] Critics and reviewers of Finley's performances observe that she defies social expectations of feminine behavior, presenting a subversive, unsocialized woman whose presence shocks the audience into confronting the degree to which women are degraded in patriarchal capitalist cultures. Stephen Watt and Gary Richardson claim that Finley "continually interrogates society's devaluation and persistent victimization of women," as she exposes the "sexuality of violence" and the "violence of sexuality" in our society (1028).

Finley is known for the explicit use of her body in performance. For example, she smears her naked body with excrement (chocolate frosting), symbolizing women's degradation and contamination. She does not shy away from inappropriate subject matter; rather, she rages against ideological systems that perpetuate the victim role for women. Timothy Wiles comments on Finley's "blatant" enactment of female rage at abuses of power, adding that her monologues "do more than depict female rage—they are part of its performance, something that Finley in turn is 'doing' to us as audience through her narration" (118). What is evident in these comments is that the rage Finley performs is transgressive because it is male-gendered rage. She is known for transgressing the boundaries of gender roles with her aggressive performance style and by using her body as an instrument of terror and presenting an image of female sexual power, rather than subscribing to the sexually submissive gender role stereotype. Ultimately, her performances subvert the traditional role of female performer and male spectator by contesting conventional audience/performer dynamics and disrupting the male gaze. In describing Finley's performances, Jill Dolan writes, "Finley does not offer herself as a passive object. She forces men to be passive in the face of her rage." She will not play the game by male spectators' rules, which consequently "leaves the male spectator nowhere to place himself in relation to her performance. He can no longer maintain the position of the sexual subject who views the performer as a sexual object" ("Dynamics of Desire" 162–63).[5]

The attributes noted by critics and reviewers of Karen Finley's work, attributes that contributed to the events related to the National Endowment for the Arts (NEA) funding for Finley, are exemplified in her performance piece *The Constant State of Desire*.

The Constant State of Desire (1986)

The Constant State of Desire is a 90-minute solo performance piece composed of three acts containing several narrative units in which Finley plays multiple characters, including two female incest survivors, a woman taking revenge on Wall Street yuppies, a dead Vietnam veteran, a woman born without a vagina, a sadistic male rapist, and a gay man who has died of AIDS. Several aspects of the play relate to the depiction of rape, rape myths, gendered sexuality, and female rage. In a review of *The Constant State of Desire*, Elizabeth Zimmer describes how Finley would "transform her body, as if undergoing demonic possession, exposing the rage, humiliation, or sadness that was boiling under her costume of femininity" (79). Finley makes full use of the disruptive and transgressive potential of performance art to unmask female rage as she refuses to assume a passive object position.

The opening monologue is entitled "Baby Bird." Finley enters in a "yellow dress" and sits in an "overstuffed chair"—stereotypically feminine and domestic images (139). She speaks in the third person, describing the dreams of a woman who first imagines herself "strangling baby birds" and then dreams of being "locked in a cage" and "singing." The woman then "dreams of falling out of a fifth-story window," and holds onto the ledge with her fingertips, calling out for help. She is ignored by her husband who walks below on the sidewalk, and ultimately her cries are only heard after the wind takes "her cries half way round the world to a child's crib, so its mother could hear her own child's cries" (139). Finley speaks of the doctors who analyzed these dreams, insisting that they were wrong, "for these were the same doctors who anesthetized her during the birth of her children…. The problem really was in the way she projected her femininity. And if she wasn't passive, well, she just didn't feel desirable. And if she wasn't desirable, she didn't feel female" (140).

This monologue highlights the gendering of sexuality (i.e., passivity equals desirability) and the power of masculine institutional forces to control women's bodies and sexuality. In the first section, when Finley describes the woman in yellow's dreams, she evokes the image of a woman as songbird, locked in a cage singing for others to judge her. She hangs from the window ledge as her unhearing husband walks below, exemplifying women's oppressed status. The fact that the woman's cries are only acknowledged when they occur in a maternal setting indicates there is only one socially prescribed role in which women's voices can be heard, the mother/wife. As Pramaggiore writes, "In contrast to the 'shot heard round the world' of the American Revolution," these cries only travel "half as far" and are only heard "within a circle of women, mothers, and children" (275). Finally, the manipulation of women's natural body by male doctors, and the socially requisite femininity, are depicted as controlling devices in this monologue.[6]

Acts Two and Three contain rage-filled depictions of sexual perversions and abuse, including patriarchal heritage being passed from father to son as nine-year-old boys eat their father's dung and chocolate covered testicles, and a man raping a woman in a laundromat by using her own baby as a dildo and then having anal sex with his own mother. "Rather than relying upon the linguistic use of 'motherfucker' as a catch-all pejorative term emptied of any relation to bodies," Pramaggiore writes, "Finley enacts the word literally, stripping it of its ability to hide behind its metaphorical status" (281). In addition, Finley also reinforces the previously discussed myth that sexuality is an uncontrollable physical force when the male character in the laundromat describes himself as being "nothing but a human penis" (147). By materializing these myths and sexual metaphors, Finley reveals their power. The myth that masculine sexuality is an uncontrollable physical force becomes a weapon used against women as it justifies the rapist's actions.

Finley's material is explicit, biting, and disturbing and one would expect audience members' reactions to be somewhat hostile and defensive as she forces them to confront uncomfortable feelings. However, more often than not, reactions to her works focus on Karen Finley, the artist, rather than focusing on her dramatic texts. I believe that the circumstances surrounding her National Endowment for the Arts funding, in addition to media and governmental reactions to her work, were an effort to demonize Finley herself. These reactions, in keeping with the antifeminist backlash of the period, constituted a strategic attempt to silence not only her rage, but more importantly the political message boiling underneath her rage.

Finley's performance texts contain vivid, stark, and shockingly brutal portraits of rape and female rage. Even though the female and male characters she depicts are brutal and may legitimately be dubbed monstrous, Finley does not demonize the characters she presents with the goal of maintaining the patriarchal status quo. Instead of seeking to silence or disempower female rage, thereby keeping women in their place, Finley unmasks female rage, giving it a voice and a venue. However, because her performances threaten to expose patriarchal political and social structures, it is not surprising that efforts were made to prevent her from continuing her artistic output. Karen Finley demonstrates why the active expression of female anger can be threatening.

In an interview with Nicholas Drake, Finley describes her work as "a reaction to my becoming aware." She recalls making "a conscious decision to exploit the feminine limitations that were given to me, and hang them over the audience's heads, the *male* audience in particular.... I started with what I felt, freeing me from what I had been imprisoned by, by exposing my gender's limitations" (12). By foregrounding and exposing the socio-cultural forces that had limited Finley due to her gender, her emotionally explosive art freed her from these imprisoning forces. However, as I will demonstrate, these patriarchal forces, as exemplified by the NEA events, persisted in their efforts to silence Finley.

Elin Diamond observes that every performance "embeds features of previous performances: gender conventions, racial histories, aesthetic traditions, political and cultural pressures that are consciously and unconsciously acknowledged" (*Performance* 1). I will focus especially on these political and cultural pressures exposed through an analysis of the reactions to Finley. An examination of the way Finley was, as Lynda Goldstein's describes, "discursively (re)produced, (re)circulated, and (re)contained" by the debate about her works in the popular media and in Congress will show the intent by many people to demonize her (104). This demonization was in keeping with the antifeminist backlash of the time.

I will present four possible motives underlying the efforts to demonize Finley: (1) Finley's works trigger homophobic reactions, (2) Finley's politics, (3) Finley's transgressive border crossings and her male-gendered rage, and (4) Finley's ability to speak the truth and confront disturbing social issues.

In an interview with Nicholas Drake, Finley said, "What was very difficult or devastating for me in the NEA experience was being looked at as if I were crazy, out of control, or unprofessional" (11). Finley herself states in an interview with Richard Schechner, "People are scared of my information. They really don't know what I'm going to do; they don't like me dealing with sexual issues or political issues" (152).

As background, I will provide a brief summary of events that took place with respect to the National Endowment for the Arts (NEA).[7] In 1989 fundamentalist Christian Minister Donald Wildmon, through his American Family Association, organized a letter-writing campaign denouncing the NEA and urging Congress to look into their policy of funding art that the American Family Association members considered blasphemous. This campaign prompted Senate conservatives Alfonse D'Amato and Jesse Helms, along with House Representative Dana Rohrabacher, to look into the matter further. In February 1990, the panel of the NEA charged with reviewing grant applications for Solo Performance Theatre Artists and Mimes, recommended approving 18 of the 95 applications they had received. Finley was among these 18 and was approved by the panel to receive $12,000.

On May 4, 1990, NEA Chairman John Frohnmayer told Philip Arnoult, chairman of the solo performance advisory board, that he had some misgivings about their recommendations. On May 11, 1990, an article appeared in *The Washington Post* by Rowland Evans and Robert Novak criticizing the NEA, specifically mentioning Karen Finley as a "nude, chocolate-smeared young woman" warning that she could become could become "the Mapplethorpe case of 1990" (A27). On May 13, 1990, the NEA postponed its decision on the solo theatre grants so it could gather more information about Karen Finley, Holly Hughes, Tim Miller and John Fleck, the four artists in question. By mid-June, Frohnmayer said certain political realities made it unlikely that all 18 solo performers would receive their recommended funding, and by the beginning of July, the NEA four—Karen Finley, Holly Hughes, Tim Miller, and John Fleck—had their grants denied.

By fall 1990, the four artists joined in a lawsuit against the NEA on the grounds that the NEA policy of enforcing decency requirements on those who ask for or receive government funding was vague and unconstitutional. In November 1991, two of the four artists, Tim Miller and Holly Hughes, had their grants reinstated, but they remained parties of the lawsuit. In the summer of 1993 the judge ruled in favor of the lawsuit, and Finley was given $8,000 of the original grant and $6,000 in damages. The government appealed the case and it ended up before the Supreme Court. Finally, in 1998 the Supreme Court upheld the constitutionality of the 1990 law requiring the National Endowment for the Arts to consider decency standards when deciding which artists should receive NEA money.

In his book, *Culture Wars: Documents from the Recent Controversies in the Arts*, editor Richard Bolton highlights the influence of the media on public opinion around the NEA situation. "Most of the public," Bolton writes, "was informed about the NEA debate through the exaggerated statements of legislators, activists, and editorialists, and through one-line 'summaries' of the works and artists in question slipped into the evening news. Unfortunately, the artists in question were not able to 'reduce their arguments to sound bites,' [consequently] artist saw their work shorn of its complexity and placed in the service of reactionary agendas" (16).

An examination of reviews and audience member reactions, as well as the political commentary related to Finley's work, is important to my analysis that she was demonized by the public, critics, and governmental officials. Long before the NEA crisis, Finley's performances were not universally welcomed. In 1987 bookings of *The Constant State of Desire* were canceled in London, when she was banned by the Westminster Council and Scotland Yard. In Los Angeles, her performance was canceled a week prior to the scheduled opening. Bookings in Miami and Atlanta were also canceled that summer. When Finley does perform, audience reaction is striking. "Her work," writes Joe Brown for *The Washington Post*, "makes audiences uncomfortable, even hostile. In New York, men dropped their pants and threw things at the stage. In San Francisco, a club offered to pay her double not to perform at all" (D2).

By 1989 there was a right-wing groundswell against left-wing artists. James Cooper noted that modern art had become "the purveyor of a destructive, degenerate, ugly, pornographic, Marxist, anti–American ideology" (*Congressional Record*, Sept. 1989, qtd. in Bolton 6). In July 1990, David Gergen wrote in *U.S. News & World Report*, "What is at issue is that some artists ... want to engage in wanton destruction of a nation's values, and they expect that same nation to pay their bills" (80). As Pat Robertson decried "tax-supported trash" on his *700 Club* one day, his co-host Shelia Walsh gravely concluded, "It's just a hellish plot to destroy this nation" (qtd. in Bolton 232).

In July 1990, CNN's program *Crossfire* host Pat Buchanan referred to Finley as "the young lady, semi-nude, who smeared herself in chocolate as a form of moral statement against what she called sexism" (qtd. in Bolton 248). Barbara Gamarekian quotes Finley in an article in *The New York Times*, "I have been made a fool in the press; I have been dismissed by William Safire, Evans and Novak and William Buckley, none of whom have seen me perform" (C15). The fact that many of Finley's more vocal critics never once saw her perform brings me to my argument that Finley herself is the female being demonized, not her work as an artist. I will now detail the five possible motives underlying efforts to demonize Finley.

Rape, Rage and Feminism in American Drama

Item One: Homophobia (or Karen, What *Do* You Do with Those Yams?)

In the mid-1980s, Karen Finley was performing a monologue entitled "Yams Up My Granny's Ass." Mary Chandler describes this piece as being about "the issue of family violence and sexual abuse, specifically a drug addict who tortured his grandmother on Thanksgiving." In the monologue, Finley "portrayed a deranged man smearing his relative with canned candied sweets." In order to depict this activity, "Finley—who used food as a prop in much of her work—turned a can of yams over her lower back and let it run down her buttocks" (E3).

The *Village Voice* cover story on June 24, 1986, by C. Carr was about Karen Finley.[8] In this article, Carr writes, "In one of Finley's more shocking routines, she pulls her pants down and smears canned yams up her ass and talks—in male persona—about sticking yams '*up my granny's butt but I never touch her twat, baby*'" ("Unspeakable" 143). Pete Hamill, a regular contributor to the *Voice*, wrote an article in the July 1, 1986, edition entitled "I Yam What I Yam," in which he took *Voice* editor Robert Friedman to task for having published Carr's cover story. He begins the article, "Last week, after reading the cover story in the *Voice*, I hurried down to the A & P to check out the yams.... I thought the adorable Karen Finley must use very small yams in her performances or have a very large anus" (10). Later, Finley wrote about this incident: "Hamill apparently never went to see the performance that he devoted so many words to excoriating, because he imagined that I actually took an uncooked yam and sodomized myself with it on stage" (qtd. in Chandler E3). The debate on the issue of whether or not Finley had inserted yams into her anus continued for weeks, as well as debates about whether someone who performed such acts should be considered an artist. Numerous statements about Finley's work were circulated in the press, including false statements that were circulated in both press accounts and academic critiques of her work. In August 1990, in an interview with Kevin Kelly of *The Boston Globe*, Finley says, "Angry? Of course I'm angry. I never put yams up my rectum, never, and that's all you hear about my performance. You hear it from people who've never seen me" (59).[9]

Lynda Hart deftly advances the argument that underlying all this talk of yams is homophobia:

> Ridiculous as these arguments sound, I think they are a text worth reading closely. This was the moment when Finley's performances became fixated in the public imagination with bodily orifices and the boundary between what is inside and outside the body. And it is important to notice that not just any bodily orifice, but her anus, the opening into the body that has historically been most associated with "unnatural" sexuality, was at issue. It is particularly worth noting that this act was read by the respondents as not only dirty and disgusting but also and most importantly as gender transgressive.... Hence in one performative gesture, Finley violated not only the boundaries of gender but also transgressed the hetero/homo binary; and in doing so she forced a response that revealed how the latter is necessary to shore up the fictive coherency of the former ["Dirty Work" 6–7].

Hart claims that Finley was often singled out as the "exception" in the NEA four (Karen Finley, Holly Hughes, Tim Miller, and John Fleck) because she is heterosexual and the others are not. But the slurry of reactions to her use of the yams, as Hart points out, suggests that the transgressions she embodies in her performances elicit homophobic reactions and in that respect, she is not the exception in the company of Hughes, Miller, and Fleck.

Finally, homophobia was evident as funded art institutions were attacked for supporting artists whose works depicted homosexual desire. On an episode of CNN's *Crossfire*, Pat Robertson was complaining that this "art" was being paid for by his tax dollars. Christopher Reeve, another guest during the program, responded, "Well, unfortunately we also paid for a Stealth bomber. I happen to think the Stealth bomber is obscene. So, we all have our different definitions of what's obscene." Robertson's reply implies the homophobia that underlies the issue of art and obscenity, "Well," he replied, "one at least keeps us free. The other one may destroy young people" (qtd. in Bolton 248).

Item Two: Finley's Politics

Robert Friedman writes, "Don't let the chocolate or the yams fool you ... it's Finley's sexual politics, not her foodstuffs that people can't digest." Actually, Friedman observes, when critics say "Finley's art isn't worthy of recognition ... they are concealing their distaste for her feminist menu behind accusations of her bad taste" (54). Obviously, a performance artist who describes castrating Wall Street yuppies is one whose political leanings probably don't bend in the same directions as the majority of those in the white male power hierarchy. Those who found the NEA's funding choices inappropriate were of the opinion that the questionable artists were promoting a progressive agenda that would undermine religious values, the current power structure, and the traditional family. The subversive potential of art and artists needed to be monitored and quelled.

Government subsidy is not necessary for art to exist, but some kind of funding *is* necessary if artists are to be freed from the financial necessity to produce works that conform to the demands of the marketplace. In a 1995 interview with Nicholas Drake, Finley said, "I wish that artists or art could become more mainstream without losing its edge, that you didn't have to compromise. I wish that becoming mainstream didn't mean that you have to lose any of your integrity. I would like to be able to reach as many people as possible" (13). In other words, artists who wish to articulate controversial or alternative worldviews cannot rely on the marketplace to fund their artistic efforts; consequently, they must seek funding elsewhere. Denying NEA grants to controversial artists (who, as Christopher Reeves pointed out, are tax payers and contribute to and support government projects that they may personally find objectionable) is an effective strategy to silence subversive voices.

As my summary of the NEA events established, the NEA four were not willing to become docile bodies and allow those who had influence over the NEA to provide them with artistic guidelines for self or even institutional patrol. Finley wrote in her May 19 response to the Evans and Novak *Washington Post* article, "I am now the latest victim of the attacks of the extremist right on freedom of expression. I see this attack as part of a larger trend of suppressing artists—especially those whose work deals with difficult social issues" (A23). Finley's work does deal with difficult social issues. The NEA debates were not so much an argument over art as they were a debate over competing views of American society and a clash over who will have the power to decide the status quo, a debate that was influenced by the antifeminist backlash of the '80s.

Item Three: Finley's Transgressive Border Crossings and Male-Gendered Rage

Finley herself has said, "I feel my work has always involved trying to break barriers and challenging taboos" (qtd. in Graham 95). Among these barriers are the culturally defined lines between male and female, and the power dynamics contained within those boundaries, especially the gendered sexuality and rage that, when contested in her performances, can provoke anxiety among audience members. Finley's enactment of the brash, abusive, and foul-mouthed characters she embodies in her performances contradicts the conventional image of the passive, polite, and clean female body. Finley subverts the patriarchal desire for this culturally determined female body by coating herself with substances that represent the abuse of women in our society, for example, excrement. But she simultaneously highlights the consumption of the female body when the substance Finley rubs on her body to represent excrement, is in fact chocolate frosting.

These disruptions of dominant representations of the female body produce an uncertainty in the expected reaction in the audience, and hence, discomfort.[10] In fact, as Michael Brenson writes, Finley is "best known for using her own naked body on stage in an effort to expose and confront male phobias and desires and their effects on the lives of women" (C13). One of the male phobias Finley enacts, the Freudian castrated woman, represents a threat to men because she embodies the possibility of castration—even being feared as a potential castrator, for example, in the section in *The Constant State of Desire* when Finley describes cutting off the balls of the Wall Street yuppies and selling them to little boys. The frequency with which one hears men refer to women as "castrating bitches" confirms this inner anxiety. The castration anxiety is undoubtedly stirred up, when Finley, a woman, depicts a man who straps on a baby as a substitute penis. In one moment, Finley assumes the male-gendered prerogative of phallus ownership, and also disrupts that status by substituting a baby for a penis, and using it in a sexually transgressive scenario with his own mother.

I believe one reason why Finley's cross-gendered performances embodying both male and female characters is unsettling for an audience, over and above the "obscene" content of her plays, lies in her performance style. As Catherine Schuler observes, unlike, for example, Lily Tomlin or Anna Deavere Smith, Finley "does not attempt to assume a 'realistic' male persona. Indeed, never during the course of *Constant State* does she transform herself physically or vocally into the series of readily distinguishable characters that are suggested by the printed text" (137). Consequently even when Finley portrays a rage-filled *male* character, she does not attempt to disguise her female status. Therefore, the performance can easily be read as the enactment, by a woman, of male-gendered rage, something unacceptable in our current social construction of anger.

In interviews Finley has described why she thinks people react to her performances the way they do: "The reason why the feminine way or the maternal way has been oppressed is because the male energy is so scared of it. And so the only way males can deal with it is to knock it down, to not allow it to come up." She notes that a woman "generates so much fear as soon as she shows her feelings or is strong. Just the words that are used—it was always that I was hysterical or that there was an out of control eroticism or unbridled sexuality, like I was some animal." In other words, strong women, with strong feelings, like rage, are out-of-control animals, monsters, demons. "People are very fearful of women showing their body or using sexual language when they're in power," explains Finley, "and when I'm on stage, I'm in a position of power. It doesn't bother anyone nearly as much if a woman shows her body when she's in a position of sexual passivity" (qtd. in Pramaggiore 284).[11] By disrupting the expectation of sexual passivity, Finley disrupts the male gaze and taps into male fear of female power.

Item Four: Finley Tells the Truth and Confronts Difficult Social Issues

Carr describes Finley's subject matter, her "territory," as being "abuse, desire, rage—their conflation." Carr notes that Finley would "take a subject like incest and push it to surreal extremes, but above all she would address it without euphemism. She would tell the awfullest truth" ("Telling" 153). The objectification and oppression of women, rape, and other forms of sexual violence against women are but some of the awfullest truths Finley confronts in her works. Finley's performances are graphic, vulgar, and shocking and they bring up intense emotions among audience members who defensively criticize Finley, rather than the societal ills she is trying to reveal. Finley is aware of the reasons why her work elicits such reactions: "What I do definitely makes people very uncomfortable" (Goldstein, "Calendar," 1). In her interview with Mifflin, Finley says the reason her work is shocking to people "is that they haven't accepted it as a reality. Part of my work is the fact that incest, rape and hostility happen in the best of families, in the best of countries" (86). Despite the onslaught of criticism, Finley feels compelled to continue. In an article for *The Los Angeles Times*, Finley writes,

> As an American artist, I have made a commitment in creating work that address social concerns. I feel it is my responsibility to apply my talents to record history and make my audience more sensitive to our country's problems. Much of my work deals with victims in our society—victims of sexism, victims of racism, victims of homophobia, economic victims, victims of sexual abuse and other violent crime—and I use the language that society commonly uses in its put-downs of these victims. I am being punished because I am a morally concerned artist, speaking about situations as they are [B7].

Karen Finley, a "morally concerned artist," was demonized by the media and Congress. She knows that speaking the truth was (and is) a dangerous proposition, especially in the era of antifeminist backlash when transgressive women were seen as legitimate targets of male outrage. As this chapter documents, evidence of antifeminist backlash can be found both in the dramatic texts written in the 1980s and in the reception of Karen Finley's work during this time period. Evidence in dramatic texts of the next waves of feminism, third-wave and postfeminism, are the subject of the next chapter.

Five

Third-Wave, Postfeminism and the Commodification of Rape

Part One: Third-Wave Feminism

Tracing movements within feminism through distinct "waves" is admittedly an imperfect approach that can result in an overly simplistic linear narrative based on generational progressions. It is, nonetheless, a common practice used to separate different phases and aspects of feminism. While first-wave and second-wave feminisms may have somewhat clearly defined timeframes and objectives, third-wave feminism is far more amorphous and has been referred to as a contested term and a movement that is confusing and one that does not lend itself to a straightforward definition.[1]

Like their second-wave foremothers, third-wave feminists value a focus on political activism, ensuring continued efforts to work against social injustices. They highlight the persistence of unequal power relations between men and women, and document the ways in which classism, homophobia, racism, fatism, and ageism contributed to the inequality they strive to eliminate. Proudly displaying their activist intentions, Shannon Liss and Rebecca Walker stress that as third-wave feminists, they intended to become part of "a national network for young feminists; to politicize and organize young women from diverse cultural and economic backgrounds; strengthen the relationship between young women and older feminists; and to consolidate a strong base of membership able to mobilize for specific issues, political candidates and events" (24).

Third-wave feminists are aware of the complex relationships among women within a global perspective. Leslie Heywood and Jennifer Drake,

Five: Third-Wave, Postfeminism and the Commodification of Rape

less naïve perhaps than the bra-burning second-wavers, openly acknowledge, "We know that what oppresses me may not oppress you, that what oppresses you may be something I participate in, and that what oppresses me may be something you participate in" (3). Such contradictions are an accepted part of third-wave feminism, and these contradictions may be most evident in the simultaneous critique of, and participation in a consumer culture. For third-wavers, there is no contradiction between working for social justice and participating in feminizing practices shunned by the second-wave feminists of the '60s and '70s. Women can run major corporations and express their femininity at the same time. The third-wave focus on sexual liberation was not for the pleasure of their male comrades; rather, it was to empower women of all shapes, sizes, and colors to appreciate and take pleasure in their own bodies. Third-wavers have dubbed their emphasis on femininity "girlie." Jennifer Baumgardner and Amy Richards declare, "Girlie says we're not broken, and our desires aren't simply booby traps set by the patriarchy. Girlie encompasses the tabooed symbols of women's feminine enculturation—Barbie dolls, makeup, fashion magazines, high heels—and says using them isn't shorthand for 'we've been duped'" (Manifesta 136). In other words, women who desire to be feminine are not traitors to the cause of social justice, and third-wave feminists seek a feminism that allows women to expresses themselves in a myriad of ways.

Finally, one of the guiding principles of third-wave feminism is the mandate for feminism to be inclusive of *all* women, often in the form of a celebration of difference. The key figures in the third-wave movement (Rebecca Walker, Jennifer Baumgardner, Amy Richards, Leslie Heywood, Jennifer Drake, and others) are for the most part the next generation of feminists—born around 1970, or at the time when second-wave feminism was strengthening. However, the foundation for this guiding principle of third-wave feminism—inclusion—was actually established by women of color who were active in second-wave feminism, and who confronted white women for their lack of racial inclusivity both in terms of membership and in terms of the priorities outlined by movement leaders. In other words, while the spokespersons of third-wave feminism may come from the next generation, the movement itself is not strictly based on a generational divide between second-wave feminists and their daughters. As Catherine Orr explains, third-wave feminism began "on the terrain of race in the early 1980s rather than age in the mid–1990s," bolstered by the criticism of feminists, including Cherrie Moraga, Gloria Anzuldua, bell hooks, Audre Lorde, and Maxine Hong Kingston (born between 1934 and 1952), who called for a "new subjectivity in what was, up to that point, white, middle-class, first world feminism" (37).

The divide among second-wave feminists over the issue of inclusion was deep. White middle-class feminists believed the category of "woman" was universal and could unite all women under an umbrella of sisterhood. However, this feeling of sisterhood was unsustainable as differences among women based on class, race, and sexual orientation became increasingly apparent. The tension between white women and women of color in second-wave feminism is evident in the writings of Linda La Rue, who wrote, "Let us state unequivocally that, with few exceptions, the American white woman has had a better opportunity to live a free and fulfilling life, both mentally and physically, than any other group in the United States, with the exception of her white husband" (36). The slogan "sisterhood is powerful" left many sisters feeling excluded, not only African American women but "Hispanic, Native American, and Asian American women of all classes, as well as many working-class women [who] have not readily identified themselves as sisters of the white middle-class women who have been in the forefront of the movement" (Dill 131). Unwilling to be defined through a white woman's lens, women of color and lesbians within the women's movement stressed the need to understand and respect the diversity of women's lives. This tension among second-wave feminists, the tension that third-wave feminists seek to alleviate, is deftly depicted by Robbie McCauley in her play *Sally's Rape*.

Sally's Rape by Robbie McCauley (1989)

Sally's Rape, by Robbie McCauley, is a theatrical reenactment of the tensions between white women and women of color surrounding the issues of race and rape—tensions that incited the goal of inclusion for third-wave feminists. *Sally's Rape* is a three-way dialogue among Robbie

Five: Third-Wave, Postfeminism and the Commodification of Rape

McCauley (an African American woman), Jeannie Hutchins (a white woman), and the audience. In the play, audience members take a very active role in the performance as they are divided into three sections, assigned loosely structured responses, and given gestural cues from Robbie and Jeannie so they know when to participate in the performance. Rebecca Schneider labels a performance as something more "akin to ritual than entertainment" (174). Raewyn Whyte describes the audience participation, writing, "At times this results in a vocal involvement similar to that of a black church congregation responding to a sermon" (289). In addition to their participation throughout the performance, the play itself ends with a discussion among audience members of the issues raised in the play.

Robbie and Jeannie (both the names of the actors and their "character" names in the script) discuss a wide range of subjects, including slavery, charm school, rape, and racial and gender discrimination. McCauley's great-great-grandmother, Sally, was a slave who was raped repeatedly by her white master. Rape was used as a method of social control which served to eliminate slave women's resistance and demoralize their men. This power hierarchy was based not only on economic domination, but also on assumed racial and gender superiority, and a belief in the overt sexuality of African women. Angela Davis argues, "One of racism's salient historical features has always been the assumption that white men—especially those who wield economic power—possess an incontestable right of access to Black women's bodies." In fact, rape was merely an extension and expression of the slave owners "presumed property rights over Black people as a whole" (175).

In the introduction to the play, McCauley writes, "Sally says, 'It wasn't nothin' to it,' when the men came down to rape them. That's a loaded statement because it means that it was done constantly and people called it other things. They didn't call it rape" (215). I believe this exemplifies Angela Harris' assertion that rape "was something that only happened to white women; what happened to black women was simply life" (16). In the play Robbie talks about the "life" her great-great-grandmother Sally and the other slave women experienced. "On the plantation you hafta stay tough and tight no matter how many times they come down there" (232). Deirdre Heddon observes, "McCauley bears and lays bare for us the wounds imprinted by the institution of slavery ... within which rape was simply another feature of the commodification of the black female body, a body—or object—that by 'right' belonged to its white owner" (71–72). Sally had two daughters by the master, one of which was Robbie McCauley's great-grandmother, and as Harvey Young explains, "four generations after the assault, McCauley exists as evidence (the stain) of the rape act.... Her experience of the body began the moment that the plantation 'master' assaulted Sally" (138–139).

Several scenes in this play reference or demonstrate the tensions between white women and women of color that surfaced during the women's movement in the '70s and '80s, and argue for productive dialogue between women. This mandate for dialogue is reflected in the way McCauley and Hutchins engage in spontaneous and often improvised conversations, difficult conversations relating to race. In the opening scene of the play, the conversation begins with Robbie stating, "Somebody said it was about cups." To which Jeannie replies, "Somebody else said it was about language." Robbie then asks, "What do you think it's about? Jennie states, "Well, that one person said it was about you and me. And I know it's not about me, but it's about you and I'm in it." Robbie insists, "It's my story, and you're in it because I put you in it." "Fair enough," Jeannie admits (219). In this brief opening exchange we see Robbie claiming her agency in relation to her white stage partner. However, a black woman in charge, a "black messenger" in McCauley's words can be "dangerous." In an interview with Vicki Patraka, McCauley explains, "There's a perception that black people getting too close to rage is dangerous.... I think people have been sold the metaphor of how bad black is and that's associated with all those other negative images that are unspeakably dangerous—you know, black is dark, black is violent, black is anger.... And I set myself up as the messenger who is black" (210). Consequently, at the start of the performance, Robbie attempts to alleviate any anxiety the audience may be feeling.

When Robbie and Jeannie are about to begin the process of dividing the audience and explaining their role in the performance, including teaching them various hand signals and chants they will use throughout the performance, Robbie says, "If oppression is at the core, then this work will never end. It's a work in progress ... a dialogue." Jeannie adds,

Five: Third-Wave, Postfeminism and the Commodification of Rape

"Otherwise, there is no progress." (The script indicates that Robbie and Jeannie alternate the following lines.)

> ROBBIE. "And we can't have a dialogue by ourselves."
> JEANNIE. "So you're in it."
> ROBBIE. "Don't worry, I won't jump in your face or down your throat."

After the audience has been shown the hand signals Robbie and Jeannie will use with them and required responses, such as "uh huh," or "That's right!" Robbie adds, "Don't worry, I'm in control" (222). Robbie explains to Patraka that as the black messenger, she is "not neutral and therefore, at that moment, you saw me saying 'Don't worry.' Some people may find that patronizing, but I think many need it" (210).

Several scenes in the play highlight what Jennifer Griffiths refers to as "collective amnesia" on the part of the dominant (white) culture in regard to the rape of women in the time of slavery. In *Sally's Rape* this amnesia is at times depicted as ignorance rather than actual memory loss, and these references harken back to the criticisms women of color voiced against their white "sisters." This amnesia/ignorance may stem from a discomfort rooted in the very real differences between women as Audre Lorde noted in 1980: "As white women ignore their built-in privilege of whiteness and define *woman* in terms of their own experience alone, then women of color become 'other,' the outsider whose experience and tradition is too 'alien' to comprehend" (117). The persistence of this inability to comprehend was acknowledged by third-wave feminists in their efforts to create a more inclusive feminism.

In a scene in which Robbie and Jeannie depict the different treatment of raped women in slavery and privileged white women, Robbie comments on the ignorance of the reality of rape in African American history, saying, "These new ones with the alligators act like they wadn't born with no memory" (233). Jennifer Griffiths contends this "collective amnesia around traumatic histories of racialized others is part of the reproduction of white privilege." She goes on to explain, "The 'alligators' suggests the label of a clothing brand worn by a certain cultural type: young, white, and affluent. Invisibility of whiteness coincides with the erasure of memory. To be born with no memory is to admit no responsibility toward the past" (7–8).

Another moment in the play that illuminates this "erasure of memory" and the racial tensions between the characters in the performance—and women within second-wave feminism—is when Robbie and Jennie recreate a conversation between Robbie and a Smith College U.S. history major working at the library. Jeannie, "playing" the college grad, says, "I never knew white men did anything with colored women on plantations." Robbie explains, "I said, 'It was rape.' Her eyes turned red. She choked on her sandwich and quit the job" (225). Jennifer Griffiths notes how "McCauley explores what it means to 'choke' on a repressed history [and] begins the process of uncovering the denial of sexual violence against black women and the damage caused by this denial." When Robbie tells the history major about the rape of slaves she "voices an alternative to the dominant historical narrative, one that contradicts the version taught at Smith College and archived within the library" (1, 14). Jeannie insists the woman was "dumb," and says to Robbie, "You have this thing that an Ivy League education could prevent her dumbness about that," adding that Robbie is "bitter" about not having been accepted into Barnard. Robbie replies, "Bitterness about Barnard I admit. But when I'm sitting around my grandmother's breakfast table, and she's telling me something that this woman who went to Smith College didn't know," Jeannie (overlapping) says, "Well, aren't you more fortunate then, that you learned so much more through your grandmother" (225).

Barbara Lewis senses that a performance of *Sally's Rape* is similar to jazz, "never the same twice, in that it repeats yet departs from a basic pattern." She describes the pattern as "two women of roughly identical age, but different races, sit and chat, drink tea. Their worlds have always been distinct. Now, they are making efforts to walk into and feel comfortable in each other's lives. They are equal, and yet not equal. Tensions rise and fall" (308). These tensions are indicative of the difficult issues raised in the play about race and rape. McCauley doesn't pretend that it is easy; she doesn't present a neat package in terms of the form or content of the dialogue. McCauley knows that any dialogue, if it will be transformative, is bound to be difficult.

The next scene in the play is an improvised section between Jeannie and Robbie during which they model the process of dialogue that they anticipate will occur between audience members at the end of the per-

Five: Third-Wave, Postfeminism and the Commodification of Rape

formance. The two women set up two chairs, face each other, and improvise a conversation centered on the reasons for their anger. The stage directions illuminate the differences between them, "*Jeannie thinks Robbie can see through her to something she can't admit. She thinks their idealism is similar. Robbie thinks admitting the difference in their histories is more important. Jeannie is concerned that she can't win. They try to reveal something to each other as if they are alone and honest about their differences*" (227–228). The improvised dialogue between Robbie and Jeannie would of course change with each performance. But in this scene the two wrestle with Jeannie's idealism and her desire to focus on their similarities, ending with Jeannie's admission that "I believed that through education, if I could change my thinking, that anything would be possible. And it just sounds so stupid" (228). In other words, the collective amnesia evidenced in the Smith College grad and the Izod Lacoste shirt-wearing yuppie, is likewise evident in the "idealism" Jeannie exhibits, and she admits that education, at least the kind received by the U.S. history major at Smith, will not solve the problem. *Sally's Rape* is a catalyst for both the actors and the audience to begin talking about race and rape. "People want answers, and I don't claim to give them," McCauley says. "I'm interested in keeping the dialogue going. People want to be healed, but it has to hurt first. And they have to talk about it." (qtd. in Hartigan 61).

McCauley writes, "I know about commonness between races, between men and women, and so forth. The commonness is easier to speak than the differences. I'm most interested in speaking about those differences. In a strange way, speaking the differences makes the connection happen" (214).

Another scene in the play that exposes racial tension and represents the differences between the experience of rape for white and black women is scene 6 of the play, titled "In a Rape Crisis Center." In this scene Robbie and Jeannie describe two different post-rape scenarios. Robbie paints the picture of Sally's frequent rape on the plantation, speaking as her great-great-grandmother, saying, "You just stay tight till they finish…. Wadn't nuthin' to it. The others watched. Sometimes they did it too…. COLD. VERY COLD. VERY VERY VERY COLD" (232). Whereas Jeannie says, "In a rape crisis center, your wounds are fresh. They can put warm clothes on you, tell you it's not your fault.... Someone would give you a cup of tea. Hot chocolate. Warm milk" (232).

In her interview with Patraka, McCauley says, "I wanted to find a way to make the point as strongly as possible that the real rape—and this is not to diminish anybody's individual experience of rape—was that we couldn't even begin to have a rape crisis center" (210). The experience of rape for Robbie/Sally and Jeannie are different; both of course denounce the pain and degradation of rape, but Jeannie is offered tea, warmth, and support, and Robbie/Sally who is taken on the ground, while others watch and participate—remains cold. The legitimization of rape in the time of slavery gives African Americans a different historical, political and personal context for rape. Ann Nymann notes how effectively McCauley "conveys the devastating effects of rape, both on the individual psyche and as a collective trauma." She also notes that the difference between Robbie/Sally's story and Jeannie's story is more than just the difference between "past and present rapes, but the difference between institutionalized and individual instances of rape" (584).

Among the other scenes that convey the differences between white women and women of color are the two auction block scenes in the play. In the first of the two scenes, Robbie voluntarily stands naked on the auction block, embodying her great-great-grandmother's experience, as well as those of other African women who were exhibited in Europe.[2] This bodily display only intensified the sexual nature of this economic exchange. Deborah Thompson notes how McCauley "manipulates the audience into gazing with colonizing/capitalist desires upon her naked body" (135). Harvey Young claims Robbie's body "becomes an example of the black captive body on display," noting how the scene "represents the black body being stripped of its individuality and displayed, as a commodity, for the highest bidder" (144). Once Robbie is on the block, Jennie starts to chant, "Bid 'em in," reminiscent of actual slave auctions, and she coaxes the audience to chant with her. Raewyn Whyte describes the impact of this scene and the chanting of the audience, "Whether or not you join the chanting you are trapped by the sympathetic magic of sound, which reanimates the past, and, no matter how much you tell yourself you had nothing to do with this scene, you are made vicariously complicit in the auction system that McCauley's staging represents"

(278). As the chanting continues, McCauley literally becomes her great-great-grandmother, who is being bought as a piece of property.

In contrast to this first auction block scene, when the duo return to the block later in the play, Robbie says to Jeannie, "Come, let's do this," and she asks the light board operator to illuminate the auction block. She then asks Jeannie to take off her dress and encourages the audience to repeat the chant, "Bid 'em in. Bid 'em in," that they had voiced when Robbie stood naked on the block. This time, however, the white woman Jeannie is on the block, and she simply lowers one strap of her dress. Robbie says to her, "Do you have something to say?" Jeannie "shakes her head 'no'" to which Robbie replies, "That's something right there." And Jeannie gets off the block and moves it out of the way (234). The scene makes clear that Sally did not have a choice when she was put on the auction block, but Jeannie does, and she will not allow herself to be treated as property. These two contrasting auction block scenes dramatize the gulf between various factions within second-wave feminism, a distance that women of color and lesbians described at the time and a distance which ultimately inspired third-wave feminists to view inclusion as a priority as they moved forward to the twenty-first century.

Part Two: Postfeminism

Definitions of and the use of the terms third-wave feminism and postfeminism often overlap; therefore, differentiating the two can be challenging.[3] While disagreement exists as to the official beginnings of both third-wave feminism and postfeminism, by the early 1990s both movements were active. In 1992, Rebecca Walker, then a student at Yale, ended her *Ms. Magazine* article entitled, "Becoming the Third Wave," with the statement, "I am not a postfeminism feminist. I am the Third Wave," making a clear distinction between the two feminisms (41). Postfeminism, much like third-wave feminism, is a disputed term and what exactly constitutes postfeminism is up for debate. It has been referred to as confusing, elusive, and incoherent. Few agree about its goals or agenda, or even if it is actually a valid movement, or only a scheme created by the media.[4]

I have divided the various interpretations of postfeminism into four reccurring themes. The first refers to the "pastness" of feminism. In this case the "post" in postfeminism could be read as "after" indicating the end of feminism. This pastness is seen as a happy release from the ideological chains of second-wave feminism that is seen as aged, redundant, and having no sense of fun. Furthermore, from this perspective, it is clear that second-wave feminism has done its job, and continuing to complain about women's victim status is out of touch. Second-wave feminism is thought to be totally anachronistic.

The second theme embraces a more active rejection of second-wave feminism, a continuation of the antifeminist backlash of the 1980s, including a belief that political correctness is a new form of tyranny. Within this theme is dismissal of the victim status of women and it is replaced with an emphasis on power feminism. These views are promoted by young conservative feminists, among the most commonly mentioned are Katie Roiphe, Naomi Wolf, Rene Denfield, and Camille Paglia.[5] In this case the "post" implies not simply "after," but "anti"—in other words, this brand of postfeminism is assumed to be antifeminist.

The third theme evident in postfeminism is the absence of aggressive political activism and a focus on the individual rather than on social institutions. In 1987, Judith Stacey wrote, "Postfeminism demarcates an emerging culture and ideology that simultaneously incorporates, revises, and depoliticizes many of the fundamental issues advanced by Second Wave feminism" (8). This depoliticizing results in the reduction of feminist *social* goals to individual lifestyle choices and threatens to ignore politics completely, leaving a movement with no political goals. In this theme it is believed that the women's movement removed all obstacles to women's advancement and notions of individual accountability along with self-serving materialism took the place of concerns for social justice. Political action is reduced to a slogan on a t-shirt. Due to the apolitical nature of postfeminist, many writers have pointed out the inversion of the famous tenant of second-wave feminism, "the personal is political," to its postfeminist incarnation, "the political is personal."[6]

The postfeminist inversion of this second-wave feminist slogan resulted in depictions of sexual violence that appears individualized and privatized. Postfeminists have replaced a critique of the patriarchy with

Five: Third-Wave, Postfeminism and the Commodification of Rape

personal/individualized statements of victimhood such as the clothesline projects. This shift is also evident in the move within organizations serving abused women from being a site of grassroots organizing to end sexual violence to organizations promoting personal healing. In the postfeminist era, the dominant perception reflected in this theme is that therapy is presented as the answer, not politics, resulting in a shift in focus from the societal causes of rape—the depolitization noted by Stacey—to the traumatic effects of rape. The expression of trauma, preferably in a therapeutic environment, allowed raped women to cope and return to their everyday lives. Abuse was no longer political as the emphasis was placed on the mental wellbeing of the raped woman rather than on the social problems that facilitated rape in the first place. Zillah Eisenstein declares that postfeminism "callously ignores how sexualized violence has historically been deployed to reinforce social hierarchies…. This mass-marketed feminism is a bit like fat-free food. Fat-free food won't make you healthy, and pop/market feminism won't make you equal or stop domestic violence" (116). While some postfeminists may feel social and political equality has been obtained and feminism is no longer needed, the sobering statistics cited in previously about the prevalence of rape in our society serves to remind us that we have a long way to go.

Finally, the fourth theme I've identified features a new definition of "woman" including a renewed focus on traditional concepts of femininity and a distinct rejection of the anti-materialism focus of the '60s and '70s. Younger women are encouraged to rebel against the dungaree-wearing, makeup-less, anti-male feminist of their mother's generation. This postfeminism is a "fun" feminism with a focus on experiencing the pleasures of being a woman, including a myriad of lifestyle choices, rather than a focus on social activism. It allows for an apolitical narcissism that includes a move away from objectification to subjectification in the ways that women are represented. It features the promise of happiness, success, and glamour as long as women choose the best improvement script. This is evident in the popularity of TV makeover shows and T-shirt ready slogans like "You go, girl!" and "Work it!" Additionally, there is a return to highlighting the sexual difference between men and women and a distinct resexualization of the female body. Instead of "Just Say No," girls and women today are encouraged to say "yes." This interpretation of postfeminism caters to young women who do not embrace the second-wave rejection of consumerism; rather, they have been convinced that being a consumer is immensely pleasurable, and they can signal their confidence and success through their purchasing power. This fourth theme of postfeminism highlights the modern consumer culture which caters to women with rising incomes, in effect selling them what it takes to have a 21st-century feminine subjectivity, and feminism is seen as a commodity. This is a pro-capitalist feminism which is promoted by corporations who are keen to exploit this new market of young women with disposable incomes. As Susan Faludi notes, "We have used our gains to gild our shackles, but not break them" (xvi).

Part Three: The Commodification of Rape in Dramatic Texts

The depolitization of rape (the third theme of postfeminism I have identified) is actually evident in dramatic texts throughout the time period under consideration in this study. This is demonstrated through the encouragement of the raped characters to express their feelings in a therapeutic environment, or at least to a trusted friend (something which can be an important feature of the path toward healing and which will be discussed further in the next chapter). It is also true that plays in which the political/social aspects of American culture that facilitate rape are highlighted and likewise were written throughout the time period under consideration. Therefore, I am not arguing that these aspects of dramatic texts about rape are tied to particular movements within feminism. However, just as most plays in which the raped woman's rage is demonized were written during the period of antifeminist backlash, the postfeminist theme of commodification (the fourth theme I have identified) is evident in plays about rape written in the postfeminist period. Ellen Riordan remarks that the "media industry uses this commodified feminism not to empower girls but, rather, to encourage their dedicated consumption to pro-girl artifacts" which translates into profit for the manufacturer of such products (291). It is perhaps not surprising that the plays I found in which characters are determined to profit in one way or another through their connection to a raped woman or a rapist were written since the advent of postfeminism. As I will demonstrate, the following four plays—*Down the Road* by Lee Blessing, *Self Defense or Death of Some Salesmen* by Carson Kreitzer, *After Ashley* by Gina Gionfriddo, and *Necessary Targets* by Eve Ensler— each written during the postfeminist era, feature characters for whom a raped woman/women or a rapist becomes a literal commodity.

Down the Road (1989) by Lee Blessing

Down the Road, which I discussed in an earlier chapter on the depiction of rapists, charts the intersection of Dan and Iris Henniman (journalists) and William Reach (rapist and serial killer). Dan and Iris are writing a book about Reach, and the ethical and financial issues swirling around the completion and publication of this book create much of the tension among the three characters. It is clear that Dan and Iris are under a lot of pressure to complete the manuscript, as Iris pleads with Dan not to do anything that might force Reach to stop talking with them, in which case they would lose the book deal. The book publisher, Scanlon, is eager for their completed manuscript. He calls repeatedly to check on Dan and Iris' progress. Dan reassures him saying Reach is cooperating, answering their questions, and is "graphic when pressed." Later, Dan tells Iris that Scanlon wanted to know "how graphic," adding, "What's he want us to do? Hype the gore?" (53). Dan considers quitting but Iris reminds him that they need the job, and their reputation as writers would be destroyed if they quit. She admits that Scanlon could easily find another writer to complete Reach's biography. "Aside from the fact that we'd never work for Scanlon again, and lose all our credibility in the business, and run away from something we've started. We can't quit our day job.... If we leave this project, Scanlon will go out and get someone who can listen to Bill Reach. He won't have to look very far" (72).

It is revealed that Iris is pregnant, which presents a financial incentive for the couple to complete the book. Reach astutely picks up on Iris's vulnerability and when she asks him questions about his employment history, he asks, "Does Scanlon know you're asking me a bunch of irrelevant questions? Do you want me to call him?" Iris quickly replies,

"No, I don't want you to call him, Bill. I'm sorry if I've offended you" (75). Iris and Dan repeatedly try to justify their choice to continue with the book and Dan admits to the seductive draw of the project when he tells Iris their job is to document what Reach did. "Make it vivid, compelling.... Write the book, get the money, get another book." Iris continues his thought, "And another book, and another." Dan states, "And support ourselves. There's nothing wrong with that." Iris says, "Iris and Dan Henniman—crime-writing couple.... Watching our names grow on the covers," Dan interrupts, "It's a business" (81–82).

The couple's anxiety about losing the job is evident when Iris informs Dan that Scanlon called, and that Reach had spoken with him. Scanlon was apparently supportive of the couple and told them to do whatever they needed to complete the job; however, Dan insists the support will last "right up until he fires us.... Scanlon can't do anything if Reach won't talk to us—we'll have to be replaced" (84–85). Iris and Dan are ultimately forced to cater to Reach's demands rather than follow their own journalistic instincts.

For the Hennimans, their professional reputation as writers is on the line, as well as the potential monetary gains, but for Reach, the commodification of rape in this play is not about a financial profit, it is about fame. He knows full well that he will not profit monetarily from the publication of the book and did not object to that stipulation. Iris reveals Reach's true motivation, noting that he didn't even exist until he began killing women. Reach himself understands this concept, he asks Iris "Who are you?" she answers, "Iris Henniman." Reach continues, "And in a hundred years, who are you going to be?" Iris replies, "Dead—that's who I'm going to be." Reach explains, "That's right. But I'll still be William Reach.... Don't talk to me about identities. You've got a chance—just a chance—to be somebody here. Stick to what Scanlon pays you for.... To write my book! Mine! Why doesn't matter. I did it—other men didn't. Besides, your theory is shit. I killed someone before Cindy Lauterber. She wasn't the first." Iris digs deeper, "Who else did you kill?" No answer from Reach. "The victim's family would like to know. It should be in the book. If we're collaborators." Finally, Reach reveals his true motivation for holding out, "*It's for the sequel, bitch!*" (78).

Five: Third-Wave, Postfeminism and the Commodification of Rape

Ultimately, Iris confronts Dan about the degree to which their participation in the project facilitates the commodification of rape. By this time in the play, Reach figuratively (and in terms of the stage picture, literally) has invaded the motel room in which Dan and Iris are staying, and he participates in their conversation. Dan insists that Reach's story needs to be told, needs in fact to be studied. Iris contends it won't be studied, it will be "consumed." Dan counters, "So what?! That's how we do it here. He kills people—we put him on the news. He's fascinating—we write about him." Iris reminds Dan that Reach has killed nineteen girls, and that through their book they are actually making it "more likely—not less—that this'll happen to someone else's daughter." Dan insists that he is does not want to "walk away from the book of my career. *Our* career," adding that he simply wants to find out the identity of the other victim Reach mentioned. Iris says she knows who the other victim is, and she tells Dan, "It's you" (94–95).

When Iris is about to leave, Reach says, "She'll stay. All I've got to say is Renee Michaels.... She's from before. She's extra. You didn't think I'd leave you high and dry? I'll add a new killing. Got to sell this thing. There's plenty of competition out there.... It's an exclusive" (96). Iris at this point in the play is caught in Reach's trap. The commodity is too powerful and she does not leave.

Self Defense or Death of Some Salesmen (2001) by Carson Kreitzer

This play was also included in the discussion of rapist characters. This drama was inspired by events in the life of Aileen Wuornos, a prostitute and female serial killer who admitted to killing seven men, but claimed it was in self-defense after the men became abusive. Aileen was sentenced to die in the electric chair for the first murder in 1992, and was ultimately executed in 2002. In the play, the Aileen Wuornos character is named Jolene Palmer.

The issue of the commodification of rape in this drama is first revealed when Annie Ames, a Hollywood producer, learns about the trial. She senses the potential in the story as a profit-making screenplay and excitedly says, "Something very intriguing is happening in Florida....

It's *Silence of the Lambs* meets *Thelma and Louise!*" (291). Annie Ames finally gets Jo on the phone and asks to make the movie of her life, stressing that "it's already happening. Those cops who arrested you are making their own movie.... So now it's your turn.... Your side of the story needs to be told. *I am offering you life everlasting*" (309).

As it turns out, not only are Annie Ames and the police interested in profiting from Jo's story, so is Jo's lesbian lover, Lu. This is revealed when Lu calls an entertainment lawyer, saying that Drums, one of the officers, said she should speak with him. "He said you could get us a better deal.... That we'd get more money than if we all signed separate deals. I just—I'd feel better knowing you were there to field the ... various offers" (299–300). Barbara Ozieblo describes the relationship between Jo and Lu as an "obsessive dedication on the part of Jo and total indifference on the part of Lu," adding that Lu's decision to "sell the rights for a movie deal" is "a cynical move to self-betterment" ("The Victim" 162).

Annie Ames reads about the trial in Seton Hill University's 2013 production of *Self Defense or, Death of Some Salesmen*; directed by Farrah Felton. Featuring Krystyn Seronka as Annie Ames (photograph by Ariel Watters).

Jo herself has an interesting reaction to the commodification of her story: "Now they got their fucking movie coming out, and I haven't even been convicted yet.... An they got me bein' played by SOMEBODY I NEVER EVEN HEARD OF. They coulda at least got Jodie Foster or something" (310). We see in this drama, written during the postfeminist era, several characters for whom Jo's life story has become a commodity and is exploited as a vehicle for potential profit.

Five: Third-Wave, Postfeminism and the Commodification of Rape

After Ashley (2006) by Gina Gionfriddo

This play depicts the events leading up to and after the rape and murder of Ashley Hammond. She is survived by her husband, Alden, and her 17-year-old son, Justin. Shortly after the rape/murder, Ashley's death was covered by *People* magazine, and Justin's 911 phone call after he discovered his mother's body in the basement of their home was not only aired repeatedly, but it was also used in a now famous rap song. Since his mother's murder, Justin has been called "the 911 kid." Alden Hammond, a former education reporter for *The Washington Post*, wrote a book chronicling the crime and tracing the impact on his family and the nation.

Alden goes on the talk-show circuit to promote the book, and he and Justin are interviewed by David Gavin on a show called *Profiles in Justice*. David Gavin's daughter was murdered when she was seventeen

Justin and Alden Hammond appear on David Gavin's TV "reality" show, Profiles in Justice in Dragon Production's 2013 production of *After Ashley*, directed by Dale Albright. Featuring Sean Gilvery as Justin (left), Dale Albright as Alden (center), and Evan Michel Schumacher as David (right) (photograph by James Kasyan).

years old, and Alden and David exchange mutual praise for each other's books. We learn that Ashley was raped and murdered by a mentally ill homeless man whom Alden had hired to work around their house. In his television interview with David, Alden says that the assailant had worked for them for two months and that there were no problems, although, Alden adds, "I know now that he was off his medications" when Ashley was murdered, and "that he was hallucinating." Alden insists that his wife's rape and murder were "taking on a sociological significance" that people who were "already doing nothing to help this population [the homeless] were latching onto my wife's death as a justification for their apathy and inaction." David adds, "You speak in the book of your wife becoming the poster girl for right-wing, conservative." Alden jumps in, "Oh, absolutely. Rush Limbaugh spoke about this crime on his radio show and his message was, basically, this is what you get. It became fodder for his anti-welfare agenda, his belief that underprivileged persons are underprivileged because they're amoral and lazy." Justin sheds light on his version of the events, saying the message of his father's book is "don't hire healthy, skilled persons for jobs a homeless person can perform for a fraction of the cost. The fact that the man we hired killed my mother should not deter anyone from bringing the homeless home." David and Alden disregard Justin's interpretation and go on to compare Ashley's murder to the events of 9/11 (28–29).

After the interview, David offers Alden the television host position since David will be out of town covering an important trial. Alden accepts. The show will have a new format, which further emphasizes the commodification of rape as it will still feature victim interviews but it will be limited to sex crimes and include reenactments. The new show will be called *After Ashley*. Alden and Justin move to Florida where the show is produced. In her article "Affecting the Audience: Gina Gionfriddo's *After Ashley*," Barbara Ozieblo points out the lure of turning rape into a commodity for both David and Alden, when she observes how "both men have suffered the consequences of violence inflicted on members of their family, and yet, in their role of talk-show hosts, they are more willing to appeal to this circumstance to capture and manipulate an audience." Ozieblo points out that "what matters is success, personal and financial" (272).

Justin's fame is predicated on his mother's murder. He is approached

Five: Third-Wave, Postfeminism and the Commodification of Rape

at a bar by Julie, and immediately knows that her approach is less than innocent:

> JUSTIN. Why did you talk to me?
> JULIE. You just looked lonely, I thought—
> JUSTIN. Bullshit.
> JULIE. I wanted to maybe get to know you—
> JUSTIN. Why?
> JULIE. Why... Do I have to have a reason?
> JUSTIN. No, but you do. (*Pause*) Let's go. (*Justin starts to leave*) Come on.
> JULIE. What do you mean—"Come on"?
> JUSTIN. Come home with me. You can tell all your friends you fucked The 911 kid. If you want, I'll slap you around, you can write a haiku.
> JULIE. That's your invitation? You think I'm gonna go for that?
> JUSTIN. Yeah, I do. You're a Goth in Central Florida. You have nothing better to do. (*Pause. Justin weighs his hands like scales.*) Creepy guy with murdered mother, rum punch and frat boys at The Sandbar. Hmmmmm... What's a sad little Goth girl to do? (*Justin walks out of the bar, confident she'll follow. After a beat, she does.*) [40].

Justin and Julie hang out in Dragon Production's 2013 production of *After Ashley*, directed by Dale Albright. Featuring Sean Gilvery as Justin and Caitlyn Tella as Julie (photograph by James Kasyan).

In addition to skillfully assessing Julie's motives, Justin understands how rape is being commodified on the new television program his father is hosting. After Justin and Julie watch one of the sex crime reenactments they discuss the program, Julie thinks, "It was rendered really tastefully." Justin says, "Well, it must have been one of those tasteful rapes." And he asks Julie why she thinks the program has reenactments. Julie guesses, "Because television is a visual medium?" Justin counters, saying, "Nonsense," and notes that on *Meet the Press*, no one is "reenacting congressional committee meetings." Julie makes Justin's point clear, saying, "That's completely different. That's not an entertainment—"Justin interrupts, "Exactly! America likes sex crimes." He goes on to explain that the way sex crimes are portrayed in the program is actually "arousing" and that "reenacted sex crimes are all about ravishing." Julie begrudgingly agrees, noting that the reenactment of the sex crime implies "a lack of participation on the woman's part. But it also implies that she enjoys it.... I mean, maybe they are lending the crimes a certain tragic beauty in the retelling. Is that so bad?" To which Justin replies, "It's appalling and unholy.... There's nothing beautiful about being raped." He goes on to describe the depths of his depression after his mother died, and that six months after her death, his father had already sold a book proposal. He explains to Julie, "My mother was murdered. I don't know what the aftermath of that is supposed to be, but I don't think it's supposed to be ... a book and a TV show and a rap song and a girl in my room" (45–46; ellipsis in orig.). In this scene, and others in the play it is clear, as Ozieblo contends, that Justin "cannot condone his father's capitalizing on the murder to promote his career on television" (271).

Necessary Targets (2001) by Eve Ensler

Eve Ensler based this play on the stories she heard in 1993 when she was interviewing female Bosnian war refugees in the former Yugoslavia. She stayed at the Center for Women War Victims, which served Muslim, Croatian, and Serbian women refugees who had been raped and made homeless by war. The play follows two American women who travel to Bosnia. The first is J.S., the play's protagonist, who is approaching fifty and a psychiatrist of twenty-six years who has been

Five: Third-Wave, Postfeminism and the Commodification of Rape

invited to go to Bosnia on a commission set up by the president. J.S. says she is the mental health expert on the team since trauma had been her area of expertise, but she now specializes in eating disorders. Since J.S. has never been to a war-torn country, she has invited Melissa, to join her. Melissa self-identifies as "a trauma counselor." She informs J.S. that she underwent specific training in order to "work with seriously traumatized populations" and that she does not consider herself a "therapist" (7–8). We learn that Melissa has been to several areas of conflict, including Haiti and Rwanda. She tells J.S. that she is currently writing a book dealing with the connections between war and trauma, focusing on "specific atrocities that traumatize women." The issue of the commodification of rape is evident as Melissa stresses, "It's my first contract with a major publisher.... It is essential that I complete the book this year. I will need to interview these women" (12).

At the refugee camp, J.S. and Melissa meet five women: Azra, an old woman from a village; Jelena, a woman in her forties who is there with her husband Dado; Nuna, an Americanized teenager; Seada, a young woman in her twenties who carries what appears to be a baby wrapped in a blanket; and Zlata, a physician near fifty who had been the head of the pediatrics unit in a hospital. J.S. and Melissa plan to conduct two group sessions with the women every day lasting two hours each. Melissa is quick to tell the women that she will be available to them at any time, and that they should not hesitate to reach out whenever they feel the need to talk.

At the first session the women resist the invitation to share their stories. Azra asks if the Americans think they are insane. The Bosnian women seem quite aware of the therapeutic mandate communicated by J.S. and Melissa, and the degree to which their stories are marketed. When Melissa says, "We are here to help you, well ... talk." Zlata replies, "There is no shortage of talking here." Nuna adds, "All we do is talk and talk." J. S. explains, "We are here to help you talk about the war, about the—"Zlata interrupts, "You flew all the way here for that? Two American doctors to 'help' a group of poor Bosnian refugees talk about the war? What did you think we were talking about before you came? Our lingerie, our dinner parties." Melissa says, "We are very moved by what you've been through. We were hoping you would talk to us. You would tell us your stories." Zlata responds, "You and everybody else. They came from everywhere at the beginning of the war to hear the gory details." Nuna adds, "We read about ourselves in the paper. They made us sound deranged." And Zlata says, "They left and they never came back." Melissa explains that she is writing a book, a collection of stories from global refugees. She asks the women if they mind if she tape records the sessions, stressing that she has no intention of exploiting "traumatized war victims." Nuna interrupts, "Is that what we're called? Traumatized war victims?" Melissa explains, "It's not a judgment." And Nuna responds, "So this is American therapy?" Azra declares, "It just feels like another terrible day to me" (25–36).

Melissa is determined to get the women to open up and when J.S. comments on the women's "rightful contempt at being patronized,"

Melissa records the counseling session in the Santa Ana College Theatre Arts Department's 2012 production of *Necessary Targets*, directed by Christopher Glenn Cannon. Featuring (from left) Amy Hallas as J.S., Sandra De Los Santos as Jelena, Ana Reyes as Zlata, Kelly Caballero as Melissa, Molly Gorman as Nuna, and Almendra Camero as Azra (photograph by Jasmin Hill).

Five: Third-Wave, Postfeminism and the Commodification of Rape

Melissa insists, "These women need an outlet for their rage and despair. We are necessary targets. I've been in other wars. It always begins like this." When J.S. asks how it will end, Melissa replies, "They tell their stories" (39). Later when Melissa tries again to tape record the sessions Zlata comments, "Recording tears, recording refugee tears—sexy business." When Azra starts to tell the story of the fate of her village, she begins to cry, Melissa asks, "Did they hurt you?" adding, "It's okay to cry." Zlata confronts Melissa saying, "Azra cries all the time. She does not get better. She just cries more and more. How does that help Azra? How does that help us to hear her cry?" (50–53). Melissa, eager to get the details, keeps pressing Azra to continue her story, but Azra never does. Zlata is firm in her determination to not be turned into a commodity. "You don't understand that this happened to us—to real people. We were just like you ... you want us to be different than you are so you can convince yourself it wouldn't happen there, where you are.... That's why you turn us into people who live in a strange country and speak a strange language—then you can feel safe, superior." Zlata identifies the way she and the others are commodified when she mimics a publisher insisting that the writer get a "raped Bosnian woman, preferably gang-raped, preferably English-speaking." She adds that ultimately the women are depicted as "freaks" (63–64).

The more Melissa presses the women, the more J.S. rejects her techniques. J.S. tells Melissa the tape recorder is an invasion into the women's lives. Melissa insists that the recorder has been helpful, "it is a device which legitimizes their experience, documents it, heals." J.S. interrupts, "It's a recorder, Melissa." And Melissa expresses her truth, saying, "We're here to trigger, provoke, release. Move in, move out" (67). As the play progresses, Melissa continues to press the women to share their stories, and J.S. warns her to slow down, but Melissa keeps up the pressure. Ultimately, Nuna tells Melissa and J.S. the secret Seada has not been able to reveal, the fact that when running away from the soldiers who shot her husband and mother, Seada accidently dropped her baby and kept on running. Unable to confront that reality, she always carries a blanket and responds to it as if it were her baby. When Seada hears her story recounted by Nuna and tape recorded by Melissa, she has an emotional breakdown. J.S. confronts Melissa saying, "Seada didn't have her terrible experience in order to serve your book.... This isn't about Seada. This is about you and your hunger for fame" (99). Seada does ultimately share her story and tells the others about her lost baby and being repeatedly raped by the soldiers. Melissa then leaves for Chechnya, gathering materials for what she hopes will be the final chapter in her book. While the play depicts Seada's emotional release as cathartic and personally healing, for Melissa it is simply a commodity that she will reproduce in her book.

In these four plays, the commodification of rape is highlighted by the playwright. While Gionfriddo, via the character of Justin; Blessing, via the character of Iris; Keitzer, via the character of Jo; and Ensler, via the character of J.S., are critical of this phenomenon, these playwrights also acknowledge the fascination a raped woman and/or rapist presents for a modern audience and therefore its commercial potential. Turning rape into a commodity for fame and profit, much like the commodification of feminism, is a feature of the dramas written during the post-feminist period.

Six

Female Rage Revisited

Part One: Recuperative Rage

Mary Valentis and Anne Devane contend that expressed rage can be a "gateway to self-assertion, deeper psychological development, and emotional well-being" (8). During the same time period that the three male playwrights, Mastrosimone, Horovitz, and Kazan, wrote the plays analyzed in my discussion of female rage demonized, two female playwrights, Marsha Norman and Julie Hebert also wrote plays in which the raped female characters actively express their rage. In these plays, however, rather than expressed rage leading to the raped women's demonization, the expression of rage is depicted as part of the characters' post-rape recuperative process, leading to their emotional well-being. These plays are *Getting Out* by Marsha Norman and *Almost Asleep* by Julie Hebert. It is interesting to note that these two texts use non-realistic staging practices and plot structures that are quite different from the previously discussed backlash plays by male playwrights which exemplify the theatrical style of realism. These non-traditional aspects support the premise expressed by many feminist theatre practitioners, that strict adherence to theatrical realism cannot adequately encompass feminist concerns.[1]

Getting Out (1977) by Marsha Norman

Getting Out was Marsha Norman's first play. It was originally produced in 1977 by the Actors Theatre of Louisville. This drama depicts the first twenty-four hours in the life of Arlene Holsclaw after she is released from the Pine Ridge Correctional Institute where she served an eight-year incarceration for the second-degree murder of a cab driver. In *Getting Out*, Arlie, a survivor of child sexual abuse by her father, and subsequent sexual mistreatment and rape by a variety of men, exhibits free-flowing rage, yet she is not depicted as a monstrous character.

There are several noteworthy features in this play, the first of which is Norman's employment of split subjectivity. Sue-Ellen Case describes how in many cases (*Getting Out* is but one example she mentions) split subjectivity includes a "male-identified" younger self and an older self "identified as woman" who must struggle with her younger self "both to overcome it and to retain its power" ("Split Subject" 132). In *Getting Out* two of the main characters, Arlene and Arlie, are actually the same person. Arlie is Arlene's younger self and they are often on stage simultaneously. Arlene's rehabilitated self is, for most of the play, in a struggle with her younger delinquent self. Norman writes in the beginning of the play, "Arlie is the violent kid Arlene was until her last stretch in

Getting Out **includes the split subjectivity of Arlie and Arlene in the Adams State University Theatre Department's 2013 production of *Getting Out*, directed by Jenna Neilsen. Featuring Clarissa McNamara as Arlene (below) and Bethany Hernandez as Arlie (above) (photograph by Linda Relyea).**

prison. Arlie's presence is not acknowledged by any of the other characters, although she may address them" (n. pag.). This split protagonist is one feature of the play that breaks from traditional realism.

A second important non-traditional aspect of the play is the non-chronological plot structure. The play contains scenes that take place in the present time as well as flashback scenes, which are often performed simultaneously. Shortly after the play begins we see Arlene enter her new home, a dingy one-room apartment where her sister, Candy, used to live. We learn, through the flashback scenes that Arlie was raped repeatedly by her father and then sent to a reform school. She subsequently became a prostitute, was subjected to dangerous situations with various Johns, got pregnant by her pimp, Carl, and gave birth to a boy, Joey, while in jail. Joey was put in the care of foster parents. Arlie's angry outbursts were unprecedented within the Alabama prison system; however, due primarily to her interactions with the prison chaplain, Arlie, who by then called herself Arlene, was ultimately deemed completely rehabilitated and was released on parole. She accepted a ride from a prison guard, Bennie, from Alabama to Louisville, Kentucky, where she intended to start her new life outside of prison.

Arlene's new life is accurately portrayed and Norman is frank in her depiction of the lower-class milieu in which Arlene now finds herself, and from which she came. Patricia Schroeder claims, "Although Arlene is legally free as the play begins, she is still surrounded by systems of enclosure" (105). These systems of enclosure are both literal (there are bars on the windows to keep the criminals out of the apartment), economic (Arlene was given twenty dollars upon her release from prison and has no marketable skills for legitimate employment), and metaphorical (her "rehabilitation" process has left her a subdued, self-contained and restricted version of her former self). Clearly for Arlene, the freedom she hoped to find on the outside is elusive.

Arlie's emotions are vividly expressed as she describes her numerous experiences of sexual abuse, her exploitation by Carl, and her sexual harassment and threatened digital rape by the prison guards. Once released from prison, Arlie is forced to fend off an attempted rape by the prison employee Bennie, discussed previously as an example of rape conflated with seduction. Both Arlie and Arlene are constantly under surveillance by the patriarchal male gaze within a culture that facilitates various forms of sexual abuse.

This patriarchal culture also insists that her release from prison is dependent on her appropriately gendered subjectivity, which victimizes Arlene once again. Jenny Spencer, for example, writes, "Arlene may get out of prison but her tragic plight involves a socially constructed identity that assigns her permanently to a powerless, passive position, to a female 'self' she hardly recognizes" (156). And Terry Curtis-Fox observes that "Norman is intent on describing a world that is a permanent prison and a prisoner who is not rehabilitated but gutted" (317). Perhaps Curtis-Fox equates Arlene's apparent passivity and domesticity upon release with being "gutted"; however, I believe this characterization overlooks two important features in the play. First, there is sufficient evidence to suggest that Arlene is not in fact the "passive figure" she may have had to play in order to gain her release. Second, Curtis-Fox and Spencer may be overlooking the split subjectivity Norman is demonstrating when she puts both aspects of Arlene's psyche on stage at once.

Admittedly Arlene's rage is a shadow of that exhibited by Arlie, and in many ways her transformation does exhibit gendered characteristics, with Arlie being the active, violent tomboy and Arlene the restrained, indecisive, good girl. I would argue, however, that her effective handling of the attempted rape by Bennie; her refusal to be exploited by Carl; her initially less than polite reception of her neighbor Ruby; and her throwing tomatoes out the car window on their ride to Kentucky, hitting the "No Littering" sign; are all signs that Arlene is hardly a docilized feminine figure.

But Arlene/Arlie's expressions of rage lead to a place of healing and hope as she is able to deal with the violence of her past. This happens at the end of the play. Frustrated by the reality of her life outside, a life she thought would be different, Arlene reaches a breaking point in a conversation with her neighbor, Ruby, who is also an ex-convict. Ruby has offered to get Arlene a minimum wage job as a dishwasher at the restaurant where Ruby works as a cook. Arlene bemoans, "I'll either be inside this apartment or inside some kitchen sweatin over the sink. Outside's where you get to do what you want, not where you gotta do some shit job jus so's you can eat worse than you did in prison." Ruby replies,

Six: Female Rage Revisited

"Well, you can wash dishes to pay the rent ... or you can spread your legs for any shit that's got the ten dollars." Arlene says, "It's just... I thought (*Increasingly upset*). Ruby interrupts her saying, "It was gonna be different. Well, it ain't." (59; ellipses in orig.). Arlene becomes progressively more agitated and angry as her identity and Arlie's identity (Arlie is on stage as well) begin to more directly affect each other. It takes Arlene re-connecting with Arlie's rage to begin the process that will lead to a unified subject.

Arlene breaks down and shares with Ruby the details of her attempted suicide while in prison. Believing the prison chaplain's statements, that Arlie was her hateful self who was hurting her, Arlene stabbed herself repeatedly with a fork, screaming, "Arlie is dead, Arlie is dead" (61). She describes her change, learning to knit, keeping things clean. In other words, adopting a more traditionally defined feminine role. "An I didn't get mad like before or nuthin... I didn't mean to do

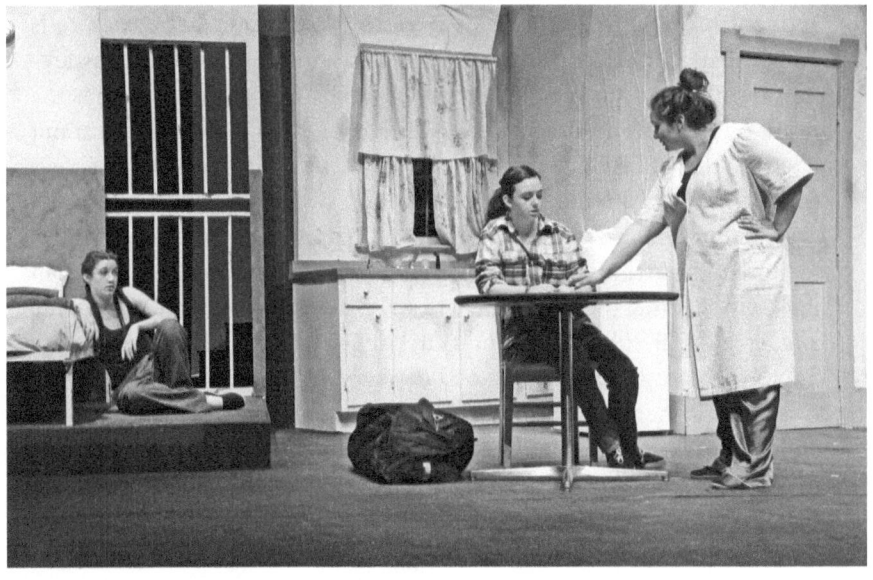

Friendships deepen in the Adams State University Theatre Department's 2013 production of *Getting Out*, directed by Jenna Neilsen. Featuring Bethany Hernandez as Arlie (left), Clarissa McNamara as Arlene (center), and Jordan Hull as Ruby (right) (photograph by Linda Relyea).

it, what I done.... I mean, Arlie was a pretty mean kid, but I did... I didn't know what I..." (61; final two ellipses in orig.). Ruby plants the seed for recuperation when she says, comforting Arlene, "You can still ... you can still love people that's gone" (61). This marks both the beginning of a friendship between Arlene and Ruby, but more importantly a friendship between Arlene and Arlie. Arlene plans to join Ruby later for a game of Old Maid. It is also clear that she will take the dishwashing job and not return to prostitution.

Left alone in the apartment, Arlene acknowledges Arlie's presence for the first time. Arlie speaks directly to Arlene, reminding her of a moment from the past when Arlie had been locked in her mother's closet. She sought revenge by urinating in her mother's shoes, and both Arlene and Arlie laugh at the memory of their transgressive act (64).

It is no accident that Norman portrays this first moment of a unified subject through an action initiated from Arlie/Arlene's rage at being locked in the closet—albeit now remembered with humor. This reenactment of the past event demonstrates what Teresa Bernardez calls "anger that liberates," noting that it is a "conscious response to an awareness of injustices suffered, of losses and grievances sustained and is the result of breaking away and defying the injunction to keep silent about it" (5). Arlie and Arlene reliving this moment of expressed rage shows the beginning of an integration and mutual awareness of past injustices.

Madonne Miner interprets the action of this play as Arlene's efforts to "to banish Arlie so as to become Arlene" (126). However, Norman makes it clear that the banishment of Arlie is not possible through Arlene and Arlie's split-subject position and Arlene's failed suicide attempt. The hope Norman portrays at the end depends on the reunification of the two parts, rather than the banishment of one. Nor, I would argue, does Norman present any kind of idealized notion of Arlene's life after this final moment. Her vivid portrayal of Arlene's class status, a portrayal that is emphasized throughout the play, does not vanish in a single moment of a shared smile between Arlene and Arlie. Many critics do not share Milner's interpretation of the final moments of the play.[2] In fact, in her interview with Elizabeth Stone, Norman said, "Arlene survives because she won't altogether relinquish the 'killer kid' she once was" (58). We are left with the impression that Arlie's refusal to be submissive will serve Arlene well in her life outside where a multitude of forces seek to keep her in her proper place. Ultimately, Arlene's survival depends in part on her acceptance, integration, and recuperation of Arlie's rage.

Patricia R. Schroeder points out two important aspects of Arlene's journey in this drama and the ultimate recuperation of her rage. First, Arlene comes to understand that while her life outside may not be what she imagined it would be, she "discovers that, on the outside, 'when you make your two nickels, you can keep both of 'em.' Second, she learns the importance of female bonding.... With Ruby's help, Arlene resolves to exercise those few options open to her and make the most of her meager economic opportunities" (108). Despite Arlene's initial rejection of Ruby's neighborly overtures, Arlene comes to value the companionship and sympathy of a woman who, like herself, has lived a lifetime of varied imprisonments, and who will not exploit or demean her as every other character in the play attempts to do. As the play ends, Arlene accepts Ruby's supportive friendship. This accepted invitation of female bonding, along with the opportunity for Arlene to open up and share her feelings, as well as the expression of both Arlie and Arlene's rage is depicted as part of her path to healing and her ability to have a successful life on the outside.[3]

Almost Asleep (1991) by Julie Herbert

This play also demonstrates how the connection between women that Norman depicts in *Getting Out* can effectively recuperate rage even if this female connection only exists within one woman. Similar to the split-subject position occupied by Arlene and Arlie in *Getting Out*, Julie Herbert divides her protagonist, Linda, into five subjects. Each of the five characters represents a different aspect of Linda's psyche as she confronts memories of having been raped by two strangers. The emotional impact and devastation of rape is brutally evident as Linda's fragmented mind excavates through layers of repressed anger and bitterness, trying to follow the bread crumbs that connect her rape to her emotions in the present. Similar to *Getting Out*, this text avoids standard conventions of modern realism. In his review of the play, Dan Hulbert describes a movement enacted on the stage, "Performers 'sleep' while pressed against the wall on platforms of staggered heights; or drift through dreams while swinging through the air in hip harnesses, gracefully skimming just inches from the floor or from each other" (D3).

Hebert describes the five characters and their functions in the script, each of the five representing different aspects of the character Linda's mind "as she falls asleep one night after a confusing, humiliating encounter earlier in the day. The encounter triggers the release of long-repressed emotion" (98). Linda's split subjectivity includes (1) The dreamer, who embodies her unconscious mind; (2) The sleeper, who thinks and remembers events through Linda's body; (3). the warrior, who protects Linda against attack; (4) the chatterer, who protects Linda against silence; and (5) the fool, who is described as an "intuitive child. She moves through the environment on ropes, suspended in air. She speaks in a high voice" (98).

Helen Smith describes the unique sensation this play evokes for the audience, "In that last moment between wakefulness and sleep, when one can feel a scary sensation of falling, disturbing emotions surface that have been repressed by the wakeful mind" (N5). And it is in these fleeting, eerie moments when the truth can slip through walls of denial that unexpressed rage can be voiced.

As the play begins, "five women in surreal dream-beds" are sleeping in "peculiar positions. They roll over in unison" (100). The movement continues, at times in unison, at times individualized. The first to speak is the chatterer, who recites a litany of apologies, noting how she "blundered" by acting "without grace." Through a conversation among the five characters we learn that earlier in the day a co-worker of Linda had grabbed her head and put it under his arm and ruffled her hair. This action was a trigger for Linda, and memories of her rape resurfaced. The dreamer says, "A foggy night in May dragged under another man's arm." The chatterer admits that her behavior at work was an overreaction that should not be repeated. The dreamer says, "My secret my secret is eating me" (100–102). This scene is an example of what Karyn Freedman describes "as though there is a traumatized part of our body that stores the experience of the trauma, and when something triggers that part, because it is not *itself* a cognitive place, no form of *rational* persuasion can effectively mitigate it" (110).

Six: Female Rage Revisited

Linda's obsessive apologizing and self-degradation are evidence of her lack of self-esteem and her acceptance of the myth that raped women are contaminated, at least with respect to the chatterer's aspect of her persona. In addition, it appears that when this incident at work happened and she "criticized" the man who grabbed her head under his arm and ruffled her hair, Linda was called a "bitch." The chatterer's compulsion to be forgiven, and to blame herself is also evidence of gendered rage. It appears that her critical reaction to the male co-worker who grabbed her, coming as it did from a woman, was criticized by the others in the room, while the actions of the head-grabbing colleague were not. In keeping with our cultural gendering of rage, the angry woman, Linda, became the bitch/monster.

Just as Arlene needs Arlie's rage in order to be whole, Linda needs to express her rage to find any sense of legitimate subjectivity. The play moves through this cycle of surfacing rage, then avoidance, as different characters attempt to submerge the memories and emotions. Over the course of the play the five aspects of Linda's persona begin to remember the rape. She is finally able to express a myriad of emotions, including doubts about her willingness to resist and fight back when attacked, despite the fact that the rapists were armed and threatened repeatedly to kill her. Once the memory of her rape vividly surfaces, Linda must voice her rage, rather than self-blame, in order to begin a healing process.

The dreamer (with help from the fool) continues prodding the others toward that goal, because she, more than any of the other characters, understands the consequences of remaining silent. "I am weak in everything save damning myself," the dreamer acknowledges. "Silence has protected me, now silence is choking me. The throat must be opened." Ultimately, the five characters re-enact moments from the rape, and this collaborative process of re-embodying the rape becomes the catalyst for the release of rage. The Warrior, declares, "I'll never let it happen again. I'd rather die." But the dreamer, to the surprise of the other characters, shouts, "NO! I choose not to die." She reminds the others of the strength Linda demonstrated the night of her rape. "Floating above my body I looked into the eyes of the rapist who feared killing. I saved my life with that look. I will not be killed now" (108–110).

"Rape exists," Sharon Marcus argues, because "interpretations, representations, and fantasies" position women in a "rape script: as paralyzed, as incapable of physical violence, as fearful" (400). Marcus discusses the imperative that women cultivate and embrace a resistive agency when confronted with an attempted rape, whether it be verbal, physical, or, in the case of Linda, a powerful look that telegraphed to the rapist her unwillingness to meekly accept the role scripted for her. Resistance can thwart an attempted rape, or, as in Linda's case, a possible murder after she was raped.

At the end of the play, the fool realizes the consequence of gendered rage as she acknowledges the weight of playing the "good little girl" and the fact that holding the secret has produced much of her sadness. The fool points out that the sadness that engulfed Linda as she began to fall asleep has now lifted, and before the fool returns to her bed, she tells the audience, "Here is Linda. Linda is not sad" (130).

Over the course of this play, while Linda is almost asleep, her rage is expressed and we sense that the process of healing has begun. She is no longer sad, she has remembered the traumatic experience, she has voiced her rage, and she can now sleep, perhaps for the first time since her rape. *Almost Asleep*, while ultimately depicting a resolution, does not do so in a simplistic manner. The resolution Linda appears to have found by the end of the play has been achieved through long-fought battles with the parts of her that want to deny the rape and deny her rage. These parts are in fact the aspects of Linda's psyche that have internalized patriarchal authority. They embody the cultural forces that seek to silence raped women and maintain masculine dominance. Celeste Miller, who directed the play, notes, "The characters gain the power to take hold of their own fates and move *forward*.... I always want audiences to leave feeling they can go through hell and come out on the other side" (qtd. in Smith N5). The overriding image is of these five women, moving and struggling together in this surreal world in order to become whole. As Helen Smith writes in her review, this piece provides the audience a well-needed "vision for recovery" (N5).

It is worth noting that this important vision for recovery in *Almost Asleep*, and in most of the plays written after the advent of postfeminism, is rooted in an individualized and depoliticized portrayal of a raped woman. This is actually true of many of the plays in this study, including those written prior to the period of postfeminism. There are, however, some plays in which the active expression of female rage is not only rooted in the experiences of the raped character, but the playwright has also vigorously highlighted the broader political, cultural, and social issues related to rape.

Part Two: Resurrecting the Personal as Political

Self Defense or Death of Some Salesmen (2001) by Carson Kreitzer

This play was previously discussed in relation to the depiction of a psychopathological rapist/murderer and also in terms of the postfeminist commodification of a raped woman. Similar to *Getting Out* and *Almost Asleep*, Carson Kreitzer employs many non-realistic dramatic strategies from a non-chronological plot structure to the use of a chorus in which actors play multiple characters to tell Jolene Palmer's story. In this play, however, Jo's rage is expressed in terms of the broader social/political issues related to rape. Reviews of productions have noted the play "lashes out at the twisted society" and examines "the legal status of Jo's self-defense claims [by situating them] against a string of unsolved prostitute murders." *Self Defense* poses a "powerful challenge to sleeping justice systems that either ignore or demean the lives of hundreds of female victims of violent assaults" and creates "a polemic about how Wuornos got a raw deal from a justice system skewed against women and the disenfranchised—particularly prostitutes."[4]

Carson Kreitzer skillfully depicts the socio-economic and familial conditions that propelled Jo into prostitution, similar to what Marsha Norman does for Arlie in her play *Getting Out*. However, the events that led to her arrest and execution are layered with an awareness of the larger political issues. For example, Jo connects America's involvement in the Gulf War to her situation, stating, "The problem was the Gulf War, see? All my regulars were getting called away to the Gulf, to go defend Uncle Sam in the desert, make sure we got enough oil to keep the semis running." And because her regular, non-threatening customers were gone, Jo "hadda get in cars with strangers that I didn't know very well. And subsequently, on several occasions, I was called upon to defend myself" (281).

As Barbara Ozieblo remarks, "Kreitzer is urging her audience to fill in the gaps presented by the judicial system" ("The Victim" 161). The audience learns through the dialogue that "self defense was mentioned a total of forty-three times in [Jo's] videotaped confession, [but] those words were never heard in the sections of the tape shown to the jury" (298). Jo points out some of the weaknesses in the judicial/police system when she declares that she has the right to defend herself. She recalls how a store owner who killed five robbers over the course of a year, because he was afraid they might kill him, was never charged with murder, and yet when she kills because she is afraid she is going to be killed, she is accused of murder. "You don't hear nobody tell him, well maybe you should stop *selling* your TVs in this bad area. Maybe you should just give up the only way you know how to make a living" (307). When her insistence that she acted in self-defense is ignored Jo observes, "There are, y'know, there are certain ... activities that are just known to carry a Death Sentence. I'm not talking about Law here I'm not talking about being illegal. I'm talking about the list a activities that, if you pursue them, these could very easily lead to death." She explains that she knew the risks involved with prostitution, and that she initially stuck to her "regulars," explaining that prostitution is "a line a work with a real high mortality rate... Alls I'm saying is *I want killing women to be added to that list...* 'Cos killing women is not on that list right now" (302).

Jo's defense team includes Cassandra Chase (Cassie), an expert witness, and two psychologists who will "contextualize" Jo's actions. The three claim that due to her abusive childhood, Jo has no concept of "what would constitute appropriate behavior" and that she suffers from "Battered Woman Syndrome" (304, 307). Jo actively refutes these women's claims. She stresses that were she to agree that she has emotional and/or mental problems that would mean the men didn't try to kill her and she simply overreacted. That she just "went nutso. Up and started shooting men. Then how come it's only seven?" she asks. "How come I'm not standing on a pile a 200 corpses?" She insists that most of the men she comes into contact with do not try to kill her, "Only some of 'em, do. Maybe seven of 'em, do" (308).

In contrast to the demonization of the raped woman who actively expresses her rage (identified in the plays written during the period of antifeminist backlash), in this play, as Ozieblo observes, "even if one has to accept that Jo has killed seven rapists, the sympathies are with her, rather than with her victims" ("The Victim" 164). Additionally, several social/political issues are foregrounded in this text, for example, the inadequate judicial system, cultural biases against prostitutes, and the trickle-down impact of the Gulf War.

The Second Coming of Joan of Arc (1988) by Carolyn Gage

Kathryn Burkman and Judith Roof document how male rage in plays is often manifested "in aggression towards and the denigration of women. However, female characters in modern drama do not always accept this denigration without putting up a mighty fight" (15). One such character is Jeanne Romee (aka Joan of Arc) in Carolyn Gage's one-woman monologue-format play, *The Second Coming of Joan of Arc*. While this play, written by an American playwright, features an iconic French protagonist and is set in France, Carolyn Gage's point of view is ripe with American feminist sentiments, and is therefore included in this study. As Carol Anne Douglas writes, "*The Second Coming of Joan of Arc* certainly told Jeanne's story from a radical feminist viewpoint, but the character sounded so much like a twentieth-century radical feminist that there seemed to be little left of the fifteenth-century French peasant girl" (20). In Gage's reimagining of Joan of Arc, the titular character becomes an effective twentieth-century spokeswoman who deftly details societal forces that facilitate rape. In this play Carolyn Gage not only depicts the expression of female rage as part of the recuperative post-rape process, but she highlights many second-wave feminist tenets about rape and patriarchal power. Joan in Gage's play says, "Rape, of course, is not the issue," highlighting Brownmiller's previously stated point that rape allows men to control women by keeping them in a state of fear. The fear of rape, as men have known for years, is just as effective as the real thing." Because of this fear a woman is "scared to live alone, scared to go places by herself, scared of the dark, waking up at the least sound in the middle of the night.... She might just as well have been raped, which of course, is the whole point" (23).[5]

In addition to documenting rape as a tool of patriarchy, Gage's play exemplifies feminist concerns about power and gender. Catherine MacKinnon claims, "A theory of sexuality becomes feminist to the extent it treats sexuality as a construct of male power—defined by men, forced on women and constitutive in the meaning of gender" ("Feminist/Political Approach" 67). "Our crime," an angry Joan says, "is our gender" (28). Gage's text makes clear that following the established patriarchal rules and performing the appropriate gendered behaviors of a peasant girl would do nothing to further Joan's cause. Joan realizes the impotence of her female status as she wonders why her request for a military escort, in order to begin the task her voices had outlined for her, had been denied. As Joan ponders her rejection she thinks about the dress she had been wearing and she says, "That dress had a voice." It spoke to the governor, informing him of Joan's feminine identity, saying, "I'm someone who chooses to wear this thing that won't let me run, fight, ride a horse, swim.... I'm someone who chooses to wear this thing that will make rape very, very easy for men" (16). When Joan returns, wearing male clothing, she is given an army, won her battles and took the king to Reims to be crowned.

Nonetheless she is subsequently abandoned, imprisoned and then, at the age of eighteen, she is turned over to the Church Inquisition. "I had broken all the rules," Joan realizes. "Here I was: A peasant, strike one. A child, strike two. And a female, strike three big time ... and I was dressed like a man" (19). Joan argues that her male clothing was actually what protected her from being raped by the guards while she was imprisoned.

After a five-month trial Joan finally broke down and renounced her voices and "promised to wear a dress" (27). Gage then returns to the issue of wardrobe, rape, and power. After having signed her confession, Joan was taken back to her cell. She was henceforth required to wear a dress, and she was immediately raped. Joan explains that if she had still been wearing male clothing it wouldn't have happened, the guard "would have had to untie forty knots and two sets of lacings with both hands.... But with a dress? One hand, one movement. That's what dresses are about, isn't it? Accessibility? Joan refers to herself as "raped, battered, [and] broken" (28–29). Joan's gender, and gendered wardrobe, is inseparable from the violence perpetrated against her.

In her drama, Gage frequently addresses the issue of representations of gender and the gendering of violence. Teresa de Lauretis contends, "Representation of violence is inseparable from the notion of gender" (*Technologies* 33). Jill Dolan claims "The female body is not reducible to a sign free of connotation. Women always bear the mark and meaning of their sex, which inscribes them within a cultural hierarchy" (*Feminist Spectator* 63). Joan notes how this inscription of women is permeated with violence as she questions the audience, "You think the days of the Inquisition are over? Every woman who's ashamed of her body is a victim of torture" (22).

Peggy Phelan discusses power and authority in patriarchy, noting that the "authority of the patriarchy depends on a hierarchical relationship between the visible and the invisible." The dominant culture "needs invisibility to survey the visible; visibility inspires surveillance and submits to the gaze of the panoptic authority" (139). In other words, the social forces that maintain masculine domination succeed in this task, in part, because the power of these forces is invisible. The power of patriarchy is naturalized, taken for granted, and in many cases internalized by the very people it seeks to dominate. The objects of patriarchy's power are often unaware that power is even being exercised over them, often because they have been trained to not only accept the authority of patriarchy, but actually carry out the task of their own discipline and punishment. Carolyn Gage takes this feminist thesis and foregrounds it in one of Joan's monologues.

Joan asks the audience if they remember Dorothy in *The Wizard of Oz* when the voice said, "Pay no attention to the man behind the curtain." She urges the women to realize that the voice of patriarchy, this powerful voice is simply "the voice of the men behind the curtain. The only reason it sounds like God is because they have been amplifying themselves for two thousand years and using a lot of special effects." Joan comes to realize that she had been a fool, wasting her time fighting to crown a king, trusting the church, and believing that she "would be saved from the actions of men by a God they had created in their own image" (31–32). In other words, she had been a fool to listen to the patriarchal voice from behind the curtain.

In addition to including many feminist concerns in her dramatic work, Gage also presents an alternative depiction of female rage—as is the case with *Getting Out* and *Almost Asleep*, the positive functions of expressed rage are evident in this text. This salutary aspect of anger, specifically the anger that accompanies rape, along with its empowering outcome, is emphasized throughout Gage's piece. Joan talks how about she dealt with the abuse she sustained while in prison, "Anger is a discipline. I practiced my anger the way some people practice piano." She describes how her anger sustained her on the days when she was tempted to feel sorry for herself. Joan tells the audience, "I would always rise to the occasion, throw back the insult, protest the abuse, and demand my rights as a human being. Of course, this had no effect on them, but it kept me alive" (23).

Joan tells the audience that a "miracle" had happened, a resurrection of her power. After having been raped, battered and broken, she no longer knew who she was, but when she was given back her male clothing, she "rose again from the dead." Joan insists she is "proof that there is life after rape" (29–30). Changed by her rape, Joan continues to rally her troops; however, this time her soldiers are the women in the audience. "We must fight for our own causes, women's causes. We must clothe ourselves in self-respect, arm ourselves with our finely-tempered rage, and obey only those voices that we women alone can hear" (32).

In *The Second Coming of Joan of Arc*, Joan's rape and the rage that ensued ultimately lead to her empowerment. Admittedly, empowerment due to rape could be taken by some to imply that rape is a "good" thing, an experience that can strengthen women. Catherine MacGregor brings up this point in her article about British playwright Howard Baker's 1986 adaptation of Thomas Middleton's Jacobean tragedy, *Women Beware Women*. MacGregor's insightful comments apply as well to Carolyn Gage's *The Second Coming of Joan of Arc*, and consequently are worth noting. In Middleton's original work, the distinction between rape and seduction is blurred. Baker, in his adaptation, adds a second rape of the character Bianca, to emphasize her raped status. After this second rape, as MacGregor remarks, "Bianca refuses to play the role that men wish her to assume" (17). She acquires a "new form of selfhood" which "can be seen as an image which breaks the idea that the characters are merely pawns at the mercy of government and forces such as lust and sin" (20).

Similar to the resurrection Joan describes in her monologue, MacGregor remarks that Bianca's rapes "could even be viewed as a resurrection of the woman as individual rather than a sublimation of woman into male society. There are problems with this analysis, as this could be read as an avocation of therapeutic rape." MacGregor wonders, "If Barker [and I will add 'if Gage'] is suggesting that rape can be beneficial does that suggest that *all* women may benefit from rape at some point in their lives?" (22–23). MacGregor's answer to this question applies equally to Gage. "Within this play, Barker is *not* saying 'rape is good,' yet, neither is he silencing the contradictions and problems that rape entails. Rape *will* change a woman's identity; more often than not her identity is changed for her by others as she is stigmatized or made a victim. In the play Bianca acts to take control of her own identity, rather than to lose it" (19). Joan also takes control of her own identity in Gage's play, as other real women in post-rape situations have done. For example, Michelle Knight, after having been held in captivity for ten years, stated, "I will not let the situation define who I am. I will define the situation" (qtd. In Timothy Williams A 16).

Additionally, Carolyn Gage's play clearly articulates feminist tenets by stressing that Joan's rape (and the rape of all women) is one of the many ways that hegemonic patriarchal forces control women's lives. Gage depicts Joan's personal transformation, but she also presents an explicit call for political transformation. As many writers have argued, we need to make the transformation of our rape culture a priority. But the positive transformational effect a woman can undergo due to having survived a rape (or by having resisted an attempted rape) and through the active expression of her rage cannot be denied.[6]

Conclusion

Lucy Nevitt writes, "Violence tells us things about the culture that produced it: the kinds of power relationship on which it is built, the attitudes and values that it takes for granted. A representation of violence can reiterate or challenge normalized social structures" (29). In this study, I have examined the ways in which contemporary American dramas have reiterated or challenged the rape culture in our society since the 1970s. I have shown the degree to which dramatic texts include characters that demonstrate a belief in rape myths within American society, as well as characters who attempt to refute these myths. The persistence of these rape myths provides evidence of the ways in which sexuality is gendered in our culture, thereby promoting a "rapist ethic" which blames the raped woman and provides a rationale for the rapists' behavior. The expression of female rage in these dramas includes examples of raped women's voices being silenced through the containment of their rage, raped characters being demonized due to their expression of extreme rage (both of which I connect to our societal gendering of rage), and depictions of the active expression of rage as part of the raped woman's healing process. It is worth repeating my contention that the containment of female rage may, in some instances, be a strategy with which playwrights attempt to actually highlight patterns in American culture, as opposed to unconsciously participating in or modeling these patterns. Finally, I have documented the influence of feminism on the portrayal of rape, beginning with the use of theatrical productions as a means of social and political activism in the period of second-wave feminism, through dramatic texts which promote antifeminist sentiments during the period of antifeminist backlash, to the commodification of rape typical of plays written during the postfeminist period.

Carolyn Gage contends that theatre creates "magic" due to its "ability to change consciousness at will," adding that "it's dangerous as hell [and] the playwright bears a lot of responsibility" (qtd. in Cramer 9). This may be especially true when dramatic texts portray rape. I would like to present three suggestions that may facilitate the change of consciousness required to transform our rape culture by tempering the power of the reccurring social forces identified in this study (rape myths, gendered rage and sexuality, the depolitization of rape, etc.), both in terms of theatrical production and in a broader context. First, we need to initiate conversations, albeit uncomfortable conversations, about all the issues involving rape and female rage that have been raised by this study. Second, we must mobilize our rage, both within a theatrical setting and in a larger political context in order to ensure that ending rape becomes as worthy a goal as ending breast cancer. And finally, we must thoughtfully examine what Sharon Marcus refers to as our culture's rape script as well as what I call our victim script.

How we speak, or don't speak, about rape and rage is scripted for us by social forces. Accomplishing these goals requires rewriting taken-for-granted scripts. These script revisions can help to dismantle the rapist ethic and denaturalize our conceptions of rape and female rage. In other words, the theatre is a place where the "unreal" of a dramatic text about rape can denaturalize the "real" of rape and female rage.

Suggestion One: Initiate Uncomfortable Conversations

Marsha Norman has stated her commitment to "the creation of unspoken dialogue—those things that are never said, or those things that are said so privately that we don't know that anyone else says them but ourselves" (Stone, "Playwright," 57). Karen Finley's work, as described by C. Carr, is "never a litany of four-letter expletives but an attempt to express emotions for which there are perhaps no words. She would expose the victimizer's monstrous impulses; she would validate feelings the victim could barely talk about" ("Telling" 153). Eve Ensler explains it's crucial "for women to tell their stories, to share them with other people," adding, "Our survival as women depends on this dialogue"

Conclusion

(*Kirkus Reviews* n. pg.) And Robbie McCauley has stated that "the monologue" is over (Soloman, "New York Theatre," 10). These women know the importance of conversations in which we speak the unspeakable. Given the demonstrated power of rape myths, gendered rage and sexuality, and the myriad of forces that control women's representations and behaviors, as theatre practitioners we have an obligation to model alternative practices if we are to transform our rape culture. Sexual assault is not an easy topic to discuss, but silence merely intensifies the rage and shame and grants agency and legitimacy to social forces that perpetuate the rapist ethic. *Sally's Rape*, which ends in an invitation to the audience to keep the conversation going, exemplifies the degree to which theatre can be an effective catalyst for dialogue.

In the early 1970s many of the plays about rape were performed within a feminist community, at theatre companies such as At the Foot of the Mountain and the Rhode Island Feminist Theatre Company. Within a community of women, these performer/activists would start the uncomfortable conversations. Their content was controversial, as was their form. Many of these companies discarded traditional theatrical conventions in order to explore alternative depictions of rape in a theatrical setting. Speaking the unspeakable may very well *require* new forms. I believe it is not merely coincidental that many of the plays within this study that subscribe to the traditional theatrical conventions of realism have been the plays that ultimately contain or demonize female rage. Dramatic texts written in a non-traditional form begin the process of denaturalizing hegemonic theatrical conventions. I believe there is a kind of fluidity, an interactive, mutually supportive dynamic between form and content. Consequently, by disrupting the expectations of audience members by presenting a non-conventional *form*, playwrights can more effectively depict non-conventional *content*. The necessary uncomfortable conversations around the issue of rape in a theatrical context may very well require new forms.

Suggestion Two: Mobilize Female Rage

Throughout the time period of this study, 1970–2007, there have been examples of plays in which an awareness of the social/political

Conclusion

forces that facilitate rape was foregrounded. While many of these were written during the period of second-wave feminism, the impulse to reinforce the philosophy that the personal is in fact political can be seen in every decade. Mobilizing our rage, as theatre practitioners, requires that we actively make visible the broader cultural environment that makes rape possible in the first place. One example of using a theatrical production to raise awareness of a variety of women's issues is Eve Ensler's *The Vagina Monologues*. As audience members and performers alike have documented, this piece combines artistic quality with a cathartic and healing experience for those seeing and participating in the production, and it has also been and continues to be a catalyst for political and social activism.[1] Ensler's play provided a vehicle through which she could bring her politics and her art together.

The Vagina Monologues touches on many issues surrounding women and their bodies, not just sexual violence. Productions have combined consciousness raising with a celebration of liberation for women who have internalized for years a sense of shame about their bodies. Ensler's V-Day College Initiative is also an effective tool for fundraising and political activism. Producers and performers alike are dedicated to these yearly performances of the piece in order to promote an awareness and understanding of the impact of oppressive conditions and sexual violence on women worldwide. Productions of *The Vagina Monologues* demonstrate the potential of theatre to instigate social and political action, but also to move people in a profound and immediate way to take action on a more personal level. For example, Rosie Perez described her cousin's reaction to a performance he attended: "He's kind of a ladies' man," Perez explained. "In the middle of the show, I looked out into the audience, and I could see him. He was crying.... Afterward I asked him if he was all right, and he said, 'I have to call my ex-wife.' I said, 'Why?' He said, 'To apologize for things I said. I had no idea I was cutting her down.' Isn't that amazing?" (qtd. in Stevens 43).

Female rage was mobilized as well in *Sally's Rape*. Raewyn White observes that for Robbie McCauley, "the space of performance is a political arena in which to contest the images of African-American men and women determined in and through dominant discourses: art is both a means by which to explore the issues and contradictions of her life and her weapon against racism" (277). Many performing artists have likewise viewed the performance space as the territory on which political battles can be fought, actively challenging the traditional discourse of representation. For example, Karen Finley declares, "All I'm doing is talking about taboos, things that we prefer to ignore in our society. I think it's the artist's duty to respond to horrific events in our society" (Goldstein, "Finley Hits," 6).

Suggestion Three: Examine Our Rape and Victim Scripts

Sharon Marcus writes, "Rape does not happen to preconstituted victims; it momentarily makes victims" (391). As I have previously explained, Marcus describes rape as a scripted interaction that facilitates rape by enhancing the rapists' power. This rape script depends to a degree on the gendering of both sexuality and rage that I have described throughout this study. Marcus contends that the more we understand this script, this narrative of rape, the more we can readjust our perceptions of rape. She warns that when the actions leading up to a rape are merged with the inevitability of rape, the gap between the two disappears, a gap in which women might thwart an imminent attack. This conflation of actions to initiate a rape with rape itself increases the likelihood of a completed rape. Consequently, in *Hush*, for example, when Kim finds her boyfriend deaf to her requests that he stop his sexual advances, the social rape script, as well as the dramatic text, closes the gap in which effective resistance could occur and allows for the completed rape to take place. The rapist ethic includes the often employed excuse "Well, sure, she said 'No' but I thought she meant 'Yes.'" The rapist's excuse is accepted and validated because resistive agency in women is effectively curtailed by the rape script. As a counter example, Arlene in *Getting Out* is finally successful in her resistive attempts when she correctly labels Benny's actions as rape. Prior to her identifying his aggressive sexuality as rape, he viewed it as seduction. Women, and female characters in dramatic texts, rarely resist to the degree that men take their resistance seriously. This speaks to the gendering of rage. I

Conclusion

do not mean to imply that women should be *obligated* to perform masculine-gendered resistance in order to be believed; rather, the current rape script does not present effective resistive alternatives for raped women.

Gendered sexuality lead to what Sharon Marcus calls grammatical positions for women in a rape script. She argues that too often women respond to the rapists' actions leading up to a rape in accordance with appropriate gendered behavior—in other words, by maintaining a communicative stance of responsiveness, in which the target stays within the limits set by the rapist, and by reacting empathetically by identifying with the rapist. This implies that when a woman/character follows the rape script, she stays within the confines of feminine-gendered rage and sexuality and identifies with the rapist rather than defend herself. As previously mentioned some writers advocate empathy as a mode of self-defense, and recommend responding lovingly as a strategy for preventing a rape. The plays in this study support the contention that these grammatical positions available to women in the rape script in fact lead to the female characters being raped. For example, in none of the rapes depicted in the plays examined for this study did "responding lovingly" thwart a rape attempt. In *Extremities*, in which the attempted rape is vividly portrayed, Raul demands that Marjorie speak to him as a lover would, saying that she loves him and wants him. It is clear in this scene that her politely complying with his demands would not have prevented her rape, or her murder, which Raul has planned. In *Almost Asleep*, when Linda first assumed her attack was just a joke, it merely prevented her from responding immediately in a way that may have averted the attack. In *Rosalee Pritchett*, Rosalee is very polite to the National Guardsmen, long after it was obvious that she was in danger.

Gendered rage also runs throughout most of the plays in this sample. Women's anger is seen as destructive and not in keeping with a feminine ideal, whereas aggression in men enhances their perceived masculinity. For example, Arlene must exorcize Arlie's masculine-gendered rage in order to be released from prison, and Yolanda, in *Under a Western Sky*, who is described as having been previously capable of voicing her rage, becomes unable to express rage after she has been raped, leaving the rage to be expressed by her husband. In *Almost Asleep*,

Conclusion

the fool's history of being a "good little girl" speaks directly to the issue of gendered rage. This aspect of Linda's persona focuses on pleasing all but herself, and the fool's feminine-gendered and contained rage does not allow for healing to take place. As I have shown, many of the raped female characters in contemporary American dramas exhibit feminine-gendered rage which prevents them from having the agency to re-write the rape script. Marcus contends, when women "cease to be grammatically correct feminine subjects" they "become much less legible as rape targets" (Marcus 396). This point is dramatized in *The Second Coming of Joan of Arc*, which makes clear that when Joan wore pants she was not perceived as rapable, but when she returned to wearing a dress, she was immediately raped. By eroticizing masculine aggression and feminine passivity, men's power and women's inferiority is made sexy. This allows for rape to be seen as an extension of normative heterosexuality, promotes the conflation between rape and seduction, and perpetuates the myth that women like rough sex and want to be raped. In *The Widow's Blind Date*, for example, Archie remembers Margie as "begging for more" while she was being gang-raped (93).

Karen Finley is one of the playwrights who disrupts these patterns by embodying female characters who will not conform to the sexually submissive standards that coincide with their assigned gender role in the rape script and in American culture. Laurie Stone observes during an interview with Finley, "Her work reminds women that there's no dividend in pleasing and obliging. Being nice hasn't earned women a bloody thing" ("Woman" 71–72). However, the visceral reaction to her performance pieces serves to document the distance we must travel before active expressions of rage will be socially acceptable for women. The gendering of rage and sexuality, as documented in this study, is but one of the components in the interwoven web of social forces that trap women and keep them silent, submissive and rapable.

Women are not only trapped by the rape script Marcus describes, but also by an equally powerful victim script. Dean MacCannell and Juliet Flower MacCannell note, "The emotional recovery of a woman whose skull is fractured by a mugger who pushes her down on the street and takes her purse is quicker and more complete than recovery from a rape which does not break the skin" (207). While these two crimes are

Conclusion

not strictly comparable, the difference in recovery time is due, in part, to the controlling forces described in this study: the hesitancy to voice rage, the feelings of contamination and shame that typically surround a raped woman's self-image, etc. However, as Sharon Lamb notes, the social script for a raped woman is culturally defined and "the expectation that an abuse victim will develop symptoms is clear. It is also clear that victims' suffering must be long and severe, or else their victimization is trivial and does not count.... For abuse to *count*, the suffering can never go away" ("Constructing the Victim" 113). Nicola Gavey finds in Sharon Marcus' description of the rape script an equally powerful directive relating to the victim script. This is the directive to "conceptualize rape differently, in a way that somehow renders it less powerful without trivializing it" ("I Wasn't Raped" 75).

Gavey's suggestions and warnings are worth noting. She argues for the importance of narratives in which women successfully avert rape as well as the need to stress the fact that "some women who are raped do not experience overwhelming psychological despair." Gavey admits that the "potential cost of this strategy is that it may do violence to the experience of women who are victimized and traumatized by rape" ("I Wasn't Raped" 75). Still others remind us that psychological trauma has not always been the reaction to rape, and that these reactions are themselves, to a degree, culturally constructed. In fact, one of the lessons from the second-wave movement was to teach women that they were not defined in terms of their oppression or their traumatic experiences, but that they had the power to act and work for social change even in the face of rape or domestic violence.[2]

As we moved into the '90s, the impact of postfeminism's return to the personalized and depoliticized world view resulted in, as Carine M. Mardorossian argues, raped women being "represented as irremediably and unidirectionally shaped by the traumatic experience of rape and hence incapable of dealing with anything but their own inner turmoil" ("Feminist Theory" 768). As a society we are suspicious if a raped woman says she is "over it." We expect suffering to persist. Sharon Lamb argues that while the connection between rape and mental anguish has kept therapists' schedules filled, she warns that "when resilience is ignored, a traditional view of women as the weaker sex, in need of protection and special services, is reinforced" ("Constructing the Victim" 116). Gavey admits, "At one extreme, some rapes occur as part of a life-threatening assault, where a women might be literally paralyzed with fear." But she also notes, "At the other end of the spectrum, a women might experience the forced sex as something that falls into a somewhat more everyday sense of 'bad life experiences.' It might not leave major psychological trauma characterized by intense ongoing fear" (*Just Sex* 229).

Final Thoughts

This leads me to my final question. Is there a way to depict a raped woman who does not conform to the victim script by meeting the social expectations of suffering, without marginalizing or, as Gavey puts it, "trivializing" raped women who are traumatized? ("I Wasn't Raped" 175). One of the few plays in this study in which a raped woman has actually moved on from any trauma is *Bovver Boys*. We learn that Joyce, the secretary at the community center in which Gene is serving his alternative service, was raped when she was sixteen. She had been going out with Danny, a famous tough boy in one of the gangs of the time. After a bovver (gang fight) he went out drinking and then found Joyce, and showed her that he "was a man." He raped her and went off to "tell the boys, ... Very manly. Very romantic," she sarcastically recalls (54). The incident in fact led to Joyce disassociating from the gang and turning her life around. As an adult she is strong and confident. Her life may not be perfect, but nor is she trapped in the victim script. In fact, when Joyce shares her own rape experience with Christine, it points the way for Christine to move on with her own life and no longer associate with the gangs.

We certainly are left with the impression at the end of both *Getting Out* and *Almost Asleep* that Arlene and Linda will recover from their abuse. Similarly, at the end of Debra Neff's play *Twice Shy*, Louise, who had been raped at a fraternity party and reluctantly slept with her boyfriend Steven so as not to be considered a "tease," is clearly portrayed as starting the process of moving on with her life. However, it is rare for the depiction of a raped woman to feature someone who has already succeeded in moving on. I'd argue that one way to disempower the victim script would be for playwrights (and writers of other forms of media) to depict raped women who span the entire spectrum of reactions to rape, including those for whom rape might not result in major psychological trauma, and those who have successfully moved on with their lives.

"By defining rape as a scripted performance," Marcus writes, "we enable a gap between script and actress, which can allow us to rewrite the script ... by resisting the physical passivity which it directs us to adopt" (392). These rewrites and the subsequent eradication of the rape script can be facilitated through a concerted effort to disempower the myths that enhance women's self-identification as rapable and men's sense of entitlement to women's bodies, and as theatre artists we can participate in this effort. Ellen Gavin, executive/artistic director of the theatre company Brava! For Women in the Arts, stresses, "Our work is to agitate, if not outright incite. Entertainment is incidental. Theatre—in the flesh, in the real moment—has to be about making a change. It's about making a change. It's about disturbing people into action" (qtd. in Fox 42). The task of transforming our rape culture is hardly complete and theatre practitioners have a role to play.

Chapter Notes

Preface

1. The issue of defining rape is discussed by numerous scholars, including, but not limited to Joanna Bourke, *Rape Sex, Violence, History* (Emeryville, CA: Shoemaker & Hoard, 2007), 8–13; Robert Golden and Fred Peterson, *The Truth About Rape* (New York: Facts on File, 2010), 5+, and Louise Gerdes (ed.), *Sexual Violence: Opposing Viewpoints* (Detroit: Greenhaven Press, 2008), 23+; Ann J. Cahill, "Sexual Violence and Objectification," in *Theorizing Sexual Violence*, ed. Renee J. Heberle and Victoria Grace, 23+ (New York: Routledge, 2009); Nicola Gavey, *Just Sex? The Cultural Scaffolding of Rape* (New York: Routledge, 2005), 10+; Martha Burt, "Rape Myths and Acquaintance Rape," *Acquaintance Rape: The Hidden Crime*, ed. Andrea Parrot and Laurie Bechhofer, 26+ (New York: John Wiley and Sons, Inc., 1991).

2. I have included two plays that do not meet the established criteria: *Selkie* by Laurie Brooks Gollobin and *The Second Coming of Joan of Arc* by Carolyn Gage. A rationale for the inclusion of these plays in this study is stated in the chapters in which the plays are discussed.

Introduction

1. The following three websites all list the same 12 percent, or 1 in 8 statistic for the incidence of breast cancer: "Breast Cancer Risk in American Women," National Cancer Institute, September 24, 2012, http://www.cancer.gov/cancertopics/factsheet/detection/probability-breast-cancer#reference; "Breast Cancer," American Cancer Society, June 10, 2015, http://www.cancer.org/cancer/breastcancer/detailedguide/breast-cancer-key-statistics; "Risk of Developing Breast Cancer," BreastCancer.org, May 15, 2015, http://www.breastcancer.org/symptoms/understand_bc/risk/understanding.jsp.

2. The figure that 20 percent of women will be raped in their lifetime comes from "Intimate Partner Violence," NISVS (National Intimate Partner and Sexual Violence Survey) 2010 Summary Report, Centers for Disease Control and Prevention, 2010, http://www.cdc.gov/violenceprevention/intimatepartnerviolence/index.html. This same percentage was found when I averaged the completed rape statistics in the following articles: Emilie Buchwald, "Raising Girls for the 21st Century," *Transforming a Rape Culture*, ed. Emilie Buchwald, Pamela R. Fletcher, and Martha Roth, 187 (Minneapolis, MN: Milkweed Editions: 1993); Arnold Kahn and Virginia Andreoli Mathie, "Understanding the Unacknowledged Rape Victim," *Sexuality, Society, and Feminism*, ed. Cheryl Brown Travis and Jacquelyn W. White, 379–380 (Washington, DC: American Psychological Association, 2000); John Stoltenberg, "Making Rape an Election Issue," in Buchwald, Fletcher, and Roth, *Transforming a Rape Culture*, 215; Mary P. Koss, "Hidden Rape," in *Rape and Society*, ed. Patricia Searles and Ronald J. Berger, 46 (Boulder, CO.: Westview Press, 1995); Robert Golden and Fred Peterson, *The Truth About Rape* (New York: Facts on File, 2010), 117; Sarah Hauffe and Louise Porter, "Interpersonal Comparison of Lone and Group Rape Offences." *Psychology, Crime & Law* 15: 5 (2009): 469; Virginia Kahn, Andreoli Mathie, and Cyndee Torgler, "Rape Script and Rape Acknowledgment," *Psychology of Women Quarterly* 18 (1994): 57; Nicola Gavey, *Just Sex? The Cultural Scaffolding of Rape* (New York: Routledge, 2005), 55; Judith Lewis Herman, "Considering Sex Offenders:

Notes—Introduction

A Model of Addiction." *Rape and Society*, ed. Patricia Searles and Ronald J. Berger, 74 (Boulder, CO: Westview Press, 1995); Peggy Miller and Nancy Biele, "Twenty Years Later: The Unfinished Revolution," in Buchwald, Fletcher, and Roth *Transforming a Rape Culture*, 49.

3. Regarding the Bill Cosby allegations, see Bill Carter, Graham Bowley, and Lorne Manly, "Comeback by Cosby Unravels as Accounts of Rape Converge," *New York Times*, 20 November 2014, final ed.: A1. Regarding the Jameis Winston allegations, see Brooks Barnes, "Unblinking Look at Sex Assaults on Campus," *New York Times*, 26 January 2015, final ed.: C.1. Regarding the Bikram Choudhury allegations, see Jack Healy, "Schism Emerges in Bikram Yoga Empire," *New York Times*, 24 February 2015, final ed.: A11. Statistics on rape and sexual assault among women in the military come from Jennifer Steinhauer, "Military Courts Are Called Outdated on Prosecutions of Sexual Assaults," *New York Times*, 9 May 2013, final ed.: A21. For information on the documentary films, see Barnes, "Unblinking Look at Sex Assaults on Campus," C1. For the report of sexual offenses on college campuses doubling, see Stacy Teicher Khadaroo. Some of the comments by Republican candidates include Senatorial candidate Todd Akin's comments that victims of "legitimate rape" can't get pregnant; Senatorial candidate Richard Mourdock's comment that "I think even when life begins in that horrible situation of rape, that it is something that God intended"; Bill Napoli, State Senator from South Dakota, who describes the only rape victim who could have a legitimate right to an abortion as someone who had been "brutally raped, savaged. The girl was a virgin. She was religious. She planned on saving her virginity until she was married. She was brutalized and raped, sodomized as bad as you can possibly make it, and is impregnated. I mean, that girl could be so messed up, physically and psychologically, that carrying that child could very well threaten her life." For articles on these and other comments, see John Eligon and Michael Schwirtz, "In Rapes, Candidate Says, Body Can Block Pregnancy," *New York Times*, 20 August 2012, final edition: A13; Jonathan Weisman, "Rape Comment Draws Attention in Indiana," *New York Times*, 24 October 2012, final ed.: A12; Sally Kalson, "Rape Is Rape, Dumb Is Dumb; The GOP Has Made a Habit of Casting Rape Victims as Evil Temptresses," *Pittsburgh Post-Gazette*, 26 August 2012, editorial B3; Molly Ivins, "The Decision Is His, not Hers," *Buffalo News*, 8 March 2006, final ed.: A7. For one of many articles documenting the horrors experienced by Gina DeJesus, Amanda Berry, and Michelle Knight, see Sandra Sobieraj Westfall, et al. "Cleveland Kidnap Survivors 'Getting Stronger Every Day,'" *People* (22 July 2013): 60–65.

4. While I find the use of Marcus' rape script useful when examining the depiction of rape in dramatic texts, Carine M. Mardorossian points out ways in which she finds Marcus' theory problematic in her book *Framing the Rape Victim: Gender and Agency Reconsidered* (New Brunswick, NJ: Rutgers University Press, 2014).

5. For discussions on the difficulty of identifying the line between rape and seduction, see Susan Estrich, *Real Rape* (Cambridge: Harvard University Press, 1987); Nicola Gavey, "I Wasn't Raped, but ... Revisiting Definitional Problems in Sexual Victimization," *New Versions of Victims: Feminists Struggle with the Concept*, ed. Sharon Lamb, 57–81 (New York: New York University Press, 1999); Susan Brownmiller, "The Myth of the Heroic Rapist," in *Against Our Will: Men, Women, and Rape*, chapter 9 (New York: Simon and Schuster, 1975); Sylvana Tomaselli and Roy Porter (eds.), *Rape: An Historical and Social Enquiry* (New York: Basil Blackwell Inc., 1986); Lois Pineau, "Date Rape: A Feminist Analysis," *Date Rape: Feminism, Philosophy, and the Law*, ed. Leslie Francis, 1–26 (University Park, PA: Penn. State University Press, 1996); Irina Anderson and Kathy Doherty, *Accounting for Rape: Psychology, Feminism, and Discourse Analysis in the Study of Sexual Violence* (New York: Routledge, 2008), 6+; Patricia L. N. Donat and Jacquelyn W. White, "Re-Examining the Issue of Nonconsent in Acquaintance Rape," in Travis and White, *Sexuality, Society, and Feminism*, 361+; Jackie Fitzpatrick, "Signifying Rape," in *Feminism, Literature and Rape Narratives: Violence and Violation*, ed. Sorcha Gunne and Zoë Brigley Thompson, 195+ (New York: Routledge, 2010); Stevi Jackson, "The Social Context of Rape: Sexual Scripts and Motivation," in *Rape and Society: Readings on the Problem of Sexual Assault*, ed. Pa-

tricia Searles and Ronald J. Berger, 20+ (Boulder, CO: Westview Press, 1995).

6. A more in-depth discussion of these various "waves" of feminism and their theatrical manifestations can be found in Chapters One, Four, and Five.

7. For more on the issue of consent see: Donat and White, "Re-Examining the Issue of Nonconsent in Acquaintance Rape," 356; and Catharine A. MacKinnon, "Sex and Violence: A Perspective," *Rape and Society*, ed. Patricia Searles and Ronald J. Berger, 30–31 (Boulder, CO.: Westview Press, 1995).

Chapter One

1. See Arnold Kahn and Virginia Andreoli Mathie, "Understanding the Unacknowledged Rape Victim," in *Sexuality, Society, and Feminism*, ed. Cheryl Brown Travis and Jacquelyn W. White, 377–403 (Washington, DC: American Psychological Association, 2000); Emilie Buchwald, "Raising Girls for the 21st Century," in *Transforming a Rape Culture*, ed. Emilie Buchwald, Pamela R. Fletcher, and Martha Roth, 179–200 (Minneapolis, MN: Milkweed Editions: 1993); Nancy MacLean, *The American Women's Movement, 1945–2000: A Brief History with Documents* (Boston: Bedford/St. Martin's, 2009).

2. This quote and information about AddVerb productions can be found at www.addverbproductions.org/

Chapter Two

1. Some of the researchers who have provided evidence that rapists believe rape myths include Kathryn Ryan, "Further Evidence of a Cognitive Component of Rape," *Aggression and Violent Behavior* 9 (2004): 579–604; David Lisak and Susan Roth, "Motivational Factors in Nonincareratead Sexually Aggressive Men," *Journal of Personality and Social Psychology* 55.5 (1988): 795–802; Christopher Kilmartin and Julie Allison, *Men's Violence Against Women: Theory, Research, and Activism* (Mahwah, NJ: Lawrence Erlbaum Associates, 2007); Neil M. Malamuth and Lisa M. Brown, "Sexually Aggressive Men's Perceptions of Women's Communications," *Journal of Personality and Social Psychology* 67.4 (1994): 699–712; Gerd Bohner, Frank Siebler, and Jürgen Schmelcher, "Social Norms and the Likelihood of Raping: Perceived Rape Myth Acceptance of Others Affects Men's Rape Proclivity," *Personality and Social Psychology Bulletin* 32.3 (2006): 286–297; Gerd Bohner, et al., "The Casual Impact of Rape Myth Acceptance on Men's Rape Proclivity: Comparing Sexually Coercive and Non-coercive Men," *European Journal of Social Psychology* 35 (2005): 819–828; Kristine M. Chapleau and Debra L. Oswald, "Power, Sex, and Rape Myth Acceptance: Testing Two Models of Rape Proclivity." *Journal of Sex Research* 47.1 (2010): 66–78; T. Walter Herbert, *Sexual Violence and American Manhood* (Cambridge, MA: Harvard University Press, 2002); Friederikek Eyssel, Gerd Bohner, and Frank Siebler, "Perceived Rape Myth Acceptance of Others Predicts Rape Proclivity: Social Norm or Judgmental Anchoring?" *Swiss Journal of Psychology* 65.2 (2006): 93–99; Virginia Greendlinger and Donn Byrne, "Coercive Sexual Fantasies of College Men as Predictors of Self-Reported Likelihood to Rape and Overt Sexual Aggression," *The Journal of Sex Research* 23.1 (1987): 1–11; William O'Donohue, Elizabeth A. Yeater, and Matthew Fanetti, "Rape Prevention with College Males: The Roles of Rape Myth Acceptance, Victim Empathy, and Outcome Expectancies," *Journal of Interpersonal Violence* 18.5 (2003): 513–531.

2. Some of the scholars who have discussed rape myths include Irina Anderson and Kathy Doherty, *Accounting for Rape: Psychology, Feminism, and Discourse Analysis in the Study of Sexual Violence* (New York: Routledge, 2008); Gerd Bohner, et al., "The Casual Impact of Rape Myth Acceptance on Men's Rape Proclivity"; Elizabeth Powell, "I Thought You Didn't Mind," in *Transforming a Rape Culture*, ed. Emilie Buchwald, Pamela R. Fletcher, and Martha Roth, 107–118 (Minneapolis: Milkweed Editions, 1993); Martha Burt, "Rape Myths and Acquaintance Rape," *Acquaintance Rape: The Hidden Crime*, ed. Andrea Parrot and Laurie Bechhofer, 26–40 (New York: John Wiley and Sons, Inc., 1991); Kathy Doherty and Irina Anderson, "Talking about Rape," *The Psychologist* 11.12 (1998): 583–587; Bettina Frese, Miguel Moya, and Jesús L. Megías, "Social Perception of Rape," *Journal of Interpersonal Violence* 19.2 (2004): 143–161; Renae Franiuk, et al., "Prevalence

Notes—Chapter Two

and Effects of Rape Myths in Print Journalism," *Violence Against Women* 14.3 (2008): 287–309; Patricia A. Frazier, "Victim Attributions and Post-Rape Trauma," *Journal of Personality and Social Psychology* 59.2 (1990): 298–304; Jacqueline M. Gray, "Rape Myth Beliefs and Prejudiced Instructions: Effects of Decisions of Guilt in a Case of Date Rape," *Legal and Criminological Psychology* 11 (2006): 75–80; Carole Goldberg-Ambrose, "Unfinished Business in Rape Law Reform," *Journal of Social Issues* 48.1 (1992): 173–185; Victoria E. Kress, et al., "Evaluation of the Impact of a Coeducational Sexual Assault Prevention Program on College Students' Rape Myth Attitudes," *Journal of College Counseling* 9.2 (2006): 148–157; Kimberly A. Lonsway and Louise F. Fitzgerald, "Rape Myths in Review," *Psychology of Women Quarterly* 18.2 (1994): 133–164; Sarah McMahon, "Rape Myth Beliefs and Bystander Attitudes Among Incoming College Students," *Journal of American College Health* 59.1 (2010): 3–11; Lisa A. Paul, et al., "Perceptions of Peer Rape Myth Acceptance," *Psychological Trauma: Theory, Research, Practice, and Policy* 1.3 (2009): 231–241; Diana L. Payne, Kimberly A. Lonsway, and Louise F. Fitzgerald, "Rape Myth Acceptance," *Journal of Research in Personality* 33.1 (1999): 27–68; Kathryn M. Ryan, "The Relationship between Rape Myths and Sexual Scripts: The Social Construction of Rape," *Sex Roles* 65 (2011): 774–782; Robin G. Sawyer, Estina E. Thompson, and Anne Marie Chicorelli, "Rape Myth Acceptance Among Intercollegiate Student Athletes," *American Journal of Health Studies* 18.1 (2002): 19–25; H. Colleen Sinclair and Lyle E. Bourne, Jr., "Cycle of Blame or Just World: Effects of Legal Verdicts on Gender Patterns in Rape-Myth Acceptance and Victim Empathy," *Psychology of Women Quarterly* 22. 4 (1998): 575–588; Elizabeth A. Yeater, et al., "Cognitive Processes Underlying Women's Rick Judgments: Associations with Sexual Victimization History and Rape Myth Acceptance," *Journal of Consulting and Clinical Psychology* 78.3 (2010): 375–386.

3. Some of the writers who discuss raped women's feeling of contamination include Kathleen Winkler, *Date Rape: A Hot Issue* (Berkeley: Enslow Publishers, Inc., 1999); Patricia Easteal, *Voices of the Survivors* (North Melbourne, Vic.: Spinifex, 1994); Andrea Parrot and Laurie Bechhoffer (eds.), *Acquaintance Rape: The Hidden Crime* (New York: John Wiley and Sons, Inc., 1991); Peggy Reeves Sanday, *Fraternity Gang Rape: Sex, Brotherhood, and Privilege on Campus* (New York: New York University Press, 1990); Leslie Francis (ed.), *Date Rape: Feminism, Philosophy, and the Law* (University Park: Penn State University Press, 1996); Charlotte Pierce-Baker, *Surviving the Silence: Black Women's Stories of Rape* (New York: Norton, 1998); Cynthia Carosella (ed.), *Who's Afraid of the Dark?* (New York: Harper Perennial, 1995); Vernon R. Wiehe and Ann L. Richards, *Intimate Betrayal* (Thousand Oaks, CA: Sage Publications, 1995); Robert Golden and Fred Peterson, *The Truth about Rape* (New York: Facts on File, 2010); and Susan Smith Nash, *Dealing with Date Rape: True Stories from Survivors* (Norman, OK: Texture Press, 1996).

4. Some of the researchers who have discussed the myth that male sexuality is uncontrollable include Judith Lewis Herman, "Considering Sex Offenders: A Model of Addiction," in *Rape and Society*, ed. Patricia Searles and Ronald J. Berger, 74–98 (Boulder, CO: Westview Press, 1995); Ann J. Cahill, "Sexual Violence and Objectification," in *Theorizing Sexual Violence*, ed. Renee J. Heberle and Victoria Grace, 14–32 (New York: Routledge, 2009); Golden and Peterson, *The Truth about Rape*; Deborah L. Laufersweiller-Dwyer and Gregg Dwyer, "Rapists," in *Sexual Assault: The Victims, the Perpetrators, and the Criminal Justice System*, ed. Frances P. Reddington and Betsy Wright Kreisel, 205–231 (Durham, NC: Carolina Academic Press, 2005); Diana Scully and Joseph Marolla, "Riding the Bull at Gillely's": Convicted Rapists Describe the Rewards of Rape," *Rape and Society: Readings on the Problem of Sexual Assault*, ed. Patricia Searles and Ronald J. Berger, 58–73 (Boulder, CO: Westview Press, 1995); and Myriam Miedzian, "How Rape Is Encouraged in American Boys and What We Can Do to Stop It," in Buchwald, Fletcher, and Roth, *Transforming a Rape Culture*, 153–164.

5. The following writers have noted the fact that women participate in nonconsensual sex because they believe the myth that men can't control their sexual urges: Jennifer M. Brown and Miranda A. H. Horvath, "Do You Believe Her and Is It Real Rape?" in *Rape: Challenging Contemporary Thinking*, ed. Miranda A. Horvath and Jennifer M. Brown

Notes—Chapter Two

(Cullompton: Willan 2009); Hannah Firth and Celia Kitzinger, "Reformulating Sexual Script Theory," *Theory & Psychology* 11.2 (2001): 209–232; and Sarah Walker, "When 'No' Becomes 'Yes': Why Girls and Women Consent to Unwanted Sex," *Applied & Preventive Psychology* 6 (1997): 157–166.

6. Some of the researchers that discuss incidents of miscommunication resulting in a rape include Laufersweiller-Dwyer and Dwyer, "Rapists"; and Malamuth and Brown, "Sexually Aggressive Men's Perceptions of Women's Communications."

7. Some of the researchers who discussed the degree to which rapists have pathological and/or psychological abnormalities include Kilmartin and Allison, *Men's Violence Against Women*; Jacquelyn White and Paige Smith, "Sexual Assault Perpetration and Reperpetration," *Criminal Justice and Behavior* 31.2 (2004): 182–202; Scully and Marolla, "Riding the Bull at Gilley's"; Herman "Considering Sex Offenders"; Paige Crosby Ouimette and David Riggs, "Testing a Mediational Model of Sexually Aggressive Behavior in Nonincarcerated Perpetrators," *Violence and Victims* 13.2 (1998): 117–130; Lisak and Roth, "Motivational Factors in Nonincarceratead Sexually Aggressive Men"; Jeffrey A. Bernat, Karen S. Calhoun, and Henry E. Adams, "Sexually Aggressive and Nonaggressive Men: Sexual Arousal and Judgments in Response to Acquaintance Rape and Consensual Analogues," *Journal of Abnormal Psychology* 108.4 (1999): 662–673; Jennifer C. Kelly, David S. Kosson, and Jacquelyn W. White, "Psychopathy-Related Traits Predict Self-Reported Sexual Aggression Among College Men," *Journal of Interpersonal Violence* 12.2 (1997): 241–255; and Karen Rapaport and Barry R. Burkhart, "Personality and Attitudinal Characteristics of Sexually Coercive College Males," *Journal of Abnormal Psychology* 93.2 (1984): 216–221.

8. Some of the researchers who discussed the degree to which rapists are psychologically and socially normal with no pathological and/or psychological abnormalities include Scully and Marolla, "Riding the Bull at Gilley's"; Stevi Jackson, "The Social Context of Rape: Sexual Scripts and Motivation," in *Rape and Society: Readings on the Problem of Sexual Assault*, ed. Patricia Searles and Ronald J. Berger, 16–27 (Boulder, CO: Westview Press, 1995); Kilmartin and Allison, *Men's Violence Against Women*; Lisak and Roth, "Motivational Factors in Nonincarceratead Sexually Aggressive Men"; Herman, "Considering Sex Offenders"; Samuel A. Rubenzahl and Kevin J. Corcoran, "The Prevalence and Characteristics of Male Perpetrators of Acquaintance Rape," *Violence against Women* 4.6 (1998): 713–725. Some of these researchers report on some studies that claim rapists are "normal" and also report on studies that claim rapists are "pathological."

9. The figure of 80 percent was obtained by averaging the research from the following sources: Golden and Peterson, *The Truth about Rape*; Louise Gerdes (ed.), *Sexual Violence: Opposing Viewpoints* (Detroit: Greenhaven Press, 2008); Jorge A. Jimenez and José M Abreu, "Race and Sex Effects on Attitudinal Perceptions of Acquaintance Rape," *Journal of Counseling Psychology* 50.2 (2003): 252–256; and Kilmartin and Allison, *Men's Violence against Women*.

10. Researchers who have discussed rape in relation to athletes and fraternity populations include Chris O'Sullivan, "Fraternities and the Rape Culture," in Buchwald, Fletcher, and Roth, *Transforming a Rape Culture*, 23–30; Sawyer, Thompson, and Chicorelli, "Rape Myth Acceptance Among Intercollegiate Student Athletes"; Andrea Parrot and Nina Cummings, "A Rape Awareness and Prevention Model for Male Athletes," *Journal of American College Health* 42.4 (1994): 179–184; Sanday, *Fraternity Gang Rape*; Patricia Yancey Martin and Robert A. Hummer, "Fraternities and Rape on Campus," in *Rape and Society: Readings on the Problem of Sexual Assault*, ed. Patricia Searles and Ronald J. Berger, 139–151 (Boulder, CO: Westview Press, 1995).

11. Researchers who have discussed gang rape, gang rapists, and the phenomenon of group think include O'Sullivan, "Fraternities and Rape Culture"; Scully and Marolla, "Riding the Bull at Gilley's"; Ryan, "Further Evidence"; Sarah Hauffe and Louise Porter, "Interpersonal Comparison of Lone and Group Rape Offences," *Psychology, Crime & Law* 15: 5 (2009): 469–491; Golden and Peterson, *The Truth about Rape*; Miranda A. Horvath, Angel Helena, and Liz Kelly, "Multiple Perpetrator Rape," *Journal of Sexual Aggression* 15.1 (2009): 83–96; and Louise E. Porter and Laurence J. Alison, "Behavioural Coherence in Violent Group Activity: An Interpersonal

Model of Sexually Violent Gang Behaviour," *Aggressive Behavior* 30.6 (2004): 449–468.

12. Interesting also are the Playwrights' Notes in which Carlton and Barbara Molettte write: "We are opposed to the idea of having the Guards played by whites. They should be played by Black men in white-face makeup. It's not that we have anything against white folks—there are some excellent white actors in the Goodoleusofa, but they just ain't capable of the kind of objectivity that is necessary in the portrayal of these roles."

Chapter Three

1. A character wishing to commit suicide is not automatically evidence of rage turned inward. For example, Marsha Norman's *'night Mother* depicts the 90 minutes Jessie and her mother spend together immediately prior to Jessie's planned suicide. Brian Clark's *Whose Life is it Anyway?* depicts the efforts of a totally paralyzed car accident victim to be released from the hospital. His release would lead inevitably to his death/suicide. In each of these plays, the choice of suicide is clearly a rational, well-thought-out decision. There is no indication that either of the protagonists is misplacing rage, clinically depressed, or in any way mentally impaired.

2. Susan Estrich, *Real Rape* (Cambridge: Harvard University Press, 1987), 57–79.

3. See, for example, Suzanne Gossett, "Best Men Are Molded Out of Faults: Marrying the Rapist in Jacobean Drama," *English Literary Renaissance* 14.3 (1984): 305–327; Lori Cidylo, "Best Men Are Molded Out of Faults: Marrying the Rapist in Jacobean Drama," *English Literary Renaissance* 14.3 (1984): 305–327; Mark Arax, "Child Brides Common Among California's Homong Refugees," *The Houston Chronicle.* 9 May 1993, star ed., sec. A: 18; Damien McElroy, "Focus on Brides for Sale," (London) *Sunday Telegraph*. 22 November 1998: 28; and Mark Franchetti, "Kingdom of the Kidnapped Brides," (London) *Sunday Times*, 7 February 1999.

4. The primary journal that publishes articles about theatre for young audiences is *Youth Theatre Journal*, published by the American Alliance for Theatre and Education. The term "theatre for young audiences" has a different meaning than the term "children's theatre." "Children's theatre" implies the production of plays in which *children* are the actors and whose target audiences are children. The term "theatre for young audiences" implies the production of plays that also have target audiences of children, but in which *adults* are the actors.

5. These quotes were taken from newspaper and magazine articles written by Kevin Sullivan, "Report of Mutilation Draws Powerful Responses," *Washington Post*, 25 January 1993, final ed.: C1; Kendall Hamilton and Marc Peyser, "The Cut Heard Round the World," *Newsweek*, 18 October 1993: 10; Daniel Wattenberg, "*Sharia* Feminists," *The American Spector* (December 1993): 62; Kris Worrell, "Bobbitt Case Rekindles the Gender Debate," *The Atlanta Journal and Constitution*, 1 December 1993: E1; Mark Sauer and Jeanne Freeman Brooks, "The Bobbitt Case," *The San Diego Union-Tribune*, 30 November 1993: E1; Judy Mann, "Beyond the Bobbitts' Battle," *Washington Post*, 13 August 1993, final ed.: E3; Maria E. Odum and Carlos Sanchez, "A Symbol of Shared Rage," *Washington Post*, 12 August 1993, final ed.: B1. Please note, often the quoted phrase was spoken by someone the writer(s) interviewed, rather than the writer's sentiments.

6. Rage when expressed by men in a fictional/dramatic context is not *always* normalized; see, for example, Curry and Allison's discussion of monstrous rage in The Incredible Hulk in Renee Curry and Terry Allison (eds.), *States of Rage: Emotional Eruption, Violence and Social Change* (New York: New York University Press, 1996).

7. See, for example, Don Braunagel, "Play Probes Issues of Rape," rev. of *Extremities*, William Mastrosimone, *The San Diego Union-Tribune*, 18 March 1985: C1; John Hayes, "Extremities Leaves Victim in Question," rev. of *Extremities*, William Mastrosimone, *Pittsburgh Post-Gazette*, 13 June 2000: D4; Walter Kerr, "Extremities and a Muffled Alice," rev. of *Extremities* by William Mastrosimone, *New York Times*, 2 January 1983, final ed.: B3; and David Richards, "None but the Brave," rev. of *Extremities*, William Mastrosimone. *Washington Post*. 21 November 1985, final ed.: C17.

8. Reviewers who have mentioned the way in which *Extremities* ultimately elicits sympathy for the rapist include Steve Bornfeld; Joe Brown, "Raw, Explosive Extremi-

ties," rev. of *Extremities*, William Mastrosimone, *Washington Post*, 4 October 1985, final ed.: Weekend 9; Anthony Del Valle; Kathy L. Greenberg; Mel Gussow, "Five Full-Length Plays," rev. of *Extremities*, William Mastrosimone, *New York Times*, 29 March 1981, final ed.: A61; Walter Kerr, "Extremities and a Muffled Alice," rev. of *Extremities* by William Mastrosimone, *New York Times*, 2 January 1983, final ed.: B3; Liam Lacey; Theodore P. Mahne; David Richards, "None but the Brave," rev. of *Extremities*, William Mastrosimone, *Washington Post*, 21 November 1985, final ed.: C17; Susan L. Rife; Megan Rosenfeld, "Chilling View of Rape," rev. of *Extremities*; Nicholas Kazan, *Washington Post*, 24 January 1985, final ed.: D2; Burke Speaker; and Jasmina Wellinghoff.

9. These descriptive adjectives were taken from the following reviewers: Mel Gussow, "Blood Moon, of Crime and Revenge," rev. of *Blood Moon*; Nicholas Kazan, *New York Times*, 14 January 1983, final ed.: C6; Mel Gussow, "In the Arts," rev. of *Blood Moon*, Nicholas Kazan, *New York Times*, 6 March 1983, final ed.: 2A3; Leah D. Frank, "How a Rape Victim Wreaks Revenge," rev. of *Blood Moon*, Nicholas Kazan, *New York Times*, 23 February 1992, final ed.: Long Island 13; Megan Rosenfeld, "Waxing Blood Moon," rev. of *Blood Moon*, Nicholas Kazan, *Washington Post*, 24 January 1985, final ed.: D2; Joe Brown, "Blood Moon: More Clamor Than Content," rev. of *Blood Moon*, Nicholas Kazan, *Washington Post*, 18 January 1985, final ed.: Weekend 13; Lisa Serene Gelb, "Of Rape and Revenge," rev. of *Blood Moon*, Nicholas Kazan, *Washington Post*, 13 January 1985, final ed.: L3; and Lawrence Christon, "Rape and Revenge in 'Moon,'" rev. of *Blood Moon*, Nicholas Kazan, *Los Angeles Times*, 22 May 1985, home ed.: Calendar 8.

10. These attributions of Manya's character come from reviews by Leah D. Frank, "How a Rape Victim Wreaks Revenge"; Gussow, "Blood Moon, of Crime and Revenge"; and Brown, "Blood Moon: More Clamor Than Content."

Chapter Four

1. See Naomi Wolf's article "Feminist Fatale," *New Republic* 206, no. 11 (March 1992): 23–25.

2. Karen Finley, along with Holly Hughes, Tim Miller, and John Fleck, came to be known as the "NEA 4" due to the denial of their NEA grants. This issue will be discussed later in this chapter.

3. "Inspired" came from John Koch, "Performance Artist Karen Finley Finds Humor in the Center of Horror," rev. of *We Keep Our Victims Ready*, Karen Finley, *The Boston Globe*. 14 September 1990, city ed.: Living 38. "Obscene" came from Stephen Holden, "Avant-Garde Antics for Fearless Audiences," *New York Times*, 5 February 1988.

4. For an interesting discussion of the challenge presented to feminist artists in terms of resisting or participating in this fantasy male-centered representation, see Chapter 2 in Peggy Phelan, *Unmarked: The Politics of Performance* (New York: Routledge, 1993).

5. My discussion of Finley's dramatic texts is based in part on the works of: Jeanie Forte, "Women's Performance Art: Feminism and Postmodernism," *Theatre Journal* 40.2 (1988): 217–235; Lynda Goldstein, "Raging in Tongues: Confession and Performance Art," *Confessional Politics: Women's Sexual Self-Representations in Life Writing and Popular Media*, ed. Irene Gammel (Carbondale: Southern Illinois University Press, 1999), 99–116; C. Carr, "Unspeakable Practices, Unnatural Acts: The Taboo Art of Karen Finley," *Acting Out: Feminist Performances*, ed. Lynda Hart and Peggy Phelan (Ann Arbor: University of Michigan Press, 1993), 141–152; C. Carr, "Telling the Awfullest Truth: An Interview with Karen Finley," Hart and Phelan, *Acting Out: Feminist Performances*, 153–160; Maria Pramaggiore, "Resisting/Performing/Femininity: Words, Flesh, and Feminism in Karen Finley's *The Constant State of Desire*," *Theatre Journal* 44.3 (1992): 269–290; Rebecca Schneider, *Explicit Body in Performance* (New York: Routledge, 1997); Timothy Wiles, "Suicide and Self-Annihilation: Marsha Norman's *'night Mother* and Karen Finley's *The Constant State of Desire*," *Staging the Rage: The Web of Misogyny in Modern Drama*, ed. Katryhn Burkman and Judith Roof (Madison: Fairleigh Dickinson University Press, 1998), 112–123; Laurie Stone, "Cameos," rev. of *We Keep Our Victims Ready*, Karen Finley, *Village Voice*, 1 May 1990: 118; Laurie Stone, "Woman of the Year—Karen Finley," *Ms.* (January/February 1998): 71–73; Jill Dolan, "The Dynamics of Desire: Sexu-

ality and Gender in Pornography and Performance," *Theatre Journal* 39.2 (1987): 156–174; Jill Dolan, *The Feminist Spectator as Critic* (Ann Arbor, University of Michigan Press, 1988); Jill Dolan, *Presence and Desire: Essays on Gender, Sexuality, Performance* (Ann Arbor: University of Michigan Press, 1993); Jill Dolan, *The Feminist Spectator in Action: Feminist Criticism for the Stage and Screen* (New York: Palgrave Macmillan, 2013); Dean Wilcox, "Karen Finley's *Hymen*," *Theatre Research International* 22.1 (1997): 31–37; Catherine Schuler, "Spectator Response and Comprehension: The Problem of Karen Finley's Constant State of Desire," *The Drama Review* 34.1 (1990): 131–145; and Phelan, *Unmarked: The Politics of Performance*.

6. In *Under The Western Sky*, an older Chicana woman describes a similar phenomenon. She links the gang rape to the medical practice of anesthetizing women during childbirth. Consequently, the boy child is not aware of the mother's pain, and therefore, is not sensitive to women's pain in general. The old woman notes this lack of sensitivity to women's pain is one of the reasons why events like gang rape can occur within their community. In other words, the medical interference in a woman's "natural" bodily functions leads to the gang rape depicted in that play.

7. The information complied in this summary of events came from the following sources: Richard Bolton (ed.), *Culture Wars: Documents from the Recent Controversies in the Arts* (New York: New Press, 1992); Hilliard Harper, "Focus on Theatre: Finley Attack on Taboo at Sushi Isn't for Timid," rev. of *The Constant State of Desire*, Karen Finley, *Los Angeles Times*, 12 February 1988, San Diego County ed.: Calendar 22; Jackie Fitzpatrick, "Finley State of Desire is Shocking, Riveting," rev. of *The Constant State of Desire*, Karen Finley, *The San Diego Union-Tribune*, 13 February 1988: B6; Joe Brown, "Art at the Outer Limits: Karen Finley, Taking Performance to a New Level," rev. of *The Constant State of Desire*, Karen Finley, *Washington Post*, 4 May 1988, final ed.: D2; Nancy Churnin, "Artist Relies on Shock Therapy to Send Message," rev. of *We Keep Our Victims Ready*, Karen Finley, *Los Angeles Times*, 12 September 1989, San Diego County ed.: Calendar 1; John Koch, "Performance Artist Karen Finley Finds Humor in the Center of Horror," rev. of *We Keep Our Victims Ready*, Karen Finley, *The Boston Globe*, 14 September 1990, city ed.: Living 38; Kevin Kelly, "Karen Finley's Vicious Fame," rev. of *We Keep Our Victims Ready*, Karen Finley, *The Boston Globe*, 31 August 1990, city ed.: Arts & Film 59; Stephen Holden, "Finley Mocks Her Critics in Her Art," rev. of *We Keep Our Victims Ready*, Karen Finley, *New York Times*, 24 July 1990, final ed.: C13; Karen Finley, "Bound and Gagged by Hearsay Evidence," *Los Angeles Times*, 11 July 1990, home ed.: B7; Karen Finley, "Chocolate-Smeared Young Woman," *Washington Post*, 19 May 1990, final ed.: A23; Barbara Gamarekian, "Frohnmayer Sid to See Peril to Theater Grants," *New York Times*, 29 June 1990, final ed.: C15; Michael Brenson, "Effects of Men's Desires on the Lives of Women," rev. of *We Keep Our Victims Ready*, Karen Finley, *New York Times*, 21 May 1990, late ed.: C13; Allan Parachini, "NEA Advisors Nix Grants," *Los Angeles Times*, 15 May 1990, home ed.: F1; William H. Honan, "U.S. Documents Said to Show Endowment Bowed to Pressure," *New York Times*, 18 September 1991, final ed.: C13; Dennis McDougal, "Despite Grants, NEA Four Presses Suit," *Los Angeles Times*, 6 November 1991, home ed.: F3; Jan Breslauer, "Body Politic: Performance Artist Karen Finley Brings Her Controversial 'Victims' to L.A.," rev. of *We Keep Our Victims Ready*, Karen Finley, *Los Angeles Times*, 8 November 1991, home ed.: F1; and Jim DeRogatis, "Finley's Denial Confirms She is a Compelling Artist," rev. of *A Certain Level of Denial*, Karen Finley, *Chicago Sun-Times*, 8 November 1994, final ed.: F39.

8. This *Village Voice* article is reprinted in Hart and Phelan, *Acting Out: Feminist Performances*. Any quotes from this article are taken from the version in *Acting Out*.

9. Immediately following the reprinted *Village Voice* cover story in *Acting Out* is an interview between C. Carr and Finley that took place in the fall of 1991. I looked to see if Carr mentioned or apologized for her original misleading comment about the yams in the 1986 *Voice* article, but no mention of it appears in the interview printed in *Acting Out*.

10. For a lengthy discussion of audience reactions to Finley's performances, see Catherine Schuler, "Spectator Response and Comprehension: The Problem of Karen Finley's

Constant State of Desire," *The Drama Review* 34.1 (1990): 131-145.

11. See interviews with Karen Finley, interview, "A Constant State of Becoming," Richard Schechner, *The Drama Review* 32.1 (1988): 152-158; Nicholas Drake, interview, *Karen Finley: What I Do Is the Feeling*, Nicholas Drake, *Art Papers* 19 (1995): 10-13; and Maria Pramaggiore, "Resisting/Performing/Femininity: Words, Flesh, and Feminism in Karen Finley's *The Constant State of Desire*," *Theatre Journal* 44.3 (1992): 269-290.

Chapter Five

1. In addition to scholars directly quoted, my summary of third-wave feminism is based on the following sources Chris Bobel, *New Blood: Third-wave Feminism and the Politics of Menstruation* (New Brunswick, NJ: Rutgers University Press, 2010); Shelley Budgeon, "The Contradictions of Successful Femininity: Third-Wave Feminism, Postfeminism, and 'New' Femininities," in *New Femininities: Postfeminism, Neoliberalism, and Subjectivity*, ed. Rosalind Gill and Christina Scharff, 279-292 (New York: Palgrave MacMillan, 2011); Sarah Gamble (ed.), *The Routledge Critical Dictionary of Feminism and Postfeminism* (New York: Routledge, 1999); June Hannan, *Feminism* (New York: Pearson Longman, 2007); Roxanne Harde and Erin Harde, "Voices and Visions: A Mother and Daughter Discuss Coming to Feminism and Being Feminist," in *Catching a Wave: Reclaiming Feminism for the 21st Century*, ed. Rory Dicker and Alison Piepmeier, 116-137 (Boston: Northeastern University Press, 2003); Leslie Heywood and Jennifer Drake (eds.), *Third Wave Agenda: Being Feminist, Doing Feminism* (Minneapolis: University of Minnesota Press, 1997); Audre Lorde, *Sister Outsider: Essays and Speeches by Audre Lorde* (Freedom, CA: The Crossing Press, 1984); Ellen Riordan, "Commodified Agents and Empowered Girls: Consuming and Producing Feminism," *Journal of Communication Inquiry* 25.3 (2001): 279-297; Kristin Rowe-Finkbeiner, *The F-word: Feminism in Jeopardy: Women, Politics, and the Future* (Emeryville, CA: Seal Press, 2004); Kayann Short, "Coming to the Table: Differential Politics of This Bridge Called My Back," *Genders* 19 (1994): n. pag.; and Sue Thornham, "Second Wave Feminism," in *The Routledge Critical Dictionary of Feminism and Postfeminism*, ed. Sarah Gamble, 29-42 (New York: Routledge, 1999).

2. The play *Venus* by Suzan Lori Parks is a compelling dramatization of the exhibition of Bartmann.

3. Ann Braithwaite's article outlines many of the ways in which third wave and postfeminism overlap. Ann Braithwaite, "The Personal, the Political, Third-Wave and Postfeminisms," *Feminist Theory* 3.3 (2002): 335-344. Additionally, several writers have illuminated the differences between third-wave feminism and postfeminism by comparing the ways in which the focus on "girl is good," advocated by third-wave feminists, and the apolitical narcissism of postfeminism was manifested in the music scene. Comparisons of the Riot Grrrl culture/groups in relation to other types of girl groups such as Spice Girls are provided in the following sources: Anna Feignbaum, "Remapping the Resonances of Riot Grrl: Feminisms, Postfeminisms, and 'Processes' of Punk," in *Interrogating Postfeminism: Gender and the Politics of Popular Culture*, ed. Yvonne Tasker and Diane Negra, 132-152 (Durham, NC: Duke University Press, 2007); Jenna Freedman, "Self-Publication with Riot Grrrl Ideals," in *Make Your Own History: Documenting Feminist and Queer Activism in the 21st Century*, ed. Lyz Bly and Kelly Wooten, 13-22 (Los Angeles, CA: Litwin Books 2012); Kate Eichhorn, "Archiving the Movement," in *Make Your Own History: Documenting Feminist and Queer Activism in the 21st Century*, ed. Lyz Bly and Kelly Wooten, 23-37 (Los Angeles, CA: Litwin Books, 2012); Kristen Schilt; "The Punk White Privilege Scene: Riot Grrrl, White Privilege, and Zines," in *Different Wavelengths: Studies of the Contemporary Women's Movement*, ed. Jo Reger (New York: Routledge, 2005); Sarah Gamble (ed.), *The Routledge Critical Dictionary of Feminism and Postfeminism* (New York: Routledge, 1999); Riordan, "Commodified Agents and Empowered Girls: Consuming and Producing Feminism"; Isabelle V. Barker, "Editing Pornography," in *Feminism and Pornography*, ed. Drucilla Cornell, 643-652 (New York: Oxford University Press, 2000).

4. My summary of postfeminism draws from the following sources: Barker, "Editing Pornography"; Jennifer Baumgardner and

Notes—Chapter Five

Amy Richards, "Feminism and Femininity: Or How We Learned to Stop Worrying and Love the Thong," in *All About the Girl: Culture, Power, and Identity*, ed. Anita Harris, 59-68 (New York: Routledge, 2004); Kellie Bean, *Post-Backlash Feminism: Women and the Media since Reagan-Bush* (Jefferson, NC: McFarland & Co., 2007); Joanna Bourke, *Rape, Sex, Violence, History* (Emeryville, CA: Shoemaker & Hoard, 2007); Braithwaite, "The Personal, the Political, Third-Wave and Postfeminisms"; Budgeon, "The Contradictions of Successful Femininity: Third-Wave Feminism, Postfeminism, and 'New' Femininities"; Ann J. Cahill, *Rethinking Rape* (Ithaca: Cornell University Press, 2001); Ann J. Cahill, "Sexual Violence and Objectification," in *Theorizing Sexual Violence*, ed. Renee J. Heberle and Victoria Grace, 14–32 (New York: Routledge, 2009); Zillah Eisenstein, *Hatreds: Racialized and Sexualized Conflicts in the 21st Century* (New York: Routledge, 1996); Karyn Freedman, "The Epistemological Significance of Psychic Trauma," *Hypatia* 21:2 (Spring 2006): 104–125; Gamble (ed.), *The Routledge Critical Dictionary of Feminism and Postfeminism*; Nicola Gavey, *Just Sex? The Cultural Scaffolding of Rape* (New York: Routledge, 2005); Nicola Gavey, "Fighting Rape," in *Theorizing Sexual Violence*, ed. Renee J. Heberle and Victoria Grace, 96–124 (New York: Routledge, 2009); Nicola Gavey, "I Wasn't Raped, but... Revisiting Definitional Problems in Sexual Victimization," in *New Versions of Victims: Feminists Struggle with the Concept*, ed. Sharon Lamb, 57–81 (New York: New York University Press, 1999); Nicola Gavey, "Women's Desire and Sexual Violence Discourse," in *Feminist Social Psychologies*, ed. Sue Wilkinson, 51–65 (Buckingham: Open University Press, 1996); Nicola Gavey, "Technologies and Effects of Heterosexual Coercion," *Feminism & Psychology* 2.3 (1992): 325-351; Stephanie Genz, *Postfemininities in Popular Culture* (New York: Palgrave Macmillan, 2009); Rosaline Gill and Christina Scharff, *New Femininities: Post Feminism, Neoliberalism, and Subjectivity* (New York: Palgrave Macmillan, 2011); Michelle Goldberg, "Feminism for Sale," *AlterNet*, http://www.alternet.org/story/10306/feminism_for_sale; June Hannan, *Feminism* (New York: Pearson Longman, 2007); Harde and Harde, "Voices and Visions: A Mother and Daughter Discuss Coming to Feminism and Being Feminist"; Anita Harris (ed.), *All About the Girl* (New York: Routledge, 2004); Anita Harris, "Jamming Girl Culture: Young Women and Consumer Citizenship," in Harris (ed.), *All About the Girl*, 163–172; Heywood and Drake, *Third Wave Agenda: Being Feminist, Doing Feminism*; bell hooks, "Selling Hot Pussy," in *The Politics of Women's Bodies: Sexuality, Appearance, and Behavior*, ed. Rose Weitz, 112–124 (New York: Oxford University Press, 1998); bell hooks, *Black Looks: Race and Representation* (Boston: South End Press, 1992); bell hooks, "Performance Practice as a Site of Opposition," *Let's Get It On: The Politics of Black Performance*, ed. Catherine Ugwu, 210–221 (Seattle: Bay Press, 1995); bell hooks, *Outlaw Culture: Resisting Representations* (New York: Routledge, 1994); bell hooks, "Feminist Opportunism or Commitment to Struggle?" *Z Magazine* (January 1994): 42–44; bell hooks, *Where We Stand: Class Matters* (New York: Routledge, 2000); Sharon Lamb, "Introduction," in *New Versions of Victims: Feminists Struggle with the Concept*, ed. Sharon Lamb (New York: New York University Press, 1999); Sharon Lamb, "Constructing the Victim Popular Images and the Lasting Labels," *New Versions of Victims: Feminists Struggle with the Concept*, ed. Sharon Lamb, 108–138 (New York: New York University Press, 1999); Carine M. Mardorossian, "Toward a New Feminist Theory of Rape," *Signs: Journal of Women in Culture and Society* 27.3 (2002): 743–775; Angela McRobbie, *The Aftermath of Feminism: Gender, Culture, and Social Change* (Los Angeles, CA: Sage, 2009); Angela McRobbie, "Post Feminism and Popular Culture," *Feminist Media Studies* 4.3 (2004): 255–263; Yvonne Tasker and Diane Negra, "Feminist Politics and Postfeminist Culture," in *Interrogating Postfeminism: Gender and the Politics of Popular Culture*, ed. Yvonne Tasker and Diane Negra, 1–26 (Durham, NC: Duke University Press, 2007); Catherine M. Orr, "Charting the Currents of the Third Wave," *Hypatia* 12.3 (1997): 29–45; Andrea L. Press, "Feminism? That's So Seventies: Girls and Young Women Discuss Femininity and Feminism in *America's Next Top Model*," *New Femininities: Postfeminism, Neoliberalism, and Subjectivity*, ed. Rosalind Gill and Christina Scharff, 117–133 (New York: Palgrave Macmillan, 2011); Rayna Rapp, "Is the Legacy of Second-Wave Feminism Postfeminism?" in *Women, Class, and the Feminist Imagination: A Socialist-Feminist Reader*, ed. Karen V. Hansen and Ilene J. Philipson, 357–362 (Philadelphia: Temple University Press, 1990); Janelle Reinelt, "Navigating Postfeminism: Writing Out of the Box," in *Feminist Futures? Theatre, Performance, Theory*, ed. Elaine Aston and Geraldine Harris, 17–33 (New York: Palgrave Macmillian, 2006); Riordan, "Commodified Agents and Empowered Girls: Consuming and Producing Feminism"; Jillian Sandell, "Adjusting to Oppression: The Rise of Therapeutic Feminism in the United States," in *Bad Girls Good Girls: Women, Sex, and Power in the Nineties*, ed. Nan Bauer Maglin and Donna Perry, 21–35 (New Brunswick, NJ: Rutgers University Press, 1996); Deborah L. Siegel, *Sisterhood Interrupted: From Radical Women to Grrls Gone Wild* (New York: Palgrave Macmillan, 2007); Deborah L. Siegel, "Reading between the Waves: Feminist Historiography in a 'Postfeminist' Moment," in *Third Wave Agenda: Being Feminist, Doing Feminism*, ed. Leslie Heywood and Jennifer Drake (Minneapolis: University of Minnesota Press, 1997), 55–82; and Tasker and Negra, "Feminist Politics and Postfeminist Culture."

5. For more in-depth analysis of the writings of the "conservative feminists" mentioned, in addition to reading their own works, I'd recommend the following authors: Chapter 4 in Gamble, *The Routledge Critical Dictionary of Feminism and Postfeminism*; Hannan, *Feminism*; Reger, *Different Wavelengths: Studies of the Contemporary Women's Movement*; Rhonda Hammer, *Antifeminism and Family Terrorism: A Critical Feminist Perspective* (Lanham, MD: Rowman & Littlefield, 2002); bell hooks, "Feminist Opportunism or Commitment to Struggle?"; Jillian Sandell, "Adjusting to Oppression: The Rise of Therapeutic Feminism in the United States"; Orr, "Charting the Currents of the Third Wave"; Gavey, *Just Sex*; and Chris Atmore, "Victims, Backlash, and Radical Feminist Theory," *New Versions of Victims*, ed. Sharon Lamb, 183–212 (New York: New York University Press, 1999).

6. The following writers have commented on the inversion of the "personal is political" to the "political is personal" from second-wave feminism to postfeminism: Dinah Luise Leavitt, *Feminist Theatre Groups* (Jefferson, NC: McFarland & Co., 1980); Char-

lotte Canning, *Feminist Theaters in the U.S.A.: Staging Women's Experience* (New York: Routledge, 1996); Peggy Miller and Nancy Biele, "Twenty Years Later: The Unfinished Revolution," *Transforming a Rape Culture*, ed. Emilie Buchwald, Pamela Fletcher, and Martha Roth, 49–54 (Minneapolis, MN: Milkweed, 1993); Mardorossian, "Toward a New Feminist Theory of Rape"; Sharon Lamb, "Constructing the Victim Popular Images and the Lasting Labels"; Braithwaite, "The Personal, the Political, Third-Wave and Postfeminisms"; Sandell, "Adjusting to Oppression: The Rise of Therapeutic Feminism in the United States"; Gavey, *Just Sex*; and Gavey, "Fighting Rape."

Chapter Six

1. Some of the primary scholars who discuss the influence of feminism on theatre practices, including but not limited to a shift away from realism, include Carol Martin (ed.), *A Sourcebook of Feminist Theatre and Performance: On and Beyond the Stage* (New York: Routledge, 1996); Elaine Aston, *An Introduction to Feminism & Theatre* (London: Routledge, 1995); Lynda Hart, "Karen Finley's Dirty Work: Censorship, Homophobia, and the NEA," *Genders* 14 (Fall 1992): 1–15; Lynda Hart (ed.), *Making a Spectacle: Feminist Essays on Contemporary Women's Theatre* (Ann Arbor: University of Michigan Press, 1989); Charlotte Canning, *Feminist Theaters in the U.S.A.: Staging Women's Experience* (New York: Routledge, 1996); Ellen Donkin and Susan Clement (eds.), *Upstaging Big Daddy: Directing Theatre as if Gender and Race Matter* (Ann Arbor: University of Michigan Press, 1993); Janet Brown, *Taking Center Stage: Feminism in Contemporary U.S. Drama* (Metuchen, NJ: Scarecrow Press, 1991); Elin Diamond, "Introduction," in *Performance and Cultural Politics*, ed. Elin Diamond, 1–12 (New York: Routledge, 1996); Elin Diamond (ed.), *Unmaking Mimesis: Essays on Feminism and Theater* (New York: Routledge, 1997); Jill Dolan, "The Dynamics of Desire: Sexuality and Gender in Pornography and Performance," *Theatre Journal* 39.2 (1987): 156–174; Jill Dolan, *The Feminist Spectator as Critic* (Ann Arbor, University of Michigan Press, 1988); Jill Dolan, *Presence and Desire: Essays on Gender, Sexuality, Per-*

formance (Ann Arbor: University of Michigan Press, 1993); Jill Dolan, *The Feminist Spectator in Action: Feminist Criticism for the Stage and Screen* (New York: Palgrave Macmillan, 2013); Helen Kirch Chinoy and Linda Walsh Jenkins (eds.), *Women in American Theatre* (New York: Theatre Communications Group, 1987); Lizbeth Goodman and Jane de Gay (eds.), *The Routledge Reader in Gender and Performance* (New York: Routledge, 2002); Elaine Aston and Geraldine Harris (eds.), *Feminist Futures? Theatre, Performance, Theory* (New York: Palgrave Macmillan, 2006); and Elaine Aston and Geraldine Harris (eds.), *A Good Night Out for the Girls: Popular Feminisms in Contemporary Theatre and Performance* (New York: Palgrave Macmillan, 2013). Additionally, Judith Stephens presents a counterargument as she proposes theatrical realism as an acceptable form in which to present feminist content. Judith Stephens, "The Compatibility of Traditional Dramatic Form and Feminist Expression," *The Theatre Annual* 40 (1985): 7–23.

2. For example, Sally Burke, "From *The Great Divide* to *The Widow's Blind Date*: Rapist Ethics in Modern American Drama," *The Mid-Atlantic Almanac* 3 (1994): 94–108; Timothy Murry, "Patriarchal Panopticism, or The Seduction of Bad Joke: *Getting Out* in Theory," *Theatre Journal* 35.3 (1983): 376–388; Gerald Weales, "Marsha Norman," *Contemporary Literary Criticism*, vol. 28 (Detroit: Gale Research Co., 1984), 319; and Patricia R. Schroeder, "Locked Behind the Proscenium: Feminist Strategies in *Getting Out* and *My Sister in This House*," *Modern Drama* 32.1 (1989): 104–114.

3. For a discussion of female bonding in other plays involving violence against women, see María Dolores Narbona-Carrión, "The Role of Female Bonding on the Stage of Violence," in *Performing Gender Violence: Plays by Contemporary American Women Dramatists*, ed. Barbara Ozieblo and Noelia Hernando-Real, 61–79 (New York: Palgrave Macmillan, 2002).

4. Review quotes are from Ed Kaufman, "Self Defense or Death," rev. of *Self Defense or the Death of Some Salesmen*, Carson Krietzer, *Hollywood Reporter* 382.26 (February 10, 2004): 51; Terri Roberts, "*Self Defense, or, Death of Some Salesmen* at the Hudson Backstage Theatre," rev. of *Self Defense or Death of Some Salesmen*, Carson Krietzer, *Back Stage West* 11.6 (5 February 2004): 28; Jeanette Toomer, "Self Defense," rev. of *Self Defense or Death of Some Salesmen*, Carson Krietzer, *Back Stage* 43.27 (5 July 2002): 19; and Graydon Royce, "Sympathetic Look at a Serial Killer," rev. of *Self Defense or Death of Some Salesmen*, Carson Krietzer, (Minneapolis) *Star Tribune* (February 9, 2002): 4B.

5. Carole J. Sheffield provides an in-depth discussion of this power to control women's behavior merely by the threat of rape. Carole J. Sheffield, "Sexual Terrorism," *Women: A Feminist Perspective*, fifth ed., ed. Jo Freeman, 1–21 (Mountain View: Mayfield Publishing Co., 1995).

6. Some writers who discuss the positive transformational effects of surviving or resisting rape are Martha McCaughey, *Real Knockouts: The Physical Feminism of Women's Self-Defense* (New York: New York University Press, 1997); Marike Lies van der Veen, "Rape and the Dichotomy of Womanhood: Empowering the Female Voice., thesis (Chapel Hill, NC: Chapel Hill University, 1991); Nicola Gavey, "Women's Desire and Sexual Violence Discourse," *Feminist Social Psychologies*, ed. Sue Wilkinson, 51–65 (Buckingham: Open University Press, 1996); chapter 7 of Ann J. Cahill, *Rethinking Rape* (Ithaca: Cornell University Press, 2001); Pauline B. Bart and Patricia H. O'Brian, *Stopping Rape: Successful Survival Strategies* (New York: Pergamon Press, 1985); and Ellen Snortland, *Beauty Bites Beast: Awakening the Warrior within Women and Girls* (Pasadena: Trilogy Books, 1998).

Conclusion

1. See Dinitia Smith, "Today the Anatomy, Tomorrow the World," *New York Times*, 26 September 1999, final ed.: sec. 2 pg. 7; and John Keenan, "Monologues Aims to Raise Awareness about Violence," *Omaha World-Herald*, 9 February 2001, sunrise ed.: living 41.

2. See Joanna Bourke, *Rape, Sex, Violence, History* (Emeryville, CA: Shoemaker & Hoard, 2007); and Carine M. Mardorossian, "Toward a New Feminist Theory of Rape," *Signs: Journal of Women in Culture and Society* 27.3 (2002): 743–775.

Bibliography

Aguirre-Sacasa, Roberto. *Good Boys and True*. New York: Dramatists Play Service, 2009.

Alive and Trucking Theatre Co. *Pig in a Blanket. Stage Left: Three Plays from Alive and Trucking's First Year*. Minneapolis: Alive and Trucking Theatre Co., 1973. 5–48.

Anderson, Irina, and Kathy Doherty. *Accounting for Rape: Psychology, Feminism, and Discourse Analysis in the Study of Sexual Violence*. New York: Routledge, 2008.

Arax, Mark. "Child Brides Common Among California's Homong Refugees." *The Houston Chronicle*. 9 May 1993, star ed., sec. A: 18.

Aston, Elaine. *Feminist Theatre Practice: A Handbook*. New York: Routledge, 1999.

———. *An Introduction to Feminism & Theatre*. London: Routledge, 1995.

Aston, Elaine, and Sue Ellen Case, eds. *Staging International Feminisms*. New York: Palgrave Macmillan, 2007.

Aston, Elaine, and Geraldine Harris, eds. *Feminist Futures? Theatre, Performance, Theory*. New York: Palgrave Macmillan, 2006.

——— and ———. *A Good Night Out for the Girls: Popular Feminisms in Contemporary Theatre and Performance*. New York: Palgrave Macmillan, 2013.

Atmore, Chris. "Victims, Backlash, and Radical Feminist Theory." *New Versions of Victims*. Ed. Sharon Lamb. New York: New York University Press, 1999. 183–212.

Austin, Gayle. *Feminist Theories for Dramatic Criticism*. Ann Arbor: University of Michigan Press, 1990.

Bailey, M.E. "Foucauldian Feminism: Contesting bodies, Sexuality and Identity." *Up Against Foucault*. Ed. Caroline Ramazanoglu. New York: Routledge, 1993.

Baker, Celia. "Theatre That Gets Under Your Skin; SLAC's 'White People' Confronts Subtle Racism Head-on." *The Salt Lake Tribune*. 24 September 2000, final ed.: D1.

Barker, Isabelle V. "Editing Pornography." *Feminism and Pornography*. Ed. Drucilla Cornell. New York: Oxford University Press, 2000. 643–652.

Barnes, Brooks. "Unblinking Look at Sex Assaults on Campus." *New York Times*. 26 January 2015, final ed.: C.1

Bart, Pauline B., and Patricia H. O'Brian. *Stopping Rape: Successful Survival Strategies*. New York: Pergamon Press, 1985.

Baumgardner, Jennifer, and Amy Richards. "Feminism and Femininity: Or How We Learned to Stop Worrying and Love the Thong." *All About the Girl: Culture, Power, and Identity*. Ed. Anita Harris. New York: Routledge, 2004. 59–68.

——— and ———. *Manifesta: Young Women, Feminism, and the Future*. New York: Farrar, Straus and Giroux, 2000.

Bean, Kellie. *Post-Backlash Feminism: Women and the Media since Reagan-Bush*. Jefferson, NC: McFarland, 2007.

Belber, Steven. *Tape. Humana Festival 2000*. Hanover, NH: Smith and Kraus, 2000. 1–46.

Benedict, Jeffrey R. *Athletes and Acquain-*

Bibliography

tance Rape. Thousand Oaks, CA: Sage Publications, 1998.

Berlatsky, Noah, ed. *Global Viewpoints: Sexual Violence.* Farmington Hills, MI: Greenhaven Press, 2014.

Bernardez, Teresa. *Women and Anger: Cultural Prohibitions and the Feminine Ideal.* Wellesley, MA: Stone Center for Developmental Services and Studies, 1987.

Bernat, Jeffrey A., Karen S. Calhoun, and Henry E. Adams. "Sexually Aggressive and Nonaggressive Men: Sexual Arousal and Judgments in Response to Acquaintance Rape and Consensual Analogues." *Journal of Abnormal Psychology* 108.4 (1999): 662–673.

Bevacqua, Maria. *Rape on the Public Agenda: Feminism and the Politics of Sexual Assault.* Boston: Northeastern University Press, 2000.

Blessing, Lee. *Down the Road: Patient A and Other Plays.* Portsmouth, NH: Heinemann, 1995. 47–89.

Bobel, Chris. *New Blood: Third-wave Feminism and the Politics of Menstruation.* New Brunswick, NJ: Rutgers University Press, 2010.

Bohner, Gerd, Frank Siebler, and Jürgen Schmelcher. "Social Norms and the Likelihood of Raping: Perceived Rape Myth Acceptance of Others Affects Men's Rape Proclivity." *Personality and Social Psychology Bulletin* 32.3 (2006): 286–297.

Bohner, Gerd, et al. "The Casual Impact of Rape Myth Acceptance on Men's Rape Proclivity: Comparing Sexually Coercive and Non-coercive Men." *European Journal of Social Psychology* 35 (2005): 819–828.

_____, et al. "Rape Myth Acceptance." *Rape: Challenging Contemporary Thinking.* Ed. Miranda A. Horvath and Jennifer M. Brown. Cullompton: Willan, 2009.

Bolton, Richard, ed. *Culture Wars: Documents from the Recent Controversies in the Arts.* New York: New Press, 1992.

Bornfeld, Steve. "Turnabout Is This Play." Rev. of *Extremities,* William Mastrosimone. *Las Vegas Review-Journal* 9 April 2010: J353.

Bourke, Joanna. *Rape, Sex, Violence, History.* Emeryville, CA: Shoemaker & Hoard, 2007.

Braithwaite, Ann. "The Personal, the Political, Third-Wave and Postfeminisms." *Feminist Theory* 3.3 (2002): 335–344.

Braunagel, Don. "Play Probes Issues of Rape." Rev. of *Extremities,* William Mastrosimone. *The San Diego Union-Tribune.* 18 March 1985: C1.

Brenson, Michael. "Effects of Men's Desires on the Lives of Women." Rev. of *We Keep Our Victims Ready,* Karen Finley. *New York Times.* 21 May 1990, late ed.: C13.

Breslauer, Jan. "Body Politic: Performance Artist Karen Finley Brings Her Controversial 'Victims' to L.A." Rev. of *We Keep Our Victims Ready,* Karen Finley. *Los Angeles Times.* 8 November 1991, home ed.: F1.

Brewer, Mary. *Race, Sex, and Gender in Contemporary Women's Theatre.* Brighton: Sussex Academic Press, 1999.

Brickman, Julie. "Female Lives, Feminist Deaths." *States of Rage: Emotional Eruption, Violence, and Social Change.* Ed. Renee R. Curry and Terry L. Allison. New York: New York University Press, 1996. 15–34.

Brown, Janet. *Taking Center Stage: Feminism in Contemporary U.S. Drama.* Metuchen, NJ: Scarecrow Press, 1991.

Brown, Jennifer M., and Miranda A. H. Horvath. "Do You Believe Her and Is It Real Rape?" *Rape: Challenging Contemporary Thinking.* Ed. Miranda A. Horvath and Jennifer M. Brown. Cullompton: Willan, 2009.

Brown, Joe. "Art at the Outer Limits: Karen Finley, Taking Performance to a New Level." Rev. of *The Constant State of Desire,* Karen Finley. *Washington Post.* 4 May 1988, final ed.: D2.

_____. "Blood Moon: More Clamor Than Content." Rev. of *Blood Moon,* Nicholas Kazan. *Washington Post.* 18 January 1985, final ed.: Weekend 13.

_____. "Raw, Explosive Extremities." Rev.

of *Extremities*, William Mastrosimone. *Washington Post*. 4 October 1985, final ed.: Weekend 9.

Brownmiller, Susan. *Against Our Will: Men, Women, and Rape*. New York: Simon & Schuster, 1975.

Buchwald, Emilie. "Raising Girls for the 21st Century." *Transforming a Rape Culture*. Ed. Emilie Buchwald, Pamela R. Fletcher, and Martha Roth. Minneapolis, MN: Milkweed Editions, 1993. 179–200.

Buchwald, Emilie, Pamela R. Fletcher, and Martha Roth. *Transforming a Rape Culture*. Minneapolis, MN: Milkweed Editions: 1993.

Budgeon, Shelly. "The Contradictions of Successful Femininity: Third-Wave Feminism, Postfeminism, and 'New' Femininities." *New Femininities: Postfeminism, Neoliberalism, and Subjectivity*. Ed. Rosalind Gill and Christina Scharff. New York: Palgrave MacMillan, 2011. 279–292.

Buhl-Dutta, Mary. "Taming the Victim: Rape in Soap Opera." *Journal of Popular Film & Television* 27.1 (1999): 34–39.

Burke, Sally. "From *The Great Divide* to *The Widow's Blind Date*: Rapist Ethics in Modern American Drama." *The Mid-Atlantic Almanac* 3 (1994): 94–108.

Burkman, Kathryn, and Judith Roof, eds. *Staging the Rage: The Web of Misogyny in Modern Drama*. Madison: Fairleigh Dickinson University Press, 1998.

Burt, Martha. "Cultural Myths and Supports for Rape." *Journal of Personality and Social Psychology* 38.2 (1980): 217–230.

———. "Rape Myths and Acquaintance Rape." *Acquaintance Rape: The Hidden Crime*. Ed. Andrea Parrot and Laurie Bechhofer. New York: John Wiley and Sons, Inc., 1991. 26–40.

Cahill, Ann J. *Rethinking Rape*. Ithaca: Cornell University Press, 2001.

———. "Sexual Violence and Objectification." *Theorizing Sexual Violence*. Ed. Renee J. Heberle and Victoria Grace. New York: Routledge, 2009. 14–32.

Canning, Charlotte. *Feminist Theaters in the U.S.A.: Staging Women's Experience*. New York: Routledge, 1996.

Carosella, Cynthia, ed. *Who's Afraid of the Dark?* New York: Harper Perennial, 1995.

Carr, C. "Telling the Awfullest Truth: An Interview with Karen Finley." *Acting Out: Feminist Performances*. Ed. Lynda Hart and Peggy Phelan. Ann Arbor: University of Michigan Press, 1993. 153–160.

———. "Unspeakable Practices, Unnatural Acts: The Taboo Art of Karen Finley." *Acting Out: Feminist Performances*. Ed. Lynda Hart and Peggy Phelan. Ann Arbor: University of Michigan Press, 1993. 141–152.

Carter, Bill, Graham Bowley, and Lorne Manly. "Comeback by Cosby Unravels as Accounts of Rape Converge." *New York Times*. 20 November 2014, final ed.: A1.

Case, Sue-Ellen. *Feminism and Theatre*. New York: Methuen, 1988.

———. "From Split Subject to Split Britches." *Feminine Focus: The New Woman Playwrights*. Ed. Enoch Brater. New York: Oxford University Press, 1989. 126–146.

———, ed. *Performing Feminisms: Feminist Critical Theory and Theatre*. Baltimore: Johns Hopkins University Press, 1990.

Chapleau, Kristine M., and Debra L. Oswald. "Power, Sex, and Rape Myth Acceptance: Testing Two Models of Rape Proclivity." *Journal of Sex Research* 47.1 (2010): 66–78.

Chandler, Mary. "Yams, No Ham: Finley Looks Back." Rev. of *A Different Kind of Intimacy: The Collected Writings of Karen Finley*, Karen Finley. *Denver Rocky Mountain News*. 7 January 2001, final ed.: E3.

Chinoy, Helen Krich, and Linda Walsh Jenkins, eds. *Women in American Theatre*. New York: Theatre Communications Group, 1987.

Christon, Lawrence. "Rape and Revenge in 'Moon.'" Rev. of *Blood Moon*, Nicholas Kazan. *Los Angeles Times*. 22 May 1985, home ed.: Calendar 8.

Churnin, Nancy. "Artist Relies on Shock

Bibliography

Therapy to Send Message." Rev. of *We Keep Our Victims Ready*, Karen Finley. *Los Angeles Times*. 12 September 1989, San Diego County ed.: Calendar 1.

Cidylo, Lori. "Women and Power: Case Study, Marriage." *Los Angeles Times*, 29 June 1993, home ed.: World Report 2.

Cline, Gretchen. "The Impossibility of Getting Out." *Marsha Norman: A Casebook*. Ed. Linda Ginter Brown. New York: Garland Publishing, 1996. 3–25.

Cochrane, Kira. "No One Talks of 'Crying Burglary.'" *New Statesman*. 18 June 2007: 22.

Conboy, Katie, Nadia Medina, and Sarah Stanbury, eds. *Writing on the Body: Female Embodiment and Feminist Theory*. New York: Columbia University Press, 1997.

Crowley, Terrence. "The Lie of Entitlement." *Transforming a Rape Culture*. Ed. Emilie Buchwald, Pamela R. Fletcher, and Martha Roth. Minneapolis, MN: Milkweed Editions: 1993. 341–350.

Cunningham, Alexandra. *No. 11 (Blue and White)*. *Humana Festival 2000: The Complete Plays*. Ed. Michael Bigelow Dixon and Amy Wegener. Newbury, VT: Smith and Kraus, 2000. 47–104.

Curry, Renee, and Terry Allison, eds. *States of Rage: Emotional Eruption, Violence and Social Change*. New York: New York University Press, 1996.

Curtis-Fox, Terry. "Marsha Norman." *Contemporary Literary Criticism*, vol. 28. Detroit: Gale Research Co. (1984). 317.

David, Miriam E. "Teaching and Preaching Sexual Morality; The New Right's Anti-Feminism in Britain and the U.S.A." *Journal of Education* 166. 1 (1984): 63–76.

Davis, Angela. *Women, Race, & Class*. New York: Random House, 1981.

Davis, Tracy. "*Extremities* and *Masterpieces*: A Feminist Paradigm of Art and Politics." *Modern Drama* 32.1 (1989): 89–103.

De Lauretis, Teresa. *Alice Doesn't: Feminism, Semiotics, Cinema*. Bloomington: Indiana University Press, 1984.

_____. *Technologies of Gender: Essays on Theory, Film, and Fiction*. Bloomington: Indiana University Press, 1987.

Del Valle, Anthony. "Director Finds Soft Edges in Little Theatre's 'Extremities.'" Rev. of *Extremities*, William Mastrosimone. *Las Vegas Review-Journal*. 14 April 2010: E6.

DeRogatis, Jim. "Finley's Denial Confirms She is a Compelling Artist." Rev. of *A Certain Level of Denial*, Karen Finley. *Chicago Sun-Times*. 8 November 1994, final ed.: F39.

De Vries, Hilary. "All the Rage." *Los Angeles Times*. 21 October 1990, home ed.: Calendar 3.

Diamond, Elin. "Introduction." *Performance and Cultural Politics*. Ed. Elin Diamond. New York: Routledge, 1996. 1–12.

_____, ed. *Unmaking Mimesis: Essays on Feminism and Theater*. New York: Routledge, 1997.

Dill, Bonnie Thornton. "Race, Class, and Gender: Prospects for an All-Inclusive Sisterhood." *Feminist Studies* 9.1 (1983): 131–150.

Doherty, Kathy, and Irina Anderson. "Talking about Rape." *The Psychologist* 11.12 (1998): 583–587.

Dolan, Jill. "The Dynamics of Desire: Sexuality and Gender in Pornography and Performance." *Theatre Journal* 39.2 (1987): 156–174.

_____. *The Feminist Spectator as Critic*. Ann Arbor, University of Michigan Press, 1988.

_____. *The Feminist Spectator in Action: Feminist Criticism for the Stage and Screen*. New York: Palgrave Macmillan, 2013.

_____. *Presence and Desire: Essays on Gender, Sexuality, Performance*. Ann Arbor: University of Michigan Press, 1993.

Donat, Patricia L. N., and Jacquelyn W. White. "Re-Examining the Issue of Nonconsent in Acquaintance Rape." *Sexuality, Society, and Feminism*. Ed. Cheryl Brown Travis and Jacquelyn W. White. Washington, DC: American Psychological Association, 2000. 355–376.

Donkin, Ellen, and Susan Clement, eds.

Upstaging Big Daddy: Directing Theatre as if Gender and Race Matter. Ann Arbor: University of Michigan Press, 1993.

Douglas, Carol Anne. "The Second Coming of Joan of Arc—Review of Collection of plays." *Off Our Backs* 25.4 (1995): 20.

Dow, Bonnie. *Prime-Time Feminism: Television, Media Culture, and the Women's Movement since 1970.* Philadelphia: University of Pennsylvania Press, 1996.

Dox, Donnalee. "Construction of Rape: Two American Musicals." *Frontiers* 17.3 (1996): 210–238.

Dworkin, Andrea. *Right-winged Women.* New York: Perigee Books, 1983.

Easteal, Patricia. *Voices of the Survivors.* North Melbourne, Vic.: Spinifex, 1994.

Eichhorn, Kate. "Archiving the Movement." *Make Your Own History: Documenting Feminist and Queer Activism in the 21st Century.* Ed. Lyz Bly and Kelly Wooten. Los Angeles: Litwin Books, 2012. 23–37.

Eisenstein, Zillah. *Hatreds: Racialized and Sexualized Conflicts in the 21st Century.* New York: Routledge, 1996.

Eligon, John, and Michael Schwirtz. "In Rapes, Candidate Says, Body Can Block Pregnancy." *New York Times.* 20 August 2012, final edition: A13. Web. 5 August 2013.

Ensler, Eve. *Necessary Targets.* New York: Villard, 2001.

———. *The Vagina Monologues.* New York: Villard, 1998, 2000.

Estrich, Susan. *Real Rape.* Cambridge: Harvard University Press, 1987.

Evans, Rowland, and Robert Novak. "The NEA's Suicide Charge." *Washington Post.* 11 May 1990: final ed.: A27.

Eyssel, Friederikek, Gerd Bohner, and Frank Siebler. "Perceived Rape Myth Acceptance of Others Predicts Rape Proclivity: Social Norm or Judgmental Anchoring?" *Swiss Journal of Psychology* 65.2 (2006): 93–99.

Fauldi, Susan. *Backlash: The Undeclared War Against American Women.* New York: Crown, 1991.

Feasey, Rebecca. *Masculinity and Popular Television.* Edinburgh: Edinburgh University Press, 2008.

Feignbaum, Anna. "Remapping the Resonances of Riot Grrl: Feminisms, Postfeminisms, and 'Processes' of Punk." *Interrogating Postfeminism: Gender and the Politics of Popular Culture.* Ed. Yvonne Tasker and Diane Negra. Durham, NC: Duke University Press, 2007. 132–152.

Filipovic, Jill. "Comment Is Free: In Brief: Remember What Lies behind Republican Rape 'Gaffes.'" *The Guardian.* 26 October 2012, final edition: 36.

"Finley, Karen." *Current Biography Yearbook.* 59.9 (1998): 16–19.

Finley, Karen. "Bound and Gagged by Hearsay Evidence." *Los Angeles Times.* 11 July 1990, home ed.: B7.

———. "Chocolate-Smeared Young Woman." *Washington Post.* 19 May 1990, final ed.: A23.

———. *The Constant State of Desire. The Drama Review* 32.1 (1988): 139–151.

———. Interview. "A Constant State of Becoming." Richard Schechner. *The Drama Review* 32.1 (1988): 152–158.

———. Interview. *Karen Finley: What I Do Is the Feeling.* Nicholas Drake. *Art Papers* 19 (1995): 10–13.

———. Interview. *An Interview with Karen Finley.* Margot Mifflin. *High Performance* 41/42 (1988): 86–87.

———. Interview. *Obsessing in Public.* Vicki Patraka. *The Drama Review* 37.3 (1993): 25–55.

———. *We Keep Our Victims Ready. American Drama.* Ed. Stephen Watt and Gary Richardson. Philadelphia: Harcourt Brace, 1995. 1026–1043.

Firth, Hannah, and Celia Kitzinger. "Reformulating Sexual Script Theory." *Theory & Psychology* 11.2 (2001): 209–232.

Fitzpatrick, Jackie. "Finley State of Desire is Shocking, Riveting." Rev. of *The Constant State of Desire,* Karen Finley. *The San Diego Union-Tribune.* 13 February 1988: B6.

———. "Signifying Rape." *Feminism, Lit-*

erature and Rape Narratives: Violence and Violation. Ed. Sorcha Gunne and Zoë Brigley Thompson. New York: Routledge, 2010. 183–199.

Fiumara, Genna Corradi. The Metaphoric Process: Connections Between Language and Life. New York: Routledge, 1995.

Forte, Jeanie. "Women's Performance Art: Feminism and Postmodernism." Theatre Journal 40.2 (1988): 217–235.

Franchetti, Mark. "Kingdom of the Kidnapped Brides." (London) Sunday Times. 7 February 1999.

Francis, Leslie, ed. Date Rape: Feminism, Philosophy, and the Law. University Park: Penn State University Press, 1996.

Franiuk, Renae, et al. "Prevalence and Effects of Rape Myths in Print Journalism." Violence Against Women 14.3 (2008): 287–309.

Frank, Leah D. "How a Rape Victim Wreaks Revenge." Rev. of Blood Moon, Nicholas Kazan. New York Times. 23 February 1992, final ed.: Long Island 13.

Frazier, Patricia A. "Victim Attributions and Post-Rape Trauma." Journal of Personality and Social Psychology 59.2 (1990): 298–304.

Freedman, Jenna. "Self-Publication with Riot Grrrl Ideals." Make Your Own History: Documenting Feminist and Queer Activism in the 21st Century. Ed. Lyz Bly and Kelly Wooten. Los Angeles: Litwin Books 2012. 13–22.

Freedman, Karyn. "The Epistemological Significance of Psychic Trauma." Hypatia 21:2 (Spring 2006): 104–125.

Frese, Bettina, Miguel Moya, and Jesús L. Megías. "Social Perception of Rape." Journal of Interpersonal Violence 19.2 (2004): 143–161.

Friedan, Betty. The Feminine Mystique. New York: W. W. Norton, 1963.

Friedman, Robert. "About Chocolate." Newsday. 7 August 1990, city ed.: Viewpoints 54.

Friedman, Sharon ed. Feminist Theatrical Revisions of Classic Works: Critical Essays. Jefferson, N.C.: McFarland, 2009.

Gage, Carolyn. Interview by Pat Cramer. Off Our Backs (January–February 2002): 9+.

_____. The Second Coming of Joan of Arc. The Second Coming of Joan of Arc and Other Plays Santa Cruz, HerBooks, 1994.

Gagliano, Laura. Hush. Boston: Baker Plays. 1993.

Gamble, Sarah, ed. The Routledge Critical Dictionary of Feminism and Postfeminism. New York: Routledge, 1999.

Gamarekian, Barbara. "Frohnmayer Sid to See Peril to Theater Grants." New York Times. 29 June 1990, final ed.: C15.

García-Crow, Amparo. Under A Western Sky. The South Texas Plays (Between Misery and the Sun). South Gate, CA: NoPassport Press, 2009. 169–280.

Gavey, Nicola. "Fighting Rape." Theorizing Sexual Violence. Ed. Renee J. Heberle and Victoria Grace. New York: Routledge, 2009. 96–124.

_____. "I Wasn't Raped, but... Revisiting Definitional Problems in Sexual Victimization." New Versions of Victims: Feminists Struggle with the Concept. Ed. Sharon Lamb. New York: New York University Press, 1999. 57–81.

_____. Just Sex? The Cultural Scaffolding of Rape. New York: Routledge, 2005.

_____. "Technologies and Effects of Heterosexual Coercion." Feminism & Psychology 2.3 (1992): 325–351.

_____. "Women's Desire and Sexual Violence Discourse." Feminist Social Psychologies. Ed. Sue Wilkinson. Buckingham: Open University Press, 1996. 51–65.

Gelb, Lisa Serene. "Of Rape and Revenge." Rev. of Blood Moon, Nicholas Kazan. Washington Post. 13 January 1985, final ed.: L3.

Genz, Stephanie. Postfemininities in Popular Culture. New York: Palgrave Macmillan, 2009.

Gerdes, Louise, ed. Sexual Violence: Opposing Viewpoints. Detroit: Greenhaven Press, 2008.

Gergen, David. "Who Should Pay for Porn?" U.S. News & World Report. 30 July 1990: 80.

Gerhard, Jane. "The Personal is Still Political: The Legacy of 1970s Feminism." *"Bad Girls"/"Good Girls": Women, Sex, and Power in the Nineties.* Ed. Nan Bauer Maglin and Donna Perry. New Brunswick, NJ: Rutgers University Press, 1996. 36–43.

Gill, Rosalind, and Christina Scharff. "Introduction." *New Femininities: Post Feminism, Neoliberalism, and Subjectivity.* New York: Palgrave Macmillan, 2011. 1–17.

Gilman, Rebecca. *The Glory of Living.* New York: Faber and Faber, 1999.

Gionfriddo, Gina. *After Ashley.* New York: Dramatists, 2006.

Goldberg, Michelle. "Feminism for Sale." *AlterNet.* http://www.alternet.org/story/10306/feminism_for_sale.

Goldberg-Ambrose, Carole. "Unfinished Business in Rape Law Reform." *Journal of Social Issues* 48.1 (1992): 173–185.

Golden, Robert, and Fred Peterson. *The Truth About Rape.* New York: Facts on File, 2010.

Goldstein, Lynda. "Raging in Tongues: Confession and Performance Art." *Confessional Politics: Women's Sexual Self-Representations in Life Writing and Popular Media.* Ed. Irene Gammel. Carbondale: Southern Illinois University Press, 1999. 99–116.

Goldstein, Patrick. "Finley Hits Below the Belt, Scores Clean KO's." *Los Angeles Times.* 17 October 1986, home ed.: Calendar 6.

Gollobin, Laurie Brooks. *Selkie. Theatre for Young Audiences: 20 Great Plays for Children.* Ed. Coleman Jennings. New York: St. Martin's Press, 1994. 582–604.

Goodman, Amy. "Rape Epidemic in Our Military." *Spokesman Review.* 10 May 2013, Main Edition: A11.

Goodman, Lizbeth, and Jane de Gay eds. *The Routledge Reader in Gender and Performance.* New York: Routledge, 2002.

Gossett, Suzanne. "'Best Men Are Molded Out of Faults': Marrying the Rapist in Jacobean Drama." *English Literary Renaissance* 14.3 (1984): 305–327.

Graham, Renee. "Karen Finley Goes Back to Nature." *The Boston Globe.* 8 September 1995, City ed.: Living 95.

Gray, Jacqueline M. "Rape Myth Beliefs and Prejudiced Instructions: Effects of Decisions of Guilt in a Case of Date Rape." *Legal and Criminological Psychology* 11 (2006): 75–80.

Greenberg, Kathy L. "Intense Extremities Shows Reality of Rape, Revenge." Rev. of *Extremities,* William Mastrosimone. *Tampa Tribune* 5 November 2010, final ed.: Friday Extra 24.

Greendlinger, Virginia, and Donn Byrne. "Coercive Sexual Fantasies of College Men as Predictors of Self-Reported Likelihood to Rape and Overt Sexual Aggression." *The Journal of Sex Research* 23.1 (1987): 1–11.

Griffiths, Jennifer. "Between Women: Trauma, Witnessing, and the Legacy of Interracial Rape in Robbie McCauley's *Sally's Rape*." *Frontiers: A Journal of Women's Studies* 26.3 (2005): 1–23.

Gussow, Mel. "Blood Moon, of Crime and Revenge." Rev. of *Blood Moon,* Nicholas Kazan. *New York Times.* 14 January 1983, final ed.: C6.

———. "Condemning an Insidious Form of Racism: Negro Ensemble Unit." Rev. of *Rosalee Pritchett.* Carlton and Barbara Molette. *New York Times.* 22 January 1971: 19.

———. "Five Full-Length Plays." Rev. of *Extremities,* William Mastrosimone. *New York Times.* 29 March 1981, final ed.: A61.

———. "In the Arts." Rev. of *Blood Moon,* Nicholas Kazan. *New York Times.* 6 March 1983, final ed.: 2A3.

———. "The Supreme Court: The Artist." *New York Times.* 26 June 1998, final ed.: A17.

———. "Women Playwrights: New Voices in the Theater." *New York Times.* 1 May 1983, final ed.: sec.6: 22.

Hamill, Pete. "I Yam What I Yam." *Village Voice.* 1 July 1986: 10

Hamilton, Kendall, and Marc Peyser. "The Cut Heard Round the World." *Newsweek.* 18 October 1993: 10.

Hammer, Rhonda. *Antifeminism and Fam-*

Bibliography

ily Terrorism: A Critical Feminist Perspective. Lanham, MD: Rowman & Littlefield, 2002.

Hannan, June. *Feminism*. New York: Pearson Longman, 2007.

Harde, Roxanne, and Erin Harde. "Voices and Visions: A Mother and Daughter Discuss Coming to Feminism and Being Feminist." *Catching a Wave: Reclaiming Feminism for the 21st Century*. Ed. Rory Dicker and Alison Piepmeier. Boston: Northeastern University Press, 2003. 116–137.

Harper, Hilliard. "Focus on Theatre: Finley Attack on Taboo at Sushi Isn't for Timid." Rev. of *The Constant State of Desire*, Karen Finley. *Los Angeles Times*. 12 February 1988, San Diego County ed.: Calendar 22.

Harris, Angela. "Race and Essentialism in Feminist Legal Theory." *Critical Race Feminism: A Reader*. Ed. Adrien Katherine Wing. New York: New York University Press, 1997. 11–18.

Harris, Anita, ed. *All About the Girl*. New York: Routledge, 2004.

_____. "Jamming Girl Culture: Young Women and Consumer Citizenship." *All About the Girl*. Ed. Anita Harris. New York: Routledge, 2004. 163–172.

Hart, Lynda. "Karen Finley's Dirty Work: Censorship, Homophobia, and the NEA." *Genders* 14 (Fall 1992): 1–15.

_____, ed. *Making a Spectacle: Feminist Essays on Contemporary Women's Theatre*. Ann Arbor: University of Michigan Press, 1989.

Hart, Lynda, and Peggy Phelan, eds. *Acting Out: Feminist Performances*. Ann Arbor: University of Michigan Press, 1993.

Hartigan, Patti. "Finding Common Ground Onstage." Rev. of *Sally's Rape*, Robbie McCauley. *The Boston Globe*. 5 March 1993, city ed.: Living 61.

Haste, Helen. *The Sexual Metaphor*. Cambridge: Harvard University Press, 1994.

Hauffe, Sarah and Louise Porter. "Interpersonal Comparison of Lone and Group Rape Offences." *Psychology, Crime & Law* 15: 5 (2009): 469–491.

Hayes, John. "Extremities Leaves Victim in Question." Rev. of *Extremities*, William Mastrosimone. *Pittsburgh Post-Gazette*. 13 June 2000: D4.

Healy, Jack. "Schism Emerges in Bikram Yoga Empire." *New York Times*. 24 February 2015, final ed.: A11.

Hebert, Julie. *Almost Asleep. Best of the West*. Ed. Murray Mednick, Bill Raden, and Cheryl Slean. Los Angeles: Padua Hills Press, 1991. 98–130.

Heddon, Dee. *Autobiography and Performance*. New York: Palgrave Macmillan, 2008.

Herbert, T. Walter. *Sexual Violence and American Manhood*. Cambridge, MA: Harvard University Press, 2002.

Herman, Judith Lewis. "Considering Sex Offenders: A Model of Addiction." *Rape and Society*. Ed. Patricia Searles and Ronald J. Berger. Boulder, CO: Westview Press, 1995. 74–98.

_____. *Trauma and Recovery*. New York: Basic Books, 1992.

Hernando-Real, Noelia. "My Home My Battleground: The Deconstruction of the American Family." *Performing Gender Violence: Plays by Contemporary American Women Dramatists*. Ed. Barbara Ozieblo and Noelia Hernando-Real. New York: Palgrave Macmillan, 2012. 39–60.

Hernando-Real, Noelia, and Barbara Ozieblo. "Introduction." *Performing Gender Violence: Plays by Contemporary American Women Dramatists*. Ed. Barbara Ozieblo and Noelia Hernando-Real. New York: Palgrave Macmillan, 2012. 1–14.

Heywood, Leslie, and Jennifer Drake, eds. *Third Wave Agenda: Being Feminist, Doing Feminism*. Minneapolis: University of Minnesota Press, 1997.

Hiber, Amanda, ed. *Opposing Viewpoints: Sexual Violence*. Farmington Hills, MI: Greenhaven Press, 2014.

Higgins, Linda, and Brenda Silver, eds. *Rape and Representation*. New York: Columbia University Press, 1991.

Holden, Stephen. "Avant-Garde Antics for Fearless Audiences." *New York Times*. 5 February 1988.

———. "Finley Mocks Her Critics in Her Art." Rev. of *We Keep Our Victims Ready*, Karen Finley. *New York Times*. 24 July 1990, final ed.: C13.

Holtzman, Willy. *Bovver Boys*. New York: Samuel French, 1991.

Honan, William H. "U.S. Documents Said to Show Endowment Bowed to Pressure." *New York Times*. 18 September 1991, final ed.: C13.

hooks, bell. *Black Looks: Race and Representation*. Boston: South End Press, 1992.

———. "Feminist Opportunism or Commitment to Struggle?" *Z Magazine* (January 1994): 42–44.

———. *Outlaw Culture: Resisting Representations*. New York: Routledge, 1994.

———. "Performance Practice as a Site of Opposition." *Let's Get It On: The Politics of Black Performance*. Ed. Catherine Ugwu. Seattle: Bay Press, 1995. 210–221.

———. "Selling Hot Pussy." *The Politics of Women's Bodies: Sexuality, Appearance, and Behavior*. Ed. Rose Weitz. New York: Oxford University Press, 1998. 112–124.

———. *Where We Stand: Class Matters*. New York: Routledge, 2000.

Horvath, Miranda A., and Jennifer M. Brown, eds. *Rape: Challenging Contemporary Thinking*. Cullompton: Willan, 2009.

Horvath, Miranda A., Angel Helena, and Liz Kelly. "Multiple Perpetrator Rape." *Journal of Sexual Aggression* 15.1 (2009): 83–96.

Horovitz, Israel. *The Widow's Blind Date*. Garden City NJ: Fireside Theatre, 1989.

Hulbert, Dan. "Almost Asleep—Rape Haunts Dreamscape in *Asleep*." Rev. of *Almost Asleep*, Julie Hebert. *The Atlanta Journal and Constitution*. 7 February 1992: D3.

Huntington, Richard. "Gender-Based Joan of Arc Story Sees Men Burned at the Stake." Rev. of *The Second Coming of Joan of Arc* by Carolyn Gage. *The Buffalo News* 25 September 1999, final ed.: C11.

Ivins, Molly. "The Decision Is His, not Hers." *Buffalo News*. 8 March 2006, final ed.: A7.

Jackson, Stevi. "The Social Context of Rape: Sexual Scripts and Motivation." *Rape and Society: Readings on the Problem of Sexual Assault*. Ed. Patricia Searles and Ronald J. Berger. Boulder, CO: Westview Press, 1995. 16–27.

Jimenez, Jorge A., and José M Abreu. "Race and Sex Effects on Attitudinal Perceptions of Acquaintance Rape." *Journal of Counseling Psychology* 50.2 (2003): 252–256.

Johnson, Allan. *The Gender Knot: Unraveling Our Patriarchal Legacy*. Philadelphia: Temple University Press, 1997.

Jones, Chris. "Don't Let The Gentle Demeanor Fool You. Her Plays Are Rife With Murder and Mayhem." *American Theatre* 17.4 (2000): 26–30.

Kahn, Arnold, and Virginia Andreoli Mathie. "Rape Script and Rape Acknowledgment." *Psychology of Women Quarterly* 18 (1994): 53–66.

——— and ———. "Understanding the Unacknowledged Rape Victim." *Sexuality, Society, and Feminism*. Ed. Cheryl Brown Travis and Jacquelyn W. White. Washington, DC: American Psychological Association, 2000: 377–403.

Kahn, Virginia, Andreoli Mathie, and Cyndee Torgler. "Rape Script and Rape Acknowledgment." *Psychology of Women Quarterly* 18 (1994): 53–66.

Kalson, Sally. "Rape Is Rape, Dumb Is Dumb; The GOP Has Made a Habit of Casting Rape Victims as Evil Temptresses." *Pittsburgh Post-Gazette*. 26 August 2012, editorial B3.

Kazan, Nicholas. *Blood Moon*. New York: Samuel French, 1984.

Kaufman, Ed. "Self Defense or Death." Rev. of *Self Defense or the Death of Some Salesmen*, Carson Krietzer. *Hollywood Reporter* 382.26 (February 10, 2004): 51.

Keenan, John. "Monologues Aims to Raise Awareness about Violence." *Omaha World-Herald*. 9 February 2001, sunrise ed.: living 41.

Kelly, Jennifer C., David S. Kosson, and Jacquelyn W. White. "Psychopathy-Related Traits Predict Self-Reported Sexual Aggression Among College Men." *Journal of Interpersonal Violence* 12.2 (1997): 241–255.

Kelly, Kevin. "Horovitz's Blind Date Gets Better Reception Overseas." *The Boston Globe*. 2 March 1990, city ed.: Arts & Film 42.

_____. "Karen Finley's Vicious Fame." Rev. of *We Keep Our Victims Ready*, Karen Finley. *The Boston Globe*. 31 August 1990, city ed.: Arts & Film 59.

_____. "This Widow Is a Stunner." Rev. of *The Widow's Blind Date*, Israel Horovitz. *The Boston Globe*. 21 July 1989, city ed.: Living 21.

Kerr, Walter. "Extremities and a Muffled Alice." Rev. of *Extremities* by William Mastrosimone. *New York Times*. 2 January 1983, final ed.: B3.

Khadaroo, Stacy Teicher. "Glimmers of Progress in Fight Against College Sexual Assault." *Christian Science Monitor*. 6 May 2015. N. pag.

Killian, Linda. "Feminist Theater." *Feminist Art Journal* 3.1 (1974): 23–24.

Kilmartin, Christopher, and Julie Allison. *Men's Violence Against Women: Theory, Research, and Activism*. Mahwah, NJ: Lawrence Erlbaum Associates, 2007.

Kimmel, Michael. "Men, Masculinity, and the Rape Culture." *Transforming a Rape Culture*. Ed. Emilie Buchwald, Pamela R. Fletcher, and Martha Roth. Minneapolis, MN: Milkweed Editions: 1993. 119–138.

Klein, Alvin. "The Birth, Death, and Resurrection of Extremities." *New York Times*. 9 January 1983, final ed.: sec. 11 p. 1.

Klein, Jeanne. E-mail message to the author. 18 November 2000.

Koch, John. "Performance Artist Karen Finley Finds Humor in the Center of Horror." Rev. of *We Keep Our Victims Ready*, Karen Finley. *Boston Globe*. 14 September 1990, city ed.: Living 38.

Koss, Mary P. "Hidden Rape." *Rape and Society*. Ed. Patricia Searles and Ronald J. Berger. Boulder, CO.: Westview Press, 1995. 35–49.

Koss, Mary P., and Mary R. Harvey. *The Rape Victim: Clinical and Community Interventions*. Newbury Pary: Sage Publications, 1991.

Kreitzer, Carson. *Self Defense or Death of Some Salesmen. Women Playwrights: The Best Plays of 2003*. Ed. D. L. Lepidus. Hanover, NH: Smith and Kraus, 2003. 273–325.

Kress, Victoria E., et al. "Evaluation of the Impact of a Coeducational Sexual Assault Prevention Program on College Students' Rape Myth Attitudes." *Journal of College Counseling* 9.2 (2006): 148–157.

Lacey, Liam. "Extremities Out of Touch." Rev. of *Extremities*, William Mastrosimone. *Globe & Mail*. 2 February 1987: C10.

Lakoff, George, and Mark Johnson. "The Metaphorical Logic of Rape." *Metaphor and Symbolic Activity* 2.1 (1987): 73–79.

_____ and _____. *Metaphors We Live By*. Chicago: University of Chicago Press, 1980.

Lamb, Sharon. "Constructing the Victim Popular Images and the Lasting Labels." *New Versions of Victims: Feminists Struggle with the Concept*. Ed. Sharon Lamb. New York: New York University Press, 1999. 108–138.

_____. "Introduction." *New Versions of Victims: Feminists Struggle with the Concept*. Ed. Sharon Lamb. New York: New York University Press, 1999.

La Rue, Linda. "The Black Movement and Women's Liberation." *The Black Scholar* 1:7 (1970): 36–42.

Laufersweiler-Dwyer, Deborah, and Gregg Dwyer. "Rapists." *Sexual Assault: The Victims, the Perpetrators, and the Criminal Justice System*. Ed. Frances P. Reddington and Betsy Wright Kreisel. Durham, NC: Carolina Academic Press, 2005. 205–231.

Leavitt, Dinah. *Feminist Theatre Groups*. Jefferson, NC: McFarland, 1980.

Lester, Neal A. "At the Heart of Shange's Feminism: An Interview." *Black American Literature Forum* 24:4 (1990): 717–730.

Levy, Carolyn. "The Date Rape Play: A Collaborative Process." *Transforming a*

Rape Culture. Ed. Emilie Buchwald, Pamela R. Fletcher, and Martha Roth. Minneapolis, MN: Milkweed Editions: 1993. 228-235.

Lewis, Barbara. "Antebellum Revisitations: Insurrectionary Interventions in *Kindred* and *Sally's Rape*." *Revisiting Slave Narratives II*. Ed. Judith Misrahi-Barak. Montpellier: Presses Université de la Méditerrané, 2007. 297-319.

Lisak, David, and Susan Roth. "Motivational Factors in Nonincarceratead Sexually Aggressive Men." *Journal of Personality and Social Psychology* 55.5 (1988): 795-802.

Liss, Shannon, and Rebecca Walker. "We Are Not Post-Feminist Feminists!" *New Directions for Women* (July-August 1992): 24.

Lonsway, Kimberly A., and Louise F. Fitzgerald. "Rape Myths in Review." *Psychology of Women Quarterly* 18.2 (1994): 133-164.

_____ and _____. "Attitudinal Antecedents of Rape Myth Acceptance." *Journal of Personality and Social Psychology* 68.4 (1995): 704-711.

Lorde, Audre. *Sister Outsider: Essays and Speeches by Audre Lorde*. Freedom, CA: The Crossing Press, 1984.

MacCannell, Dean, and Juliet Flower MacCannell. "Violence, Power, and Pleasure." *Up Against Foucault*. Ed. Carolline Ramazanoglu. New York: Routledge, 1993. 203-238.

MacGregor, Catherine. "Undoing the Body Politic: Representing Rape in *Women Beware Women*." *Theatre Research International* 23.1 (1998): 14-25.

MacKinnon, Catharine A. "Feminism, Marxism, Method, and the State: An Agenda for Theory." *Signs* 7.3 (1982): 515-544.

_____. "Feminism, Marxism, Method, and the State: Toward Feminist Jurisprudence." *Signs* 8.4 (1983): 635-658.

_____. *Feminism Unmodified: Discourses on Life and Law*. Cambridge, Harvard University Press, 1987.

_____. "A Feminist/Political Approach: Pleasure under Patriarchy." *Theories of Human Sexuality*. Ed. James H. Geer and William T. O'Donohue. New York: Plenum Press, 1987. 65-90.

_____. "Rape: On Coercion and Consent." *Writing on the Body*. Ed. Katie Conboy, Nadia Medina, and Sarah Stanbury. New York: Columbia University Press, 1997. 42-58.

_____. "Sex and Violence: A Perspective." *Rape and Society*. Ed. Patricia Searles and Ronald J. Berger. Boulder, CO.: Westview Press, 1995. 28-34.

_____. "Sexuality." *The Second Wave: A Reader in Feminist Theory*. Ed. Linda Nicholson. New York: Routledge, 1997. 158-180.

MacLean, Nancy. *The American Women's Movement, 1945-2000: A Brief History with Documents*. Boston: Bedford/St. Martin's, 2009.

Mahne, Theodore P. "Going to Extremes." Rev. of *Extremities*, William Mastrosimone. *Times-Picayune*. 30 April 2010: A9.

Malamuth, Neil M., and Lisa M. Brown. "Sexually Aggressive Men's Perceptions of Women's Communications." *Journal of Personality and Social Psychology* 67.4 (1994): 699-712.

Mann, Judy. "Beyond the Bobbitts' Battle." *Washington Post*. 13 August 1993, final ed.: E3.

Marcus, Sharon. "Fighting Bodies. Fighting Words: A Theory and Politics of Rape Prevention." *Feminists Theorize the Political*. Ed. Judith Butler and Joan W. Scott. New York: Routledge, 1992. 385-403.

Mardorossian, Carine M. *Framing the Rape Victim: Gender and Agency Reconsidered*. New Brunswick, NJ: Rutgers University Press, 2014.

_____. "Toward a New Feminist Theory of Rape." *Signs: Journal of Women in Culture and Society* 27.3 (2002): 743-775.

Martin, Carol, ed. *A Sourcebook of Feminist Theatre and Performance: On and Beyond the Stage*. New York: Routledge, 1996.

Martin, Patricia Yancey, and Robert A. Hummer. "Fraternities and Rape on

Bibliography

Campus." *Rape and Society: Readings on the Problem of Sexual Assault.* Ed. Patricia Searles and Ronald J. Berger. Boulder, CO: Westview Press, 1995. 139–151.

Mastrosimone, William. *Extremities.* Garden City, NY: Nelson Doubleday Inc., 1978.

_____. "Interview." *William Mastrosimone Author of Extremities. Sexual Coercion & Assault* 1.3 (1986): 105–107.

McCaughey, Martha. *Real Knockouts: The Physical Feminism of Women's Self-Defense.* New York: New York University Press, 1997.

McCauley, Robbie. Interview. *Obsessing in Public.* Vicki Patraka. *The Drama Review* 37.3 (1993): 25–55.

_____. *Sally's Rape: Moon Marked and Touched by the Sun.* Ed. Sydne Mahone. New York: Theatre Communications Group, 1994. 211–238.

_____. "Thoughts on My Career, *The Other Weapon*, and Other Projects." *Performance and Cultural Politics.* Ed. Elin Diamond. New York: Routledge, 1996. 265–282.

McDonough, Carla. *Staging Masculinity: Male Identity in Contemporary American Drama.* Jefferson, NC: McFarland, 1997.

McDougal, Dennis. "Despite Grants, NEA Four Presses Suit." *Los Angeles Times.* 6 November 1991, home ed.: F3.

McElroy, Damien. "Focus on Brides for Sale." (London) *Sunday Telegraph.* 22 November 1998: 28.

McMahon, Sarah. "Rape Myth Beliefs and Bystander Attitudes Among Incoming College Students." *Journal of American College Health* 59.1 (2010): 3–11.

McRobbie, Angela. *The Aftermath of Feminism: Gender, Culture, and Social Change.* Los Angeles, CA: Sage, 2009.

_____. "Post Feminism and Popular Culture." *Feminist Media Studies* 4.3 (2004): 255–263.

Merriam, Eve. *And I Ain't Finished Yet.* New York: Samuel French, 1982.

Messner, Michael A. *Taking the Field: Women, Men, and Sports.* Minneapolis: University of Minnesota Press, 2002.

Miedzian, Myriam. *Boys Will Be Boys: Breaking the Link between Masculinity and Violence.* New York: Doubleday, 1991.

_____. "How Rape Is Encouraged in American Boys and What We Can Do to Stop It." *Transforming a Rape Culture.* Ed. Emilie Buchwald, Pamela Fletcher, and Martha Roth. Minneapolis, MN: Milkweed, 1993. 153–164.

Miller, Peggy, and Nancy Biele. "Twenty Years Later: The Unfinished Revolution." *Transforming a Rape Culture.* Ed. Emilie Buchwald, Pamela Fletcher, and Martha Roth. Minneapolis, MN: Milkweed, 1993. 49–54.

Miner, Madonne. "What's These Bars Doin' Here? The Impossibility of *Getting Out.*" *The Theatre Annual* 40 (1985): 115–136.

Molette, Carlton, and Barbara Molette. *Rosalee Pritchett.* New York: Dramatists, 1972.

Moore, Michael Scott. Rev of *No. 11.* "Head of the Class: A Drama About a Rich Teen Rapist Feels Surprisingly Like Everyday life." *San Francisco Weekly.* 28 January 2004, Culture/Stage: n. pag.

Moss, Mark. *The Media and Models of Masculinity.* Lanham, MD: Lexington Books, 2011.

Murry, Timothy. "Patriarchal Panopticism, or The Seduction of Bad Joke: *Getting Out* in Theory." *Theatre Journal* 35.3 (1983): 376–388.

Narbona-Carrión, María Dolores. "The Role of Female Bonding on the Stage of Violence." *Performing Gender Violence: Plays by Contemporary American Women Dramatists.* Ed. Barbara Ozieblo and Noelia Hernando-Real. New York: Palgrave Macmillan, 2002. 61–79.

Nash, Susan Smith. *Dealing with Date Rape: True Stories from Survivors.* Norman, OK: Texture Press, 1996.

Neff, Debra. *Twice Shy. Ten out of Ten.* Ed. Wendy Lamb. New York: Dell Publishing, 1992.

Norman, Marsha. *Getting Out.* Garden City, NY: Nelson Doubleday, 1979.

Bibliography

———. *'night mother*. New York: Hill and Wang, 1983.

Norris, Bruce. *The Pain and the Itch*. Evanston, IL: Northwestern University Press, 2008.

Nymann, Ann. "Sally's Rape: Robbie McCauley's Survival." *African American Review* 33.4 (1999): 577–587.

O'Donohue, William, Elizabeth A. Yeater, and Matthew Fanetti. "Rape Prevention with College Males: The Roles of Rape Myth Acceptance, Victim Empathy, and Outcome Expectancies." *Journal of Interpersonal Violence* 18.5 (2003): 513–531.

Odum, Maria E., and Carlos Sanchez. "A Symbol of Shared Rage." *Washington Post*. 12 August 1993, final ed.: B1.

Orr, Catherine M. "Charting the Currents of the Third Wave." *Hypatia* 12.3 (1997): 29–45.

O'Sullivan, Chris. "Fraternities and the Rape Culture." *Transforming a Rape Culture*. Ed. Emilie Buchwald, Pamela R. Fletcher, and Martha Roth. Minneapolis: Milkweed Editions, 1993. 23–30.

Other Theatre Company. *Obadiah's Image: The Training of a Rapist*. 1982.

Ouimette, Paige Crosby, and David Riggs. "Testing a Mediational Model of Sexually Aggressive Behavior in Nonincarcerated Perpetrators." *Violence and Victims* 13.2 (1998): 117–130.

Ozieblo, Barbara. "Affecting the Audience: Gina Gionfriddo's *After Ashley*." *Violence in American Drama: Essays on Its Staging, Meanings, and Effects*. Ed. Alfonso Ceballos Muñoz, Ramón Espejo Romero, and Bernardo Muñoz Martínez. Jefferson, NC: McFarland, 2011. 267–278.

———. "The Political and the Personal in American Drama." *Staging a Cultural Paradigm: The Political and the Personal in American Drama*. Ed. Barabara Ozieblo and Miriam Lopez-Rodriguez. New York: Peter Lang Publishing. 2002. 13–29.

———. "The Victim and the Audience's Pleasure." *Performing Gender Violence: Plays by Contemporary Women American Dramatists*. Ed. Barbara Ozieblo and Noelia Hernando-Real. New York: Palgrave Macmillan, 2012. 155–172.

Ozieblo, Barbara, and Noelia Hernando-Real, eds. *Performing Gender Violence: Plays by Contemporary Women American Dramatists*. New York: Palgrave Macmillan, 2012.

Paglia, Camille. *Vamps & Tramps*. New York: Vintage Books, 1994.

Parachini, Allan. "NEA Advisors Nix Grants." *Los Angeles Times*. 15 May 1990, home ed.: F1.

Parrot, Andrea, and Laurie Bechhofer, eds. *Acquaintance Rape: The Hidden Crime*. New York: John Wiley and Sons, Inc., 1991.

Parrot, Andrea, and Nina Cummings. "A Rape Awareness and Prevention Model for Male Athletes." *Journal of American College Health* 42.4 (1994): 179–184.

Paul, Lisa A., et al. "Perceptions of Peer Rape Myth Acceptance." *Psychological Trauma: Theory, Research, Practice, and Policy* 1.3 (2009): 231–241.

Payne, Diana L., Kimberly A. Lonsway, and Louise F. Fitzgerald. "Rape Myth Acceptance." *Journal of Research in Personality* 33.1 (1999): 27–68.

Pearson, Alyn. "Cultural Messages Contribute to the Prevalence of Date Rape." *Date Rape*. Ed. James Haley. San Diego: Greenhaven Press, 2003. 62–71.

Pedro, Laura. "Society Should Not Blame the Victim for Sexual Violence." *Sexual Violence: Opposing Viewpoints*. Ed. Louise I. Gerdes. Detroit: Greenhaven Press, 2008. 100–103.

Pershing, Linda. "His Wife Seized His Prize and Cut It to Size: Folk and Popular Commentary on Lorena Bobbitt." *National Women's Studies Association Journal* 8.3 (1996): 1–35.

Phelan, Peggy. *Unmarked: The Politics of Performance*. New York: Routledge, 1993.

Pierce-Baker, Charlotte. *Surviving the Silence: Black Women's Stories of Rape*. New York: Norton, 1998.

Pineau, Lois. "Date Rape: A Feminist Analysis." *Date Rape: Feminism, Philos-*

ophy, and the Law. Ed. Leslie Francis. University Park, PA: Penn State University Press, 1996. 1–26.

Porter, Louise E., and Laurence J. Alison. "Behavioural Coherence in Violent Group Activity: An Interpersonal Model of Sexually Violent Gang Behaviour." *Aggressive Behavior* 30.6 (2004): 449–468.

Powell, Elizabeth. "I Thought You Didn't Mind." *Transforming a Rape Culture.* Ed. Emilie Buchwald, Pamela R. Fletcher, and Martha Roth. Minneapolis: Milkweed Editions, 1993. 107–118.

Pramaggiore, Maria. "Resisting/Performing/Femininity: Words, Flesh, and Feminism in Karen Finley's *The Constant State of Desire*." *Theatre Journal* 44.3 (1992): 269–290.

Press, Andrea L. "Feminism? That's So Seventies: Girls and Young Women Discuss Femininity and Feminism in *America's Next Top Model*." *New Femininities: Postfeminism, Neoliberalism, and Subjectivity.* Ed. Rosalind Gill and Christina Scharff. New York: Palgrave Macmillan, 2011. 117–133.

Projansky, Sarah. *Watching Rape: Film and Television in Postfeminist Culture.* New York: New York University Press, 2001.

Proulx, Jean, et al., eds. *Pathways to Sexual Aggression.* New York: Routledge, 2014.

Quinn, Nicole. *Information. Great Short Plays,* vol. 3. New York: Playscripts Inc., 2007. 49–58.

Rae, Charlotte. "Women's Theatre Groups." *The Drama Review* 16.2 (1972): 79–89.

Rapaport, Karen, and Barry R. Burkhart. "Personality and Attitudinal Characteristics of Sexually Coercive College Males." *Journal of Abnormal Psychology* 93.2 (1984): 216–221.

Rapp, Rayna. "Is the Legacy of Second-Wave Feminism Postfeminism?" *Women, Class, and the Feminist Imagination: A Socialist-Feminist Reader.* Ed. Karen V. Hansen and Ilene J. Philipson. Philadelphia: Temple University Press, 1990. 357–362.

Reger, Jo, ed. *Different Wavelengths: Studies of the Contemporary Women's Movement.* New York: Routledge, 2005.

Reinelt, Janelle. "Navigating Postfeminism: Writing Out of the Box. *Feminist Futures? Theatre, Performance, Theory.* Ed. Elaine Aston and Geraldine Harris. New York: Palgrave Macmillian, 2006. 17–33.

Rhode Island Feminist Theatre. *Persephone's Return. Frontiers* 3.2 (1978): 60–74.

Richards, David. "None but the Brave." Rev. of *Extremities,* William Mastrosimone. *Washington Post.* 21 November 1985, final ed.: C17.

Rife, Susan L. "Extremities' Tense, Thought-Provoking." Rev. of *Extremities,* William Mastrosimone. *Sarasota Herald Tribune.* 31 May 2005: E3.

Riordan, Ellen. "Commodified Agents and Empowered Girls: Consuming and Producing Feminism." *Journal of Communication Inquiry* 25.3 (2001): 279–297.

Roberts, Terri. "*Self Defense, or, Death of Some Salesmen* at the Hudson Backstage Theatre." Rev. of *Self Defense or Death of Some Salesmen,* Carson Kreitzer. *Back Stage West* 11.6 (5 February 2004): 28.

Rogers, J. T. *White People.* New York: Dramatists, 2006.

Roiphe, Katie. "All the Rage." *New York Times.* 29 November 1993, late ed.: A17.

_____. "Lorena Bobbitt Exposed the Raw Hostility Between the Sexes." (Minneapolis) *Star Tribune.* 2 December 1993, metro ed.: A29.

_____. *The Morning After: Sex, Fear, and Feminism on Campus.* Boston: Little, Brown and Co., 1993.

Rooney, Ellen. "Criticism and the Subject of Sexual Violence." *MLN* 98.5 (1983): 1269–1278.

Rosenfeld, Megan. "Chilling View of Rape." Rev. of *Extremities,* William Mastrosimone. *Washington Post.* 25 June 1981, final ed.: F8.

_____. "Waxing Blood Moon." Rev. of *Blood Moon,* Nicholas Kazan. *Washington Post.* 24 January 1985, final ed.: D2.

Rowe-Finkbeiner, Kristin. *The F-word: Feminism in Jeopardy: Women, Politics, and the Future*. Emeryville, CA: Seal Press, 2004.

Royce, Graydon. "Sympathetic Look at a Serial Killer." Rev. of *Self Defense or Death of Some Salesmen*, Carson Krietzer. (Minneapolis) *Star Tribune* (February 9, 2002): 4B.

Rubenzahl, Samuel A., and Kevin J. Corcoran. "The Prevalence and Characteristics of Male Perpetrators of Acquaintance Rape." *Violence against Women* 4.6 (1998): 713–725.

Rubik, Margaret. "A Sisterhood of Women: Marsha Norman's *Getting Out* and *The Laundromat*." *Gramma: Journal of Theory and Criticism* 2.2 (1994): 141–147.

Russell, Dianna. *Dangerous Relationships: Pornography, Misogyny, and Rape*. Thousand Oaks, CA: Sage Publications, 1998.

———. *The Epidemic of Rape and Child Sexual Abuse in the United States*. Thousand Oaks, CA: Sage Publications, 2000.

———. *The Politics of Rape*. New York: Stein and Day, 1975.

Ryan, Kathryn. "Further Evidence of a Cognitive Component of Rape." *Aggression and Violent Behavior* 9 (2004): 579–604.

———. "The Relationship between Rape Myths and Sexual Scripts: The Social Construction of Rape." *Sex Roles* 65 (2011): 774–782.

Sandell, Jillian. "Adjusting to Oppression: The Rise of Therapeutic Feminism in the United States." *Bad Girls Good Girls: Women, Sex, and Power in the Nineties*. Ed. Nan Bauer Maglin and Donna Perry. New Brunswick, NJ: Rutgers University Press, 1996. 21–35.

Sandstrom, Karen. "Entertaining, Enlightening Production." Rev. of *The Second Coming of Joan of Arc*, Carolyn Gage. *The Plain Dealer*. 27 January 1998: E7.

Sanday, Peggy Reeves. *Fraternity Gang Rape: Sex, Brotherhood, and Privilege on Campus*. New York: New York University Press, 1990.

———. "The Socio-Cultural Context of Rape." *Journal of Social Issues* 37.4 (1981): 5–27.

Sauer, Mark, and Jeanne Freeman Brooks. "The Bobbitt Case." *The San Diego Union-Tribune*. 30 November 1993: E1.

Sawyer, Robin G., Estina E. Thompson, and Anne Marie Chicorelli. "Rape Myth Acceptance Among Intercollegiate Student Athletes." *American Journal of Health Studies* 18.1 (2002): 19–25.

Schilt, Kristin. "The Punk White Privilege Scene: Riot Grrrl, White Privilege, and Zines." *Different Wavelengths: Studies of the Contemporary Women's Movement*. Ed. Jo Reger. New York: Routledge, 2005.

Schneider, Rebecca. *The Explicit Body in Performance*. New York: Routledge, 1997.

Schroeder, Patricia. "Locked Behind the Proscenium: Feminist Strategies in *Getting Out* and *My Sister in This House*." *Modern Drama* 32.1 (1989): 104–114.

Schuler, Catherine. "Spectator Response and Comprehension: The Problem of Karen Finley's Constant State of Desire." *The Drama Review* 34.1 (1990): 131–145.

Scully, Diana, and Joseph Marolla. "'Riding the Bull at Gilely's': Convicted Rapists Describe the Rewards of Rape." *Rape and Society: Readings on the Problem of Sexual Assault*. Ed. Patricia Searles and Ronald J. Berger. Boulder, CO: Westview Press, 1995. 58–73.

Seham, Amy. *One Night at Alta Bates*. Berkeley: University of California Press, 1993.

Shange, Ntozake. *boogie woogie landscapes*. *Three Pieces: Ntozake Shange*. New York: St. Martin's Press, 1978.

———. *For Colored Girls Who Have Considered Suicide When the Rainbow is Enuf*. New York: MacMillian, 1977.

Sheffield, Carole J. "Sexual Terrorism." *Women: A Feminist Perspective*, fifth ed. Ed. Jo Freeman. Mountain View: Mayfield Publishing Co., 1995. 1–21.

Shepard, Alan Clarke. "Aborted Rage in Beth Henley's Women." *States of Rage*. Ed. Renee R. Curry and Terry L. Allison. New York: New York University Press, 1996. 179–194.

Short, Kayann. "Coming to the Table: Differential Politics of This Bridge Called My Back." *Genders* 19 (1994): n. pag.

Siegel, Deborah. "Reading between the Waves: Feminist Historiography in a 'Postfeminist' Moment." In *Third Wave Agenda: Being Feminist, Doing Feminism*. Ed. Leslie Heywood and Jennifer Drake. Minneapolis: University of Minnesota Press, 1997. 55–82.

_____. *Sisterhood Interrupted: From Radical Women to Grrls Gone Wild*. New York: Palgrave Macmillan, 2007.

Sinclair, H. Colleen, and Lyle E. Bourne, Jr. "Cycle of Blame or Just World: Effects of Legal Verdicts on Gender Patterns in Rape-Myth Acceptance and Victim Empathy." *Psychology of Women Quarterly* 22. 4 (1998): 575–588.

Smith, Dinitia. "Today the Anatomy, Tomorrow the World." *New York Times*. 26 September 1999, final ed.: sec. 2 p. 7.

Smith, Helen C. "Audience Gives Insights into the Emotions of *Almost Asleep*." Rev. of *Almost Asleep*, Julie Hebert. *The Atlanta Journal and Constitution* 2 February 1992: N5.

Smith, Susan Harris. "En-Gendering Violence." *Public Issues, Private Tensions: Contemporary American Drama*. New York: AMS Press, 1993. 115–131.

Snortland, Ellen. *Beauty Bites Beast: Awakening the Warrior within Women and Girls*. Pasadena: Trilogy Books, 1998.

Solomon, Alisa. "How Robbie Do." Rev. of *Sally's Rape*, Robbie McCauley. *Village Voice*. 19 November 1991: 10, 103.

_____. "A New York (Theater) Diary, 1992." Rev. of *Sally's Rape*, Robbie McCauley. *Theater* 24.1 (1993): 7–18.

_____. "Weeping for Racist, Rapists, and Nazis." *Performing Arts Journal* 7.1 (1983): 78–83.

Solomonson, Michael. "Rebecca Gilman's Exploration of Gender Conditioning as a Factor in Violence Against Women." *Violence in American Drama: Essays on Its Staging, Meanings, and Effects*. Ed. Alfonso Ceballos Muñoz, Ramón Espejo Romero, and Bernardo Muñoz Martínez. Jefferson, NC: McFarland, 2011. 200–211.

Sonnega, William. "Beyond a Liberal Audience." *African American Performance and Theater History: A Critical Reader*. New York: Oxford University Press, 2001. 81–98.

Speaker, Burke. "Button-Pushing Play Extremities is Disturbing, Intriguing." Rev. of *Extremities*, William Mastrosimone *Star News*. 5 October 2006: Currents 4.

Spencer, Jane. "Introduction: Genealogies." *Third Wave Feminism: A Critical Exploration*. Ed. Stacy Gillis, Gillian Howie, and Rebecca Munford. New York: Palgrave Macmillan, 2004. 9–12.

Spencer, Jenny. "Marsha Norman's She-Tragedies." *Making a Spectacle*. Ed. Lynda Hart. Ann Arbor: University of Michigan Press, 1989. 147–168.

Spillane, Margaret. "The Culture of Narcissism." *The Nation*. 10 December 1990: 737–740.

Stacey, Judith. "Sexism by a Subtler Name? Postindustrial Conditions and Postfeminist Consciousness in Silicon Valley." *Socialist Review* 96 (November–December 1987): 7–28.

Steinhauer, Jennifer. "Military Courts Are Called Outdated on Prosecutions of Sexual Assaults." *New York Times*. 9 May 2013, final ed.: A21.

Stevens, Alexander. "Monologues Affect Actresses Personally." *The Boston Herald*. 13 May 2001: Arts & Life 43.

Stephens, Judith. "The Compatibility of Traditional Dramatic Form and Feminist Expression." *The Theatre Annual* 40 (1985): 7–23.

Stoltenberg, John. "Making Rape an Election Issue." *Transforming a Rape Culture*. Ed. Emilie Buchwald, Pamela R. Fletcher, and Martha Roth. Minneapolis: Milkweed Editions, 1993. 213–224.

Stone, Elizabeth. "Playwright Marsha Norman: An Optimist Writes about Suicide, Confinement, and Despair." *Ms*. (July 1983): 56–59.

Stone, Laurie. "Cameos." Rev. of *We Keep Our Victims Ready*, Karen Finley. *Village Voice*. 1 May 1990: 118.

_____. "Woman of the Year—Karen Finley." *Ms*. (January/February 1998): 71–73.

Bibliography

Sullivan, Dan. "Padua Hills B Series is Grade A." Rev. of *Almost Asleep*, Julie Hebert. *Los Angeles Times*. 25 July 1989, home ed.: Calendar 1.

Sullivan, Kevin. "Report of Mutilation Draws Powerful Responses." *Washington Post*. 25 January 1993, final ed.: C1.

Superson, Anita. "Welcome to the Boys' Club: Male Socialization and the Backlash against Feminism in Tenure Decisions." *Theorizing Backlash: Philosophical Reflections on the Resistance to Feminism*. Lanham, MD: Rowman & Littlefield Publishers, Inc., 2002. 89–118.

Superson, Anita, and Anne Cudd, eds. *Theorizing Backlash: Philosophical Reflections on the Resistance to Feminism*. Lanham, MD: Rowman & Littlefield Publishers, Inc., 2002.

Tasca, Jules. *The God's Honest: An Evening of Lies*. New York: Samuel French, 1987.

Tasker, Yvonne, and Diane Negra. "Feminist Politics and Postfeminist Culture." *Interrogating Postfeminism: Gender and the Politics of Popular Culture*. Ed. Yvonne Tasker and Diane Negra. Durham, NC: Duke University Press, 2007. 1–26.

Thomas, Sandra, ed. *Women and Anger*. New York: Springer Publishing Co., 1993.

Thompson, Deborah. "Blackface, Rape, and Beyond: Rehearsing Interracial Dialogue in *Sally's Rape*." *Theatre Journal* 48.2 (1996): 123–140.

Thornham, Sue. "Second Wave Feminism." *The Routledge Critical Dictionary of Feminism and Postfeminism*. Ed. Sarah Gamble. New York: Routledge, 1999. 29–42.

Tomaselli, Sylvana, and Roy Porter, eds. *Rape: An Historical and Social Enquiry*. New York: Basil Blackwell Inc., 1986.

Toomer, Jeanette. "Self Defense." Rev. of *Self Defense or Death of Some Salesmen*, Carson Krietzer. *Back Stage* 43.27 (5 July 2002): 19.

"The Vagina Monologues." *Kirkus Reviews*. 1 December 1997 n. pag.

Van der Veen, Marike Lies. "Rape and the Dichotomy of Womanhood: Empowering the Female Voice." Thesis. Chapel Hill University, 1991.

Valentis, Mary, and Anne Devane. *Female Rage: Unlocking Its Secrets, Claiming Its Power*. New York: Carol Southern Books, 1994.

Walker, Rebecca. "Becoming the Third Wave." *Ms.* (January/February 1992): 39.

Walker, Sarah. "When 'No' Becomes 'Yes': Why Girls and Women Consent to Unwanted Sex." *Applied & Preventive Psychology* 6 (1997): 157–166.

Watt, Stephen, and Gary Richardson, eds. *American Drama Colonial to Contemporary*. Philadelphia: Harcourt Brace, 1995.

Wattenberg, Daniel. "*Sharia* Feminists." *The American Spector* (December 1993): 62.

Weales, Gerald. "Marsha Norman." *Contemporary Literary Criticism*, vol. 28. Detroit: Gale Research Co., 1984. 319.

Webb, Jeannie. "The Glory of Living at the Victory Theatre Center." Rev. of *The Glory of Living*. *Back Stage West*, 22 November 2007: 21.

Weisman, Jonathan. "Rape Comment Draws Attention in Indiana." *New York Times*. 24 October 2012, final ed.: A12. Web. 5 August 2013.

Welllinghoff, Jasmina. "Extremities a Tense Tale." Rev. of *Extremities*, William Mastrosimone. *San Antonia Express-News*. 27 August 2010: F2.

Westfall, Sandra Sobieraj, et al. "Cleveland Kidnap Survivors 'Getting Stronger Every Day.'" *People* (22 July 2013): 60–65.

White, Jacquelyn W., and Paige Hall Smith. "Sexual Assault Perpetration and Reperpetration." *Criminal Justice and Behavior* 31.2 (2004): 182–202.

Whyte, Raewyn. "Robbie McCauley: Speaking History Other-Wise." *Acting Out: Feminist Performances*. Ed. Lynda Hart and Peggy Phelan. Ann Arbor: University of Michigan Press, 1993. 277–294.

Wiehe, Vernon, and Ann Richards. *Intimate Betrayal*. Thousand Oaks, CA: Sage Publications, 1995.

Wilcox, Dean. "Karen Finley's *Hymen*."

Bibliography

Theatre Research International 22.1 (1997): 31–37.

Wiles, Timothy. "Suicide and Self-Annihilation: Marsha Norman's *'night Mother* and Karen Finley's *The Constant State of Desire*." *Staging the Rage: The Web of Misogyny in Modern Drama*. Ed. Katrhyn Burkman and Judith Roof. Madison: Fairleigh Dickinson University Press, 1998. 112–123.

Williams, Tennessee. *Vieux Carre*. New York: New Directions Pub, 1979.

Williams, Timothy. "Freed Captives in Cleveland Issue Messages of Resolve." *New York Times*, 10 July 2013: A 16.

Wilson, August. *Ma Rainey's Black Bottom*. New York: New American Library, 1985.

Wilson, Margo, and Martin Daly. "Till Death Us Do Part." *The Politics of Women's Bodies*. Ed. Rose Weitz. New York: Oxford University Press, 1998. 207–220.

Winkler, Kathleen. *Date Rape: A Hot Issue*. Berkeley: Enslow Publishers, Inc., 1999.

Wolf, Naomi. "Feminist Fatale." *New Republic* 206.11 (March 1992): 23–25.

Wolfe, Lauren. "The Silencing Crime: Sexual Violence and Journalists." *Committee to Protect Journalists*. 6 June 2011. https://www.cpj.org/reports/2011/06/silencing-crime-sexual-violence-journalists.php

Worrell, Kris. "Bobbitt Case Rekindles the Gender Debate." *The Atlanta Journal and Constitution*, 1 December 1993: E1.

Yeater, Elizabeth A., et al. "Cognitive Processes Underlying Women's Rick Judgments: Associations with Sexual Victimization History and Rape Myth Acceptance." *Journal of Consulting and Clinical Psychology* 78.3 (2010): 375–386.

Index

Abide in Darkness 18
abortion 91, 99, 168*n*3
acquaintance rape 16–17, 21–22, 25, 28, 31, 38, 167*pref.n*1, 168*n*5
Adams State University Theatre Department 81, 140, 143
Add Verb Productions 24
After Ashley 127–134
Aguirre-Sacasa, Roberto 41–45, 52
Albright, Dale 131, 133
Alive and Trucking Theatre Company 17–18
Almost Asleep 139, 145–149, 154, 162, 165
And I Ain't Finished Yet 61–63
antifeminist backlash 11, 83–113, 139, 157
Aston, Elaine 17, 177*n*4, 177*n*1, 178*ch*6*n*1

Baumgardner, Jennifer 115
Baumgartner, Rebekah 85, 86, 88
Belber, Steven 45–47, 52
bell hooks 116, 176*n*4
Bernardez, Teresa 67, 68, 144
Berry, Amanda 5, 168*n*3
Besler, Colleen 55
Blessing, Lee 53–54, 127–129
Blood Moon 84, 90–91
Bobbitt, Lorena 83, 100, 172
Bolton, Richard 106, 107, 109, 174*n*7
boogie woogie landscapes 21–22
Bourke, Joanna 25, 28, 167*pref.n*1, 176*n*4, 178*conc.n*2
Bovver Boys 39–45, 52, 58, 74, 165
Boy Gets Girl 56
Brava! For Women in the Arts 166
Brownmiller, Susan 15, 18, 151, 168*n*5
Bryant, Kobe 36
Bubin, Amelia iv, 49, 51
Buchanan, Pat 107, 109

Buckley, William 107
Burke, Sally 6, 61, 91, 94, 178*ch*6*n*2
Burt, Martha 25–26, 167*pref.n*1, 169*ch*2*n*2

Caballero, Kelly 136
Camero, Almendra 136
Campbell, Matt 55
Canning, Charlotte 27, 177*n*6, 177*n*1
Cannon, Christopher Glenn 136
Carr, C. (Cynthia) 108, 112, 158, 173*n*5, 174*n*9
Carr, Jonathan iv, 49, 51
Choudhury, Bikram 5, 168*n*3
clothesline project 125
commodification of rape 126–138
consciousness raising groups 14–17, 20–21, 23–24
consent 30, 37, 169*intro.n*7
The Constant State of Desire 102, 107, 111, 173*n*5, 174*n*7, 175*n*11
Cornpropst, Matt 85, 86, 88
Cosby, Bill 5, 168*n*3
Crossfire 107, 109
Cunningham, Alexandra 48–52

date rape 16–24, 46–47, 67–70, 168*n*5, 170*n*2, 170*n*3
date rape drugs 24
Davis, Angela 59, 87, 117
definition of rape 2, 11–12, 15–16, 39, 167*pref.n*1
DeJesus Gina 5, 168*n*3
De Lauretis, Teresa 9–10, 101, 153
Delia, Marlee 49
De Los Santos, Sandra 136
demonization of raped women 83–95
Denfield, Rene 124
Diamond, Elin 105, 177*n*1

197

Index

Dick, Kirby 5
Dolan, Jill 45, 102, 153, 174n5, 177n1, 178n1
Down the Road 53–54, 127–129
Dragon Productions Theatre Company 131, 133
Drake, Jennifer 115, 175n1, 176n4, 177n4
Dworkin, Andrea 98

Ensler, Eve 23, 127, 130–134, 138, 158, 160
Estle, Cody 20, 43, 44
Estrich, Susan 75, 168n5, 172n2
Evans, Rowland 106, 107, 110
Extremities 29, 84–90, 91, 94, 96, 98, 100, 162, 172n7, 173n8

Faludi, Susan 96, 99, 126
Felton, Farrah 130
female rage 65–95
feminism 10, 13–14, 157; antifeminist backlash 11, 83–113, 139, 157; first-wave 13; postfeminism 3, 123–126, 175n3, 175n4, 177n5; second-wave 11, 13–17, 24, 115–124, 151, 160, 164; third-wave 11, 114–123, 175n1, 175n3
feminist theatres 17–18, 139, 159
Ferguson, Lisa Cesnik 85, 86, 88
Finley, Karen 34, 100–113, 158, 161, 163, 173n2, 17n3, 173n5, 174n5, 174n7, 174n9, 174n10, 175n11
Firehouse Theatre Project 93
first-wave feminism 13
Flannagan, Ford 93
Fleck, John 106, 109, 173n2
For Colored Girls Who Have Considered Suicide When the Rainbow Is Enuf 21
Friedan, Betty 13

Gage, Carolyn 151–155, 157, 167pref.n2
Gagliano, Laura 66, 67–70
Gallobin, Laurie Brooks 76–79
gang rape 19, 57–64, 98
Garcia-Crow, Amparo 60–61, 67, 72–74
Gavey, Nicola 2, 9, 16, 164–165, 167pref.n1, 167intro.n2, 168n5, 176n4, 177n5, 177n6, 177n1, 178n6
gendered rage 1, 7–10, 62, 65–67, 73–74, 83–84, 89, 99, 102, 109, 111–112, 142, 147–148, 154, 158–159, 161–163, 166
gendered sexuality 1, 6–7, 9, 16, 33, 37–38, 56, 69, 75, 89, 102–103, 111–112, 158–159, 161–163
gendered violence 6, 7, 56, 153, 178n3
Gergan, David 107
Getting Out 75, 76, 79–82, 139–145, 149, 154, 161, 165
Gilman, Rebecca 54–56
Gilvery, Sean 131, 133
Gionfriddo, Gina 127–134
The Glory of Living 54–56
The God's Honest: An Evening of Lies 30
Golden, Robert 19, 53, 62, 167pref.n1, 167intro.n2, 170n3, 170n4, 171n9, 171n11
Goldstein, Lynda 105, 113, 161, 173n5
Gollobin, Laurie Brooks 75–79, 167pref.n2
Good Boys and True 41–45, 52
Gorman, Molly 136
group think 60–62
Guither, Pete 55
Gussow, Mel 71, 90, 173n8, 173n9

Hallas, Amy 136
Harper, Milton 47
Hart, Lynda 1, 109, 177ch6n1
Hebert, Julie 136, 145–149
Herman, Judith 89, 167intro.n2, 170n4, 171n7, 171n8
Hernandez, Bethany 140, 143
Hernando-Real, Noelia 6, 41, 82, 178n3
Heywood, Leslie 114, 175n1, 177n4
Hill, Jasmin 136
Holtzman, Willy 39–45, 52, 58, 74, 165
Horovitz, Israel 61–62, 81–84, 91–98, 139
Hughes, Holly 106, 109, 173n2
Hull, Jordan 143
Humana Festival 48
The Hunting Ground 5
Hush 66–70, 82, 161

Information 24, 36–37
The Invisible War 5
It's All Right to Be a Woman Theatre Company 17

Jackson, Stevi 9, 83, 168n5, 171n8
Johnson, Allan 34, 45, 60, 61, 74, 97

Kasyan, James 131, 133
Kazan, Nicholas 84, 90–91, 139, 173n8, 173n9

Index

Kiley, Will 43, 44
Kilmartin, Christopher 8, 169*ch*2*n*1, 171*n*8, 171*n*9
Kirwin, Meghan 47
Klein, Jeanne 79, 86
Knight, Michelle 5, 155, 168*n*3
Kreitzer, Carson 56–57, 127, 129–130, 149–151

Lakoff, George 84
Lamb, Sharon 164, 168*n*5, 176*n*4, 177*n*5
Landers, Ann 27, 31
La Prairie, Dean 20, 43, 44
Levitt, Dinah 17, 18, 177*n*6
Levy, Carolyn 22–23
Lewis, Barbara 120
Lilac City Performing Arts 47
Limbaugh, Rush 132
limitations of the study 1–2
Lorde, Audre 116, 119, 175*n*1

Ma Rainey's Black Bottom 61–63
MacKinnon, Catherine 16, 169*n*7
male bonding 39–42, 45, 59–61
male competition 45–47, 92
male gaze 60, 84, 102, 112, 142
Mamet, David 84
Man of La Mancha 75
Marcus, Sharon 7–9, 24, 54, 67, 69, 72, 80–81, 89–90, 147–148, 158, 161–166, 168*n*4, 168*n*5, 169*ch*2*n*1, 170*n*2*n*4, 171*n*5, 171*n*8
Mardorossian, Carine 164, 168*n*3, 176*n*4, 177*n*5, 178*conc.n*2
marital rape 17, 20–21, 100
Marolla, Joseph 38, 170*n*4, 171*n*7, 171*n*8, 171*n*11
masculinity and rape 39, 53–54, 58, 60, 64
Massey, Jennifer 93
Mastrosimone, William 29, 84–90, 139, 172*n*7, 173*n*8
McBurnett, Nora Lindsay iv, 49, 51
McCauley, Robbie 116–123, 159, 160
McNamara, Clarissa 81, 140, 143
Menendian, Sophia 43
Merriam, Eve 63
Middleton, Thomas 154
Miller, Tim 106, 109, 173*n*2
Molette, Barbara 58–60, 70–72
Molette, Carlton 58–60, 70–72

monstrous female metaphor 83–95, 99–100, 147
Moraga, Cherrie 116
Ms. magazine 17, 123

Nagel, Landon 93
National Endowment for the Arts (NEA) 100, 102, 105–107, 110, 173*n*2, 174*n*7, 177*n*1
National Organization of Women (NOW) 13
Necessary Targets 127, 134–138
Neff, Debra 29–30, 165
Neilsen, Jenna 81, 140, 143
Nicholls, Blaine 47
No. 11 (Blue and White) 48–52
Norman, Marsha 79–82, 139–145, 149, 158, 173*n*5, 178*n*3, 178*ch*6*n*2
Norris, Bruce 27
Northeastern University iv, 49, 51
Nourse, Chris 51
Novak, Robert 106, 107, 110

Obadiah's Image: The Training of a Rapist 22, 32–34
Oklahoma 75
Olson, Cori 47
One Night at Alta Bates 23, 34–36
Other Theatre Company 22, 32–34
Ozieblo, Barbara 6, 17, 132, 134, 150, 151, 178*ch*6*n*3

Paglia, Camille 98, 124
The Pain and the Itch 27
Parks, Ken 85, 86, 88
Patraka, Vicki 118, 119
patriarchy 74–75, 97, 101, 103–104, 142, 152–155
Patton, Bill 93
Paul, Jay 93
performance art 100, 102
Persephone's Return 18–20
Peterson, Fred 19, 53, 62, 170*n*4, 171*n*9, 171*n*11
Phelan, Peggy 45, 76, 153, 173*n*4, 173*n*5, 174*n*8
Pig in a Blanket 18
Plourde, Cathy 24
postfeminism 3, 123–126, 175*n*3, 175*n*4, 177*n*5; and commodification of rape 126–138
Pramaggiore, Maria 103, 112, 173*n*5

199

Index

Quinn, Nicole 24, 36–37

Rabe, David 84
rage 65–95; and African American Women 118–119; appropriated 66, 73–74; contained 65–70, 157; contamination 65–68, 72, 74, 83; demonization of women 83–95, 157; demonized 66, 83–95, 98–100; gendered 1, 7–10, 62, 65–67, 73–74, 83–84, 89, 99, 102, 109, 111–112, 142, 147–148, 154, 158–159, 161–163, 166; pathologized and trivialized 70–73; recuperative 139–149, 157; turned inward 67–68, 70
Randolph College 85, 86, 88
rape: and abortion 91, 99, 168n3; acquaintance 16–17, 21–22, 25, 28, 31, 38, 167pref.n1, 168n5; and African American women 117–122; and athletes 41, 48–52; on college campuses 5, 19, 23–24, 32, 37, 48, 168n3; commodification 126–138; and consent 30, 37, 169intro.n7; and contamination 34, 50, 65–68, 72, 74, 83, 147, 164, 170n3; date 17–24, 46–67, 67–70, 168n5, 170n2, 170n3; definition 2, 11–12, 15–16, 39, 167pref.n1; and demonization of women 83–95; depolitization 126, 148, 158, 164; and depression 67–78; as entertainment 134; gang rape 19, 57–64, 98; and group think 60–62; and homophobia 44; and male bonding 39–42, 45, 59–61; and male competition 45–47, 92; marital 17, 20–21, 100; and masculinity 53–54, 58, 60, 64; and power 53, 61–62, 81; and race 21–22, 51, 58–63, 70–72, 116–123, 159–162; and seduction 36, 66, 75–83, 161, 168n5; and self-blame 40, 83, 92; and shame 40, 50, 68; and slavery 117–123; statistics 5, 41, 167intro.n2, 168n3; stranger 19–21; and suicide 68; survivor vs. victim 2–3; and theatrical activism 17–18; unacknowledged 41–42
rape culture 5, 15, 24, 69, 117, 153, 155, 157–160, 166, 169ch1n1, 169ch2n2, 171n10, 171n11, 177n6
rape myths 1, 3, 7, 19–20, 25–64, 157–159, 169ch2n2; and contamination 34, 50, 65–68, 72, 74, 83, 147, 164, 170n3; definition 25–26; examples 26–27; and rapists 27, 38, 169ch1n1; refuting myths 28–29, 32, 35; and shame 27; and uncontrollable male sexuality 27–29, 31, 48, 61, 77, 83, 98–99, 104, 170n4, 170n5; women invite rape 29–30, 32–36, 52, 61, 92, 97–99; women lie about rape 30–31, 35–36, 51–52, 61, 71–72; women want to be raped 33–35, 70, 75
The Rape of Emma Bunche 30–31
rape script 7–9, 24, 54, 67, 69, 72, 80–81, 89–90, 147–148, 158, 161–166, 168n4, 168n5, 169ch2n1, 170n2, 170n4, 171n5, 171n8
Rape-in 18
rapist ethic 6, 157, 159, 161
rapists 25–64, 75–79; "boy next door," normal men 38, 48–52; murderers 53–57; psychopathological 38, 52–57, 87, 127; and rape myths 27, 38, 169ch1n1; sympathetic depiction of 87, 92, 94, 99
The Raven Theatre 20, 43, 44
Reeve, Christopher 109
Reeves Sanday, Peggy 19, 32, 40, 170n3
Reitsma, Joel 20
Relyea, Linda 81, 140, 143
Reyes, Ana 136
Rhode Island Feminist Theatre Company 18–20, 159
Richards, Amy 115, 176n4
Riordan, Ellen 126, 175n1, 175n3, 177n4
Robertson, Pat 107
Rogers, J. T. 62
Roiphe, Katie 8, 124
Rosalee Pritchett 58–60, 70–72, 162
Russell, Dianna 27
Ryan, Kathryn 48, 58, 169ch2n1, 170n2, 171n11

Safire, William 107
Sally's Rape 116–123, 159, 160
Santa Ana College Theatre Arts Department 136
Schneider, Rebecca 117, 173n4
The School of Theatre and Dance at Illinois State University 55
Schroeder, Patricia 141, 145, 178ch6n2
Schuler, Catherine 112, 174n5, 174n10
Schumacher, Evan Michael 131
Scully, Diana 38, 170n4, 171n7, 171n8, 171n11

Index

The Second Coming of Joan of Arc 151–155, 163, 167*pref.n*2
second-wave feminism 11, 13–17, 20–24, 115–124, 151, 160, 164
Seham, Amy 23, 34–36
Self Defense or Death of Some Salesmen 56–57, 127, 129–130, 149–151, 178*n*4, 178*n*6
Selkie 75–79, 167*pref.n*2
Seronka, Krystyn 130
Seton Hill University 130
sexual revolution 16
sexual script 8–9
sexuality, gendered 1, 6–7, 9, 16, 33, 37–38, 56, 69, 75, 89, 102–103, 111–112, 158–159, 161–163
Shange, Ntozake 21–22
Shepard, Sam 84
Smith, Anna Deavere 112
Solomon, Alisa 87
Sound Off Theatre 24
Spencer, Jenny 142
split subjectivity 140–141, 144–146
Stoughton, Eliza 20
stranger rape 19–21

Tape 45–47, 52
Tella, Caitlyn 133
Theatre for Young Audiences 76
Thelma and Louise 130
There's Something About Mary 28
third-wave feminism 11, 114–123, 175*n*1, 175*n*3
Tinker, Zachary 47
Tomaselli, Sylvana 11, 168*n*5
Tomlin, Lily 112
Tosca, Jules 30–31
Twice Shy 29–30, 165

Under a Western Sky 60–61, 67, 72–74, 162
Until Someone Wakes Up 22–23

The Vagina Monologues 23, 160
victim script 163–166
Vieux Carré 20–21

Walker, Dolores 18
Walker, Rebecca 114, 115, 123
Watters, Ariel 130
We Keep Our Victims Ready 34, 173*n*3, 173*n*5, 174*n*7
Webb, Jack 81
Westbeth Feminist Collective 17–18
White People 61–62
Whyte, Raewyn 117, 122
The Widow's Blind Date 61–62, 75, 76, 79, 82–84, 91–98, 100, 163, 178*n*2
Williams, Tennessee 20–21
Wilson, August 63
Winston, Jameis 5, 168*n*3
Wolf, Naomi 124, 173*n*1
Wolfe, Lauren 63
Women Artists in Revolution (WAR) 13
Women's Interart Center 17
Women's International Terrorist Conspiracy from Hell (W.I.T.C.H.) 13
Women's Strike for Equity 13
Wuoros, Aileen 56, 129, 149

You the Man 24
Young, Harvey 18, 122

Ziering, Amy 5
Zimmer, Elizabeth 102

www.ingramcontent.com/pod-product-compliance
Lightning Source LLC
Chambersburg PA
CBHW032059300426
44116CB00007B/819